PORNO? CHIC!

'Brian McNair has done more than almost anyone to reframe how we look at the relations between sex and the media and the ways that sex is represented in a wide range of cultural forms. *Porno? Chic!*, his latest contribution to the debate, is a response to the increasingly hyperbolic claims that are made about the effects of pornography and pornified culture. This is a brave and forthright book which is to be welcomed in the current climate of fear and panic about both sex and the media.'

Feona Attwood, *Sheffield Hallam University, UK*

Porno? Chic! examines the relationship between the proliferation of pornography and sexualised culture in the West and social and cultural trends which have advanced the rights of women and homosexuals.

Brian McNair addresses this relationship with an analysis of trends in sexualised culture since 2002 linked to a transnational analysis of change in sexual politics and sex/gender relations in a range of societies, from the sexually liberalised societies of advanced capitalism to those in which women and homosexuals remain tightly controlled by authoritarian, patriarchal regimes.

In this accessible, thought-provoking book, Brian McNair examines why those societies in which sexualised culture is the most liberalised and pervasive are also those in which the socio-economic and political rights of women and homosexuals have advanced the most.

Brian McNair is Professor of Journalism, Media and Communication at Queensland University of Technology. He is the author of *Mediated Sex, Striptease Culture* and *Cultural Chaos*.

PORNO? CHIC!

How pornography changed the world and made it a better place

Brian McNair

Routledge
Taylor & Francis Group

LONDON AND NEW YORK

First published 2013
by Routledge
2 Park Square, Milton Park, Abingdon, Oxon OX14 4RN

Simultaneously published in the USA and Canada
by Routledge
711 Third Avenue, New York, NY 10017

Routledge is an imprint of the Taylor & Francis Group, an informa business

British Library Cataloguing in Publication Data
A catalogue record for this book is available from the British Library

Library of Congress Cataloging in Publication Data
McNair, Brian, 1959–
Porno? Chic!: how pornography changed the world and made it a
better place / Brian McNair.
p. cm.
Includes bibliographical references and index.
1. Pornography–Social aspects. 2. Sex–Social aspects. 3. Pornography
in popular culture. 4. Sex in popular culture. I. Title.
HQ471.M386 2013
363.4'7–dc23
2012011934

ISBN: 978-0-415-57290-3 (hbk)
ISBN: 978-0-415-57291-0 (pbk)
ISBN: 978-0-203-13415-3 (ebk)

Typeset in Bembo
by Taylor and Francis Books

CONTENTS

LIST OF FIGURES

ACKNOWLEDGEMENTS

For encouragement, support and advice in thinking and writing about porn I would like to thank Feona Attwood, Clarissa Smith, Anne-Frances Watson, Angela White, Alan McKee, Catharine Lumby and Kath Albury. For research assistance thank you to Marina Dekavalla in Scotland, and Jess Rodgers in Brisbane. For putting up with the dirty old man working away in his study, night after night in the sticky heat of a Queensland summer, I express my gratitude to, and love for, my wife Kathy.

Brian McNair, Brisbane, March 2012

PREFACE

This is my third book about pornography and mediated sex, and I will preface it by restating a point made in the previous two — that sex and sexual culture matter like few other elements of our lives, in ways both personal and political; that sexuality and its representation are therefore of great importance at the individual and societal levels, and should be studied in a serious and sustained manner by sociologists of culture.

If the prevalence of pornography within individual lives and social structures is not enough to justify a book like this one, I need only point out that sexual culture (including pornography) is one of the largest sectors of the culture industries, worth billions and consumed by hundreds of millions of people every day all over the world. That fact alone would justify the proliferation of research and writing on porn studies we have seen in the last twenty years or so. If the study of culture is to be driven by the scale of its penetration into and impact on everyday life and the political economy of media, 'porn studies' is a no-brainer.

The fact that much of this consumption, and indeed production, even in the current era, is still shrouded in secrecy and shameful masking, hidden from public view, its dynamics and practices masked in rumour, speculation and anecdote, only makes it more fascinating to the student of media. Many do it (consume pornography), but few feel able to admit to it. That paradox was and remains one of the main motivations for my scholarly interest in porn.

As to the others? When I made my first book-length contribution to the field with *Mediated Sex* in 1996 my motivations were both personal *and* political. Lauren Rosewarne's 2011 study of *Part-time Perverts* — an example of the sex-confessional, *striptease culture* I identified in 2002 — observes that 'academic work has many functions; it would be amiss to pretend that the capacity for arousal is not one of the rationales underpinning research topic choice' (p.96). For myself I would say, not that researching and writing about porn are never arousing (of course they can be), but that this was not my principal motivation in summoning the energy and effort required to write a book on the subject. The scholarly project by its nature requires discipline, distance and detachment, and porn can be accessed easily enough if one wants it, without having to put in the effort demanded by a book project.

So, no. In writing about mediated sex, striptease culture, pornographication and porno chic I have been *primarily* driven by my awareness of the importance of sexuality and sexual culture in my own life. Steeped in Catholicism as I had been at school, sexuality and its representation were from an early age central to my experience and thinking. In addition to the impact of a religion which plays heavily on notions of guilt and sin, it was also the case that many of the pop performers and movements which most influenced me in my teens and early twenties – Roxy, Bowie, glam rock, punk and Patti Smith in the 1970s; the British synth bands such as the Human League and the Pet Shop Boys in the 1980s – were highly sexualised, and often perversely so, transgressing all manner of sexual and cultural categories, boundaries and taste hierarchies. For me, as for many others, the feelings and emotions associated with religion, sex, pop culture and art were all intertwined.

Sexual culture was all the more significant to me, because I had spent my university years in the company of radical feminists who taught me that the personal is political, and for whom in the early 1980s pornography was unquestionably and inherently wrong. This I understood intellectually, and at the political level endorsed, but could not help how I felt when I looked at or read sexually explicit texts. Arousal was a visceral, irresistible sensation. For me, for these reasons, my personal relationship to sexual culture became a valid research question (McNair, 2009b), its relevance and interest enhanced further as I encountered women who expressed their interest in consuming pornography. Befriending gay men, throughout university and after, it became clear that many of them also consumed pornography, matter of factly as part of their sexual lives, and without apparent guilt.

Today, in the era of same-sex marriage and gay adoption, this may sound sweetly naïve, but the late 1970s and early 1980s were different times, in which homosexuality was much less visible in public than now, anti-pornography feminism much more combative and hegemonic within the field of radical sexual politics, and me much younger and less sure in my responses to the competing political and cultural influences around me. As both a lapsed Catholic and a pro-feminist I struggled to reconcile what I believed to be right politically with what I felt emotionally. This disjunction posed fascinating questions for me as a young researcher and then into the 1990s, as a research academic.

How could it be that sexual desire was so paradoxical and contradictory a presence in my life (and of course in that of many others)? The answer is, of course, precisely that – sexuality *is* paradoxical and contradictory, and therefore compelling. Eroticism is rooted not least in the transgression of social conventions about what is forbidden and what should be hidden from view. Sexuality is and always has been in large part about the exploration of *fantasy*, and in fantasy rules are broken, sins committed, boundaries crossed, including those put in place not just by the predatory barons of patriarchy, but by a then still-hegemonic strand of radical feminism which was in those days uncomfortably close to the religiously-inspired moral conservatism of the US anti-porn, anti-gay and anti-women's rights lobbies.

That hegemony broke down in the 1990s. When researching and writing *Mediated Sex* I was able to draw upon many writings by women who, although feminist in their outlooks, challenged these anti-porn positions. By the early 2000s and the project which became *Striptease Culture* there were many more to take into account, such as Laura Kipnis and Nadine Stroessen in the United States, and Catharine Lumby in Australia. Feminism had fractured and fragmented, and the anti-porn orthodoxy was no longer uncontested. As part of that process the messiness of sexual desire, and the full range of meanings to be found in the pornographic representation of sex, fuelled a widening debate which coincided with the early manifestations of second-wave 'porno chic' (see Chapter 3).

In the period between the publication of *Striptease Culture* and this book, there have been still more additions to this strand of feminist literature, exemplified by the work of Clarissa Smith, Feona Attwood, Susanna Paasonen, Lauren Rosewarne and others. All proceed from the premise that women, in contrast to the biological determinism of earlier feminist perspectives, are not so very different in their sexualities from men, and often share with them an interest in the transgressive, and in the visual, objectifying dimensions of the erotic. The expanding output of this strand of feminist writing about pornography helps, I believe, to explain the fact that *Striptease Culture*, which had been attacked by one academic reviewer on the grounds that I was a man,[1] and by a red-top tabloid-newspaper pundit on the grounds that I was both 'a dirty old man', and a 'sad porn loser',[2] came to be seen as a valid reading of the cultural trends.

Another reason for writing this book was, however, my sense that the arguments are not yet won. If there is indeed what Feona Attwood calls a 'new paradigm' (2010) available for the study of pornography and sexual culture, the 'old' paradigms of moral conservatism and anti-pornography feminism have made comebacks in the period since 2004 or so – what I characterise below as a resurgence of *porno fear* (Chapter 4).[3] There has been, at least in the three countries which provide the bulk of the material discussed in this book – the United States, the United Kingdom and Australia – a discernible backlash against the shifting sands of sex and gender studies.

More serious than the anti-porn backlash (since, for all the opposition to pornographication and cultural sexualisation, it has had very little impact on the progress evident in the sexual politics of those societies where these trends are most obvious) is the pressing political fact that there are still many places in the world where female (and homosexual) assertion of sexual autonomy is extremely dangerous to individual life and liberty, and where pornography as well as most forms of sexual culture are banned. That concerns me as a supporter of sexual citizenship, and so I wish in this book to make a clear statement about what I assert to be the *progressive power and positive impact of the pornographic*. I will also defend cultural sexualisation more broadly, in the context both of the advanced liberal democracies where women's and gay rights have advanced remarkably fast and far in four decades but where continuing progress cannot be taken for granted; and in the remaining theocracies and authoritarian regimes of the world, where control of sex and its representation is a key weapon in the denial of human rights, to women and gays above all.

To assert such power and impact for pornography is not to defend all of its sub-genres and niches. I share McKee *et al.*'s recognition that there is still 'some horrible and upsetting stuff' in the market (2008, p.71). Nor do I dispute the form's hetero-sexist, patriarchal roots; but wish to say that, after all and everything is taken into account, in the key indicators of progress in sexual politics we are better off as societies which permit pornography and sexual liberalisation than those which do not. As former porn producer Anna Arrowsmith put it in October 2011, and I will try to demonstrate in this book, 'porn is good for society'.[4]

PART I

Porno? Chic!

1

INTRODUCTION

This is a book about the relationship between sexual culture (the spheres of mediation and representation of the sexual) and sexual politics (the system of socio-sexual stratification which characterises late patriarchy). How, if at all, have trends in one sphere shaped and influenced the evolution of the other?

Porno? Chic! explores, first, the *pornographication* of mainstream capitalist culture, that process whereby the once heavily stigmatised and marginalised cultural form we call pornography has become not only more plentiful, and more visible, but also fashionable, or 'chic'; routinely referenced, pastiched, parodied, analysed and paid homage to in a host of non-pornographic cultural forms and genres, as well as being more plentiful and accessible than ever before in human history. Not only has the *pornosphere* – that cultural space where the sexually explicit texts we call pornography circulate – expanded dramatically (Chapter 2); pornography has, as the authors of *The Porning Of America* put it, 'become the dominant influence shaping our culture' (Sarracino and Scott, 2008, p.9).

The influence of pornography on mainstream culture is certainly substantial, part of that wider set of trends often referred to as *cultural sexualisation*. The sexualisation of culture has unfolded in parallel with what has been substantial progressive change in the position of women, gays and other sexually-defined groups since the 'sexual revolution' of the 1960s and 1970s. That the two processes have occurred, and coterminously, are demonstrable facts. But has one influenced or impacted on the other, and if so, how?

The question is important, because we live in a time of widespread anxiety about sexual culture, reflected in the pressure to roll back the tide of what some view as degenerate filth, or at least as the excessive visibility of inappropriate sexual imagery in mainstream culture. As Chapter 4 describes, since 2004 or so we have seen in many liberal democracies a backlash to the preceding two decades of pornospheric expansion and the steady spread of porno chic into many areas of cultural practice and production. As in the Dworkin-MacKinnon anti-porn campaigns of the 1980s, the post-2004 resurgence of that movement has united sections of the feminist movement with moral conservative forces in anti-sexualisation and anti-porn campaigns. These traditional opponents of cultural sexualisation have been joined by other voices roused by what are genuinely new features of the media environment, most notably the historically unprecedented ease of access to pornography enabled by the internet.

There have probably always been these anxieties, let us concede, which appear to be nearly universal in human culture. But the convergence of three sets of factors has, after a period of relative sanguinity around sexual culture in the 1990s and early 2000s, acted to place them high on the public agenda again. The first of these factors is *political* change, and the transformed political economy of desire that change has encouraged. By this I mean that sexual liberalism in general, and the growing social acceptance of feminism and gay rights in particular, have generated a societal demand for more sexual culture, and for forms of sexual culture that deviate in various ways from those long associated with established or traditional patriarchy because they are desired not just by men but by women, and not just by heterosexuals but also by homosexuals of both sexes, as well as bisexuals, transsexuals, and all the other sexually-oriented consumer sub-cultures which now inhabit the marketplace. These forms deviate, too, from what traditional feminists thought they were fighting for when they campaigned against sexist imagery in advertising and pornography in the 1970s and 1980s. Much of the resistance to pornographication and cultural sexualisation described in this book comes not from the churches and moral lobbies but from feminist women, directed against other, often self-identified feminist women such as Lady Gaga.

Much of this anxiety is focused, as always was true, on the growing visibility of homosexuality in culture, even (or especially) when the images are softened and sweetened for mass consumption, as in Britney Spears' kissing of Madonna on a 2004 MTV awards show. Representations of homosexuality in mainstream culture remain vulnerable to criticism and attack despite, or perhaps because of, the real transformations which have been occurring in the lives of gay men and women. There is backlash because there *has* been progress, and the homophobes know it (although they are on the retreat: Chapter 7 shows how breathtakingly rapid the advance of gay rights in liberal capitalist societies has been since the 1970s).

Progressive sex-political change has produced specific forms of cultural sexualisation, which have in turn generated political reaction. From one side – moral conservative and religiously fuelled perspectives – pornographication and cultural sexualisation are feared because they are perceived as threatening to male heterosexual hegemony and the stability of the nuclear family. From the other – anti-porn feminism – they are opposed because they allegedly reinforce patriarchy and heterosexist hegemony. The obvious contradiction between these two perspectives is one reason why we may justifiably scrutinise the political response they share. If both the moral conservatives and the anti-porn feminists cannot be correct in their reasons for opposing these cultural shifts, then perhaps neither is?

The second anxiety-inducing factor is the emergence of digital communication technology as the main means of pornographic production and, more importantly, distribution. The internet has transformed the consumption and production of sexual culture, breaking down boundaries and barriers here as it has in journalism, music, book publishing and other spheres. The *pornosphere* has emerged and expanded from the shadows of the patriarchal underground into a vast, highly visible global network, most of it open and accessible to anyone with a computer and an internet connection. This is unprecedented, and poses different problems for democratic and authoritarian societies respectively.

The politics of pornographication

The implications of digitisation and cultural globalisation for authoritarian regimes accustomed to controlling the information circulating in their societies are particularly serious, although concern about who is watching porn also drives current anxieties in the liberal capitalist world.

In the former, mass access to sexually explicit material subverts the female subordination and institutionalised homophobia present in all of them without exception and which their leaders may view, rightly or not, as essential to regime maintenance. For religiously legitimised patriarchal regimes especially, the notions of sex as a resource for autonomous female pleasure and individual expression, or of the legitimacy of same-sex love for purely hedonistic reasons and without regard to the holy books and theological dogmas, cannot be tolerated. In these countries, typically, the pornosphere is heavily and often brutally policed (although many who live in these dictatorships find ways of bypassing state censorship and accessing restricted sexual material, see Chapter 9).

As for the non-religious despotisms, from Stalin's Soviet onwards, all 'socialist' regimes have sought to control and restrict the expression of sexuality amongst the 'people', correctly understanding it to be an anarchic and potentially subversive force in human action, undermining the Party's need for ideological and behavioural conformity. If some contemporary dictatorships, such as that which exists in China, have a more complicated and ambivalent attitude to sexuality and its pornographic representation (Jacobs, 2011), and to the concept of individual freedom in general, they still find the internet intensely threatening and constantly seek ways to limit the general population's online access to sexually explicit material.

For the liberal democracies, meanwhile, where mass access to pornography on the internet is practically unconstrained, anxiety has been focused on the vulnerability of those who might view sexual images without the emotional maturity to process them safely. The sexualisation of children, girls and young women is of particular concern, echoing earlier waves of anxiety around prostitution in the *fin de siècle*. Concern is also focused on adults who may become 'addicted' to the limitless supply of porn now available to them and thus inflict harm on themselves and their families. From this perspective, pornography consumption is viewed as an activity open to psychological dependence and abuse, like gambling or drug taking.

In addition to these two sets of qualitatively new factors – a transformed political economy of desire, and a digital, globally networked technology to service it – both of which fundamentally alter the dynamics of sexual culture in a democratising and decentralising but also potentially threatening direction, we can view current anxieties about cultural sexualisation as a consequence of *familiar economic factors* driving the production and consumption of commodities in general. These include the profit imperative, and the efficiency of the market as a distribution *mechanism*, which have been active on cultural processes for nearly two centuries, when mass publics comprised of increasingly affluent and educated people first began to emerge as cultural consumers. Much contemporary debate around cultural sexualisation is centred on notions of the 'commercialisation' and 'commodification' of sex, and premised on the belief that sex is somehow too precious to be the object of market relations. Commerce is coarse and crude, goes the lament, whereas sex should be, if not sacred (and for many with religious beliefs, of course, it is precisely that), about the authentic expression of pure love, removed from the cash nexus.[1]

This book rejects that view of the market's coarsening effects, and the related assumption that commercialisation/commodification are bad things in themselves, even when applied to the most intimate of human activities and emotions. The impact of sexual commerce on political, socio-economic and cultural status has self-evidently not been negative in respect of the position of women and other sexually defined groups. I agree with Rosemary Hennessey's observation that

> capitalism is progressive in the sense that it breaks down oppressive and at times brutally constraining traditional social structures and ways of life. In this progressive capacity capitalism's need for raw materials and markets has always enacted a quest for the new through a modernising impulse that is in many ways quite liberatory.
>
> *(2000, p.29)*

This vision of how markets may promote or distribute social progress extends to sexuality and sexual orientation. She adds that

> just because capitalism has made use of heteronormativity [in the maintenance and reproduction of the nuclear family and working class, as well as the regulation and protection of property rights through inheritance] doesn't mean that it is necessary for capitalist production.
>
> *(p.105)*

The role of sexual culture as an agent of sex-political progress is possible because 'it is in the interests of global capitalism to celebrate and enhance awareness of local communities, cultures and forms of identification' (p.29). Capitalism does not require any particular set of social relations to function, as long as there is consumption and systemic reproduction. The undermining of heteronormativity, and the advance of women's and gay rights in particular, has proceeded further and faster in advanced capitalist societies than in any other type of social organisation precisely because of the adaptive features of the system.

Capitalism, moreover, in generating unprecedented economic surplus, produces what Hennessey calls a 'widespread acceptance of pleasure, self-gratification and personal satisfaction that easily translates to the province of sex' (p.103). The logic of cultural capitalism is to call forth, address and make visible, through acts of consumption and often in complex and contradictory ways, previously marginalised, subordinate or invisible sexual categories and communities.[2] It can be argued that in these contexts the commodification of sex is ethical. The exercise of enhanced economic power through cultural consumption reflects changes in the socio-economic status of previously marginalised groups, but it also helps to secure and advance that change by fusing it with the economic interests of service providers and industries dependent on its sustainability.

And then there is the demonstration effect. The commodities which signal 'gayness', for example, are also visible to the non-gay consumer, who may be educated, attracted or perhaps repelled (although the social survey evidence explored in Chapter 7 suggests not: reported levels of tolerance and acceptance of homosexuality have doubled in the US and other countries since 1995). Markets are blind, and commodities do not have morals. They are rather mechanisms for the distribution of material and ideas, and since their emergence human societies have on average advanced hugely in terms of economic affluence, range of consumer choice, and the quality of life associated with those advances (Ridley, 2010). One can go further and state that the erosion of heteronormativity and patriarchy, as measured in the gains made by the women's and gay liberation movements over 40 years or so, has proceeded further and faster in liberal democratic societies of the type where cultural sexualisation and pornographication have been most visible. Capitalism, on this evidence, appears to be the optimal mode of production for the generation not only of economic wealth and cultural liberalism, but of sexual equality and progress. Capitalism is not perfect, of course, and there is some way to go before equality is achieved between genders, sexual orientations, different approaches to families and relationships, and so on. But even in an era of economic crisis such as that seen since 2008, no other type of society has gone as far in this regard, so fast, as the advanced capitalist societies which have experienced the greatest degree of pornographication.

This should not be surprising. Cultural capitalism identifies, calls forth and serves new markets for commodities of all kinds. A Cycle of Liberalisation seems to operate, whereby subcultural lifestyles move from the avant garde margins into the mainstream, through processes of assimilation, popularisation and commodification as illustrated in Figure 1.1. Capitalism wants to sell things, and wants this more than it cares about the sexual orientation or gender or ethnicity of the purchaser. Capitalism's drive for profit has been fused to the political and technological changes noted above, as the advance of female and gay liberation has produced markets for new kinds of sexual goods and services. The result is the commodification and widespread diffusion into mainstream commercial culture of sexual images which are both more explicit and politically challenging of traditional patriarchy than any we have ever

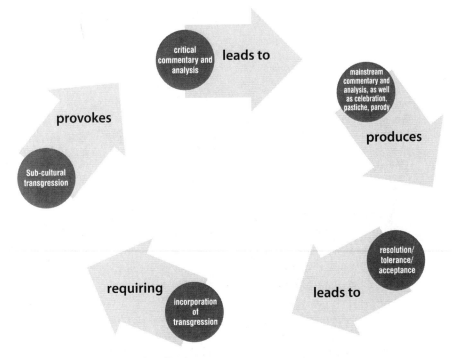

FIGURE 1.1 The cycle of liberalisation

seen. For this reason the commodification of sex which threatens some liberates others, in giving them access to a quality of life, a *sexual citizenship*, never available to any previous generation.

Whatever one's moral judgment of the commercialisation of sex, however, there can be no doubt that the consumer commodity market has fuelled the sexual revolution in countries where sexual citizenship is recognised (here I mean societies in which, while there may certainly be homophobia, there is no law preventing a gay man or woman from expressing his or her sexual identity in the high-street store or the theatre venue, and in which public institutions recognise and officially promote equal rights in the spheres of sex and gender). Cultural capitalism has been progressive in this respect since, to repeat, free markets are unconcerned with gender and sexual orientation, as long as you can pay for the things you want to consume. The successes of feminism and gay liberation have enhanced the economic power of women and gays in recent decades, creating new markets for sexual commodities including pornography for women and gay users, dildos and sexy underwear as sold in the hugely successful Ann Summers chain in the UK.

And the growing mainstream visibility of these artefacts has fed back into 'straight' heterosexual culture, pushing it in new directions. Thus we have the phenomenon of the 'metrosexual', and the self-conscious blurring of traditional masculine/feminine gender divisions seen in a celebrity figure such as David Beckham. Identities and behaviours once marginal, perhaps perceived as subversive or threatening to mainstream patriarchy, become visible, then tolerated, then themselves mainstream through cultural commodification. Commodities become the *memetic* vehicles for sex-political progress.

So sexual culture *has* changed, of that there is no doubt, reflecting changes in the socio-sexual structures of liberal capitalism, and fuelled by forces which, of themselves, have little to do with sexuality and sexual politics, such as the impact of digital networks and markets, but which have put new forms and iterations of all kinds of sexualities in places of unprecedented visibility and accessibility. The consequent anxieties are intelligible, because change is often threatening. They are misplaced, however, if, as this book argues, the sexual culture we inhabit today is inseparable from the positive sex-political changes of the last four decades; if pornography, and porno chic, and the commodification of sex, and cultural sexualisation, are all bound together, informing the complex environmental conditions which have permitted real, meaningful, positive change in gender relations and sexual rights over that same period. You cannot have one, I will argue, without the other.

The argument must be made, because the battle for human rights in the sexual sphere is not yet won in the liberal capitalist world, and certainly not in the developing and authoritarian world. If we live in an era of global pornographication and cultural sexualisation, we live also in a time of continuing resistance to the advances of feminism and homosexuality, which are not irreversible and certainly cannot be taken for granted, even in the liberal democratic countries where they are most apparent. The last few years of the first decade of the twenty-first century saw constant debate and negotiation around such issues as gay marriage and adoption rights in the capitalist world (granted in some US states and some countries, denied in others, and fiercely debated in the Australian general election of 2010), women's right to choose abortion, and the right of gays to serve in the armed forces. While the direction of sex-political change has been broadly progressive, the forces of reaction are never far away. In the second decade of the twenty-first century they have made pornographication and cultural sexualisation their battleground.

In the world beyond liberal capitalism, meanwhile, homosexuality is still in many countries viewed as criminal or heretical, punishable by imprisonment and even death. Young men have been publicly hanged in Iran, jailed in Botswana, and discretely silenced by anti-gay laws in Singapore. The position of women is equally shocking, subject as they are to all manner of mental and physical abuses in the name of patriarchal and religious authority. Robert Fisk's harrowing article for the *Independent* in July 2010[3] presented a list of sadistic tortures, murders and other brutalities inflicted on women by men in the developing world. While most of these crimes were inspired by an extreme reading of Islam, other religions were included in the roll call of perpetrators of misogynistic violence. And let us not forget the paedophile epidemic at the heart of the Catholic church globally, which has led to the sexual abuse of hundreds of thousands of children over many decades by men and women supposedly serving their god while proclaiming loudly on the sexual moralities and behaviours of others.

Is there any connection between the prevalence of these abuses and the social tolerance they are afforded, and the fact that the societies and communities where they occur are nearly always illiberal in their approaches to sexual culture and politics? It will be my argument that there is, and that the trends of cultural sexualisation attacked by these forces should be seen by supporters of women's and gay rights, not to mention the protection of children against abuse, as a vehicle, sometimes a weapon, of progressive socio-sexual change in societies which have resisted it. It should be defended and its critics replied to, though, with civility and respect and in full recognition of the points on which criticism of cultural sexualisation is justified (and there are a few). But it *should* be defended, without apology or hesitation, and with as much vigour as is deployed by the opponents of sexual liberalisation.

Outline

The book begins with an account of the evolution of what I call the *pornosphere*, or that sphere of culture in which sexual imagery and discourses circulate, from its origins in prehistoric cave-dwelling societies to the hyperconnected, globalised world of the internet. In Chapter 3 I show how the narrow cultural category of pornography influenced and became part of mainstream culture in the form of *porno chic*. Chapter 4 explores the resurgence of anxieties around this 'pornographication', and also the critique of cultural sexualisation. In the chapters which make up Part II I will counter those criticisms with an account of the evidence on impacts, and suggest five ways in which pornography can be argued to have changed the world and made it a better place:

- Its role in the evolution of communication technologies and media industries, where it has, time and time again, been the killer application which leads to commercialisation and broad adoption (in particular, digitised, networked, globalised communication);
- Its role in the articulation and making visible of hitherto marginalised or supressed sexual identities;
- By making sex and sexuality visible, pornography has often educated its users, about the mechanics of sex in general, and safe sex in particular;
- Pornography has provided a safe outlet for sexual desires which for various reasons it may not be possible to satisfy within a real relationship; which can therefore help keep couples together, and enable sexual release for people who can't or don't want to have real partners; and
- Its role in the inspiration of art and culture, much of it made by women, gay men, and artists identifying with other minority sexual orientations.

There are downsides to pornographication, of course. If porn can be defined as the representation of sex for the purpose of sexual arousal, then it is also the representation of sexualities which may offend, violate and invade. Some men are misogynistic.

The porn they use may be misogynistic too. My point in Part II, though, will be this: we cannot reduce porn to the subset of its most offensive types, to the misogynistic porn made by misogynists for misogynists. Just as we cannot cite Mel Gibson's *The Passion* as a reason to critique all cinema as anti-Semitic (nor even all of Mel Gibson's films as evangelical nonsense – *Apocalypto* and *Braveheart* demonstrate that, for all his personal flaws, he is a talented film director), we cannot cite Max Hardcore as representative or exemplary of porn in general.

Nor can we say that only misogynistic men like what is often called 'extreme' porn. Some women enjoy hetero S&M material; many lesbians and gay men enjoy the representation of S&M and other fetishistic sexual practices – the 'degrading' types of images often cited as the embodiment of patriarchal misogyny by anti-porn critics. In the end, I will argue, there is no meaningful 'pro-' or 'anti-porn' position, just as there can be no pro-/anti-prose fiction position, or pro-/anti-narrative film or TV drama position. Porn is no more nor less than a type of culture, a frame or formal category used to describe a particular kind of content (sex), with a particular intention (arousal), and a particular place in the hierarchy of taste and status. The value and ethical legitimacy of pornographic content and pornographic intent is determined, as with all culture, by who makes it, and for what ends.

Defining terms

Throughout this book I will use as neutral descriptors terms which are commonplace in critical discourses around the sexualisation of culture, although usually in those contexts employed without explanation or consideration of their actual meanings. Before proceeding any further, therefore, I will briefly define what *I* mean by them, and how they fit into the model of culturally driven sex-political change which underpins the book (pornography and porno chic are defined in Chapters 2 and 3 respectively).

Objectification

First is the concept of objectification. This term has customarily been used as a reference to the process by which a human subject is reduced to a sexual object, thereby losing a key element of her humanity (and it is usually a 'she', although of course men can be objectified too). My starting point in this book is that everything can be and often is objectified, merely by being perceived by another. This includes people. And contrary to the assumption that objectification is in and of itself a bad thing, there are many circumstances in which we want to be viewed, observed and objectified – not all the time, and not in circumstances of predation or powerlessness, but in a variety of quite normal, healthy contexts. We dress to be noticed for parties, weddings, job interviews or going on holiday. We often dress to be noticed for our sexuality, and hope to proceed from that moment of objectification to a sexual relationship or contact. To fail to be noticed is often to be disappointed.

Objectification, in this sense, is not a patriarchal imposition on women, but an aspect of human sexuality which encompasses all genders and sexual identities. Its association with patriarchy and sexism reflects the power relations which have traditionally favoured men, but lesbians and gay men objectify each other every bit as much as straight men and women. Fortunes are spent on hair and clothes, and elaborate grooming rituals endured, in order to maximise the chances of being objectified. And so, while unwanted looking is rightly condemned, sexual objectification in itself is often invited and welcomed by those to whom it is directed. I share female porn producer Starla Haze's assessment that 'the clumsy application of feminist ideas of "objectification" has oversimplified men and women to the point where both sexes are anxious to enter the bedroom'.[4]

Sexualisation

Much of culture, including sexual culture, is designed to prelude or accompany the moment of objectification, and the sexual contacts and intimacies which might follow from it; to celebrate and heighten those moments, as in the pop song and video, or the romantic comedy in cinema. Cultural sexualisation includes those moments, alongside all the other articulations and reflections of human sexuality contained in the variety of cultural forms to which we are daily exposed. And it is the case, oft noted, that as sexual liberalisation has proceeded in the advanced capitalist world since the 1950s, mainstream culture has become more overtly and directly sexual.

As we shall see, cultural sexualisation has come to be perceived as a problem by critics of the trends explored in this book; deemed inappropriate because, for these viewpoints, most sexual discourse itself is unacceptable in public cultural arenas, and especially in those arenas occupied by the young and the 'vulnerable'. To make a judgement of that kind requires that one interpret the meanings of sexual representation as harmful in some way or another. This book, by contrast, views such representations as expressions of sex-political trends which are, in most if not all respects, positive.

I will argue that cultural sexualisation has been a vehicle for progressive sex-political change, as much a condition as an index of change. Yes, there can be inappropriate sexualisation, such as the parading of young girls in beauty pageants, for which they are groomed to look and behave like sexually active adults, for audiences of adults. The protection of children from inappropriate sexual display and imagery is, and always has been, a legitimate issue. Most sexual abuse of children resides not in the inappropriately sexualised advertisement, but much more often in the home, or the church, or the care home. Cultural sexualisation, as I use the term here, has no automatic negative connotation, but refers to the growing visibility of sexual signifiers in all forms of culture, a trend evident since the 1950s.

Commodification/commercialisation

Capitalist culture is largely commodified culture. Sexual culture in capitalism is thus the commodification of sexuality – its embodiment in goods and services which are exchanged in the market, generating profits. Sex itself can be a commodity, in the form of prostitution, and any kind of sexual representation intended to produce sexual arousal and leisure (such as pornography). Sex toys, intended to substitute for human bodies and sex organs, are commodities. Romantic fiction is a commodity, as are clothes intended to facilitate sexual objectification.

There is a presumption in some quarters, as noted above, that human sexuality should not be commodified. My argument to the contrary is that markets cannot be viewed as degenerate or shallow by definition, but function simply to distribute goods and services, and the ideas often underpinning them, in ways which expand their reach or democratise them. Matt Ridley writes in *The Rational Optimist* (2010) that commodity exchange is the engine of economic growth. By extension, cultural exchange can be viewed as the engine of progressive ideological change, or political growth. Through the circulation of cultural commodities, including sexual commodities, progressive ideas and concepts circulate amongst those who would otherwise not be exposed or receptive to them, in contexts where they are received as 'entertainment' or 'art' or 'recreation'. Commodification, in this sense, can be the agent of social progress and not its enemy.

2

PORNOSPHERE

The concept of the public sphere is a familiar one in media and cultural studies. Originated by German sociologist Jürgen Habermas in his classic work *The Structural Transformation of the Public Sphere* (1989),[1] it refers to a communicative space where information and debate circulate, allowing public opinion to be formed and deliberative democracy to be exercised. The public sphere underpins democratic political culture – indeed, it is a precondition for democracy to exist – because the information it permits to circulate enables citizens to know about the world around them, and to debate the issues which that world presents to them.

In the early days of bourgeois democracy, Habermas explains, the public sphere was a restricted cultural space, accessible only to those educated, wealthy, male elites who had political and economic power – the gentlemen habitués of the seventeenth-century European coffee-houses, who in their thinking and conversation brought forth much of Enlightenment philosophy, liberal capitalism and democracy as we know it. They were the readers of, and writers for, early newspapers and periodicals, in which news, analysis and commentary informed the transition from feudalism to capitalism, and all the political and cultural trends associated with that movement. Over decades and centuries, more and more people became educated enough to read, the right to vote was gradually extended to cover the entire population (although this process was not completed until the mid-twentieth century in several European countries), and the public sphere expanded with it. Elite media became mass media, and public opinion a mass phenomenon. And in the late twentieth century and into the twenty-first, as satellite TV and the internet emerged to break down geo-temporal boundaries, the public sphere was globalised. As this book went to press the democratic implications of that cultural globalisation were being felt in the Arab countries of north Africa and the Middle East.

If the Habermasian public sphere can be viewed as a space for the circulation and exchange of political discourse, the *pornosphere* of this chapter can be viewed as the

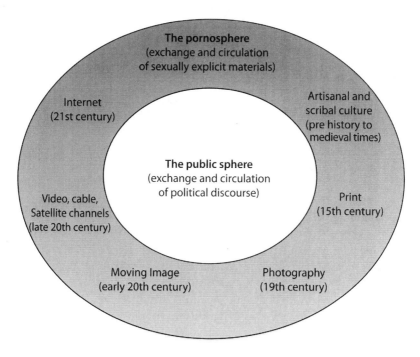

FIGURE 2.1 The pornosphere and the public sphere

space in which explicit sexual discourse is circulated (Figure 2.1). By this I mean the written word, as well as pictures, photography, moving images and sound – all the forms in which pornography and explicit sexual representation are produced and consumed by *sexual citizens* (Evans, 1992). The production, distribution and consumption of these texts comprises a significant part of the sexual lives of many individuals in society. As the public sphere is to democratic politics, the pornosphere is to sexuality and sexual behaviour. What the public sphere is to democracy, the pornosphere is to the libido – the source of knowledge, information and imagery which will facilitate arousal and sexual expression; the means of self-empowerment.

The latter's expansion, like that of the public sphere in relation to democratic politics, accompanies and is a precondition for the *democratisation of desire* (McNair, 2002), meaning the entry of traditionally excluded or marginalised groups into sexual citizenship. The rise of feminism and the advance of women's rights, like gay liberation and the mainstreaming of homosexuality we have seen in the liberal democracies since the 1970s, have taken place alongside the expansion of the pornosphere, and the emergence of hitherto absent or hidden categories such as women's porn, gay porn, lesbian porn and so on. The Habermasian public sphere was the province of elite, educated males. Only over time did it become a more fragmented and popularised cultural space available for mass debate and the discussion of politics by all regardless of gender, sexual orientation, ethnicity or class. The pornosphere, similarly, was until recently a narrow zone of sexual imagery practically monopolised by heterosexual men – the 'ruling class' of patriarchy. Over time – the decades since the onset of the sexual revolution in particular – heterosexist male porn has been joined in an evermore segmented sex-cultural marketplace by a diversity of pornographies, catering to what might seem to be every taste and desire.

The parallels between the porno and public spheres are not coincidental. The expansion of the pornosphere is a process which has been coterminous with the evolution of the public sphere. Both communicative zones have been part of the cultural environment of liberal democratic capitalism as it has evolved over four centuries. Of course they service very different aspects of individual and social life – the public and the private, the political and the personal, which, although they increasingly overlap in contemporary culture (coverage of the '*bunga bunga*' exploits of the former Italian leader Silvio Berlusconi, for example, comprised a wealth of explicit sexual imagery and discourse involving prostitutes, underage girls and drug-fuelled orgies in Italian palazzos) retain their distinctive features and functions.

I will note in passing that as the public sphere has evolved, its core form of journalism – especially popular journalism – has taken on qualities shared with pornography. Journalism, as it has been popularised and made more accessible to mass readerships, has often been viewed in the same way as pornography (the core form of the pornosphere). Both reveal things previously hidden or unseen: news is about things we do not know, in places we cannot be; porn is about sex we have not had, or cannot have, and is thus the object of fantasy. As Knudsen *et al.* observe, after Foucault, 'it is in pornography that we find information about the hidden, the forbidden and the taboo' (2007, p.39). Both can be the subject of public condemnation and outrage (as in the 2011 scandal affecting the popular red-top newspaper *The News Of The World* in the UK), at the same time as being consumed by millions of people, who feel more or less shameful even as they consume.

Both forms transgress, or shock, and deploy this transgressive quality as a key part of their appeal. Both have for centuries generated heated public debates about the morality and ethics of their content (and of the people who produce the content). Both became more controversial, more contested, as they became more popular and accessible from the nineteenth century onwards. Both have been at various times the foci of culture wars around taste hierarchies, so that the serious/sensational, high/low culture divide seen frequently in the public discussion of journalism, which usually corresponds to the division between elite and popular media (with the latter being seen as debased, dumbed down, distasteful, etc.), parallels the erotica/pornography divide, where erotica is the respectable form of sexual representation, and porn the pariah.

There are of course many important points of difference between the pornosphere and the public sphere. The former is a communicative space within which circulates a very particular and narrowly defined type of content: explicit sexual representation. The public sphere, by contrast, contains a huge breadth of informational content addressing all of the issues which comprise a society's political and civic life, including at times 'porno chic' and the discussion of pornography (see Chapters 3 and 4).

Pornography is defined by its intention to sexually arouse the user through the explicit, transgressive representation of sex. It does not invite debate, or seek to shape opinion (although it regularly provokes heated debate in the public sphere), but instead to arouse, stimulate and then satisfy sexual desire. As a mode of communication it is highly instrumental, aiming to make the consumer feel and do quite specific things – get turned on, masturbate or have sex with a partner, climax. But the analogy is useful, and this chapter will pursue it in the form of an account of the *structural transformation* of the pornosphere. The themes of that account will include:

- The part played by pornography as a driver of communications technology and media infrastructure, including the business models underpinning the evolution of the cultural market since medieval times and early modernity;
- The expansion of access to pornography over time, and the entry of mass publics into sexual culture;
- The diversification and democratisation of the cultural space in which pornography resides, to include most notably women (where the pornosphere had initially been a male preserve); homosexuals of both sexes (where it had been heterosexist); and other sexually-defined groups, such as fetishists and paraphiliacs of various kinds, transsexual and transgendered people; and also categories such as the disabled and the elderly;
- The relationship between access to sexual culture through the pornosphere and the acquisition of sexual power and citizenship;
- The emergence of interactivity and participation as important elements of the pornosphere, paralleling the digitally-enabled growth of user-generated content in the public sphere. I will characterise this as an explosion of user-generated *citizen porn*, comparable in many ways to the more familiar notion of 'citizen journalism' in its shattering of traditional distinctions in media production between professional and amateur, producer and consumer; and
- The impact of these trends – expansion, diversification, democratisation and increased participation – on the form and content of pornography.

Before telling that story, however – what *is* pornography?

Defining pornography

The question has been asked many times, and many different answers given. For anti-porn feminists, pornography is the record of abusive, violent acts committed against female performers in the moment of production, and against women as a whole at the point of (straight male) consumption. Or, it is perceived as the propaganda of male heterosexual rape, the *ur-text* of misogyny, leading directly to violence against women and children.

For some religious people – not all, since being religious does not necessarily mean hostility to the consumption of sexual representation – pornography is a blasphemous insult to the sanctity of sex and the inviolability of marriage. For some kinds of aesthetes and lovers of fine art it is the trashy opposite to erotica – an insult not to God but to human decency and taste.

We could work through the various definitions of pornography for the rest of this book. Instead I will briefly restate my own take on the matter, first set out in *Mediated Sex* (1996), which sought to identify the essential elements in the many other definitions out there, and to avoid moral evaluation. Pornography, I argued there, is a cultural form defined by its content (sex), its intention (to sexually arouse), and its *transgressive* relationship to prevailing codes of sexual display and representation. Pornography tends to be 'explicit' sexual representation, although what is viewed as explicit is culturally variable.

In relation to the first element of this definition – and although one often hears references to 'war porn' and 'torture porn' in relation to news footage and horror movies respectively, with the attendant implication that something nasty is being made to look nice in an inappropriate and possibly harmful manner – we can say with certainty that *pornography is always about sex*. Sex is always its content, the diversity of that content being a reflection of the variety of human sexualities. Pornography is the representation of sex, *out of context*. Context-*less* sexual content. Sex for its own sake, for the sheer hell of it, and all the more transgressive in being so, because the cultural preference for sex within marriage and stable, loving relationships remains powerful, even for those who would not identify themselves as religious believers. Umberto Eco has observed of pornography that:

> Its typical characteristic is dead time, time in which nothing happens. In order to mark the transgression of moral (and aesthetic) norms as such and to awake an interest, the sexual interaction has to be distinguished from the everyday, from normality, from the unexpected. Similarly the performances of sex depicted in pornographic photographs are conventionally situated within rather banal and often bare if not dreary environments to draw the attention to the act rather than the surroundings.
>
> *(Umberto Eco, quoted in Kerstin, 2007, p.92)*

Typically, the sexually arousing effect of the pornographic text is realised without recourse to other aspects of creative construction, such as quality of script (assuming there is dialogue at all – in most contemporary pornographic videos, the soundtrack is little more than a series of moans and crudely dubbed exclamations), acting ability or production values. We access porn not to admire the sets or the lighting design, but to consume sex.[2]

Porn made for women has traditionally been viewed as distinct from heterosexual male porn in that it places greater emphasis on the sensual surroundings of the sex act, as opposed to explicit images of sexual penetration and so on. Whether this stylistic trait has been a reflection of social convention, which says that female sexuality is different from that of men (and porn for women must therefore be 'dressed up' in soft focus camerawork and candles for decoration – made 'warm, humane, funny, dangerous, psychedelic, with wholly different parameters to male porn', as one feminist commentator puts it (Moran, 2011, p.35)), is an open question, given the increasingly visceral porn made by women in more recent times (see Chapter 6). Desire is complex, and heavily contextual, and it may be that in the past women have perceived these kinds of pornographic images – often referred to as 'erotica' to separate them from the more visceral form of pornography – to be the only kind they could respectably access.[3] Anecdotal evidence from a number of female commentators suggests that women are just as turned on by the 'hard' in pornography as the 'soft', if not more so.

It is true as a generalisation, nonetheless, that pornography nearly always lacks the aesthetic elements of other kinds of sexual representation. In pornography, story, script, sets and the rest of the apparatus of non-pornographic image-making are merely obstacles to the pursuit of arousal and orgasm. In the era of video and streaming, especially, even short films are typically scrolled through at speed, until the sex is arrived at.

The purpose of porn

Pornography, then, as *explicit sexual representation*, is distinct from a movie such as *The Mother* (Roger Michell, 2003) where actor Daniel Craig has sex with an older woman (thus transgressing a western cultural norm which tends to avoid the representation of older people, and women in particular, as having sexualities which require to be satisfied). The film contained a number of relatively explicit sex scenes, but it was not pornography.

Intentionality is crucial to a robust definition of pornography. Many kinds of text are described as porn which are not, and which are excluded from that category because they are not intended to provoke sexual arousal in the reader/viewer/user. This is true of *The Mother*, and many of the sexually explicit artworks considered in Chapter 8, where the effect may be to repel or repress the viewer's sexual feelings rather than turn him or her on.

To be pornographic, a representation of sex has to be made with the principal aim of arousing the reader/viewer/user. Arousal must be its intention, its desired effect, its *raison d'etre*, next to which all other objectives are secondary. People can be turned on by images which are not intended to be arousing, and which are not therefore pornographic, but the effect in that case is accidental. The difference between, say, the underwear or swimwear sections of a chain-store catalogue (not pornography, though quite possibly sexually arousing to some viewers) and very similar images made for the swimsuit and underwear categories of the tubegalore.com porn site is that the latter are made with sexual arousal as their goal. A film like *Sleeping Beauty* (Julia Leigh, 2011), with its frequent images of a young woman (Emily Browning) nude or in her underwear, is not pornography, even if it may be arousing for some sections of the audience. In Leigh's film the sex serves a story about a woman's search for identity, about power and control, and about the nature of prostitution as a job. Steve McQueen's *Shame* (2011), an explicit cinematic study of sexual obsession and dysfunction, likewise, is not pornography.

The relativism of porn

Pornography is not merely explicit sexual representation intended to arouse. It tends also to be *transgressive*, which means that it cannot be defined absolutely or objectively, once and for all, by its content alone. It is an historical category, *culturally specific*, always defined in the context of and in opposition to what is socially and morally acceptable within a given society at a given time, and determined by the range of cultural, moral, social and political factors which have shaped that particular society's evolution. The Saudi clergy's definition of pornography is very different from that of the youthful western consumer of Lady Gaga pop videos. For the former, a picture of Gaga in concert, even fully dressed, would by the nature of her sexualised bodily display be viewed as pornographic. For the teenage Gaga fan in London or New York, on the other hand, she is a pop star who uses sexuality as a device in her work, which may often qualify as 'porno chic' because it refers to or draws from pornography (see Chapter 3) but is not in itself pornographic. Where both perspectives will agree is on the matter of transgression, and the necessity of its being present in a text for that text to be deemed 'pornographic'.

Definitions of what pornography is also change within a given society, over time. Knudsen *et al.*'s study of pornography in the Nordic countries observes that

> many of the images that appear in mainstream media today – images depicting nakedness or explicit sexual activity and situations – would have been defined as pornography some twenty to thirty years ago. Conversely, much of what was then regarded as 'indecent' would most likely not be considered as such by the majority of people today.
>
> *(2007, p.8)*

Pornography transgresses a given society's prevalent codes of acceptability in sexual representation, which will vary significantly from those prevailing elsewhere.

The structural transformation of the pornosphere – prehistory

The content of pornography as I have defined it here hasn't changed very much since the days of the Marquis de Sade. Pornography – or forms of explicit sexual representation that look very like it, even if they have been called by other names – has been around for ever, or at least since human beings first began to make their marks on cave walls and rock formations: primitive but instantly recognisable representations of animals and people fighting and fucking. The term is derived from the ancient Greek words *porno* and *graphos*,[4] and indeed the Greeks decorated their plates and vases with explicit representations of sexual activity between men and women, men and men, and even men and boys, not having a concept of paedophilia as understood today.[5]

When the ancient Roman towns of Pompeii and Herculaneum were reclaimed from layers of volcanic ash in the nineteenth century, archaeologists found the interior walls of some of the houses decorated with painted representations of men and women having sex. Their exact purpose and function are unknown, but on the opening to public view in 2006 of Pompeii's *Lupanese*, the ancient city's only purpose-built brothel, it was reported that 'researchers believe the *Lupanare*'s celebrated wall paintings each depicting a different position, were intended to advertise the various specialities on offer'.[6]

  These images were not coy in the repertoire of sex acts they depicted, but in many respects identical to the style and content of modern pornography, so much so that they were hidden away from the public gaze in what Walter Kendrick called 'secret museums' (1987). The discovery of this explicit sexual imagery was indeed, he argued in his ground-breaking book, the beginnings of what we today think of as pornography and its associated sanctions. The paintings were deemed transgressive by the moral guardians of the time, and thus forbidden to the ordinary, uneducated masses, who in their childlike innocence and naïveté (as they were presumed to be) could not be trusted to handle them responsibly or without doing themselves moral damage.

  This response set the template for all subsequent efforts to police sexually explicit representation in the Judaeo-Christian world. Patriarchal elites, who themselves may access and 'study' the offending images, at the same time exercise the power to restrict access to others, on grounds of moral and spiritual vulnerability. Within this regulatory paradigm, which remains firmly in place in many countries even where sexual culture has been substantially liberalised, pornography is not just transgressive, it is dangerous to both body and mind.

  Long before the nineteenth century, sexually explicit images intended to arouse their readers and viewers were in circulation across the world. Japanese *shunga* paintings depicting sexual activity in explicit terms were common in the seventh and eight centuries, and in the eighteenth century *ukiyo-e-shunga* circulated widely – 'booklets of woodblock prints depicting sexual activity in graphic detail. They were ostensibly erotic, for women as well as men' (Watkins, 2005, p.22).

  Sexually explicit artefacts can be traced back to first century AD China, and the production of erotica/pornography reached its peak with the Ming dynasty in the seventeenth century, coinciding with the rise of the mercantile middle-classes in big cities such as Guangzhou. One source notes that these 'pornographic artworks' were known as *chungong hua* (spring palace paintings), 'a reference to the presumed debauchery that occurred behind the walls of the Forbidden City'.[7] The Indian *Kama Sutra*, dating back to the second century AD is familiar all over the world. Aretino's *Postures* were produced in the late sixteenth century. The writings of the Marquis de Sade and the satirical, sexually explicit etchings of the early modern era in France circulated in the late eighteenth century (Hunt, 1993).

  These images predated the widespread use of the term pornography which, according to some sources, was first recorded in the early nineteenth century in French and in 1838 in English. A published reference to the 'new pornographie' allegedly abundant in the London of 1638 is attributed to English publisher Nathanial Butter in a history of the Fleet newspaper industry (Boston, 1990, p.20). Regardless of the roots of the term, and the precise moment of its birth as a widely understood reference to transgressive, sexually explicit materials, porn is what these materials were. They were intended to sexually arouse their readers and viewers, and were widely sought after for that reason. They comprised, as contemporary pornography does, images of people having sex in various positions and combinations, for the purpose of inducing sexual arousal.

In some of those societies these images were policed, with greater or lesser ferocity, precisely because they transgressed moral codes. Other societies seem to have been comfortable with their presence, or were at least prepared to tolerate them. All had one thing in common, however. They, and the embryonic pornosphere they established, were exclusive, elite and inaccessible to the people as a whole, who had neither the resources nor the education required to, for example, purchase and read a copy of Aretino's *Postures* (Renaissance-era sexually explicit poems illustrated with engravings).

If the history of pornography as a popular (as opposed to elite) cultural form begins with the spread of literacy and the invention of photography in the nineteenth century, the emergence of the pornosphere as a space accessible to mass audiences – as a mass medium – goes back only a few decades, to the launch of *Playboy* magazine, perhaps, in 1953, with its now-iconic images of a nude Marilyn. From that point on pornography was not under- but overground, not elite but popular culture, not artisanal but industrial.

What has not changed over time is the content of explicit sexual representation, which is shaped and bounded by human sexuality and thus to an extent universal. One is struck, for example, when viewing early pornographic photographs and films, by the presence even then of contemporary fetishisms and perversions such as uroglania and bestiality. Oral sex, anal sex, group sex, gay sex – all were practiced, and all were represented in these images from an earlier era. What *has* changed are the means of communication of the pornographic, its reach and penetration into mass culture, and its social and cultural meanings. Latterly, and over the last four decades in particular, these have proliferated, to embrace the positive and the approving as well as the negative and the denunciatory.

The remainder of this chapter explores that evolution. It is a process in which the demand for access to a cultural form drives the development of the means of communicating that form, as well as limiting communication within certain socio-economic categories. The desire to distribute explicit sexual representation is one of the key, though of course not only, impulses behind the process of technological advance which brought humanity from handmade artisanal culture to the globalised, digitised, networked environment of the internet. Pornography has been what Patchen Barss calls an 'erotic engine … a powerful source of creativity and innovation that has spurred the development of many new media' (2010, p.1). 'Throughout history', he adds, 'across cultures, and in every part of the world, whenever a new means of communication emerged, people adopted it and used and adapted it so as to find new ways to produce, distribute and consume pornography' (Ibid., p.4). As one observer put it in 2002, 'the sex industry places itself at the leading edge of every new technology'.[8] Gail Dines notes that 'the demand for porn has driven the development of core cross-platform technologies for data compression, search, transmission and micro-payments'.[9] Sarah Neely has written about the role of sex in *Second Life* (2010), observing that 'developments in technology are continually led by the sex industry' (p.90).

Tom Hodgkinson writes that

> pornography is sometimes characterised as the symptom of a degenerate society, but anyone even noddingly familiar with Greek vases or statues on ancient Hindu temples will know that so-called unnatural sex acts, orgies and all manner of complex liaisons have for millennia past been represented in art for the pleasure and inspiration of the viewer everywhere. The desire to ponder images of love-making is clearly innate in the human – perhaps particularly the male – psyche.
>
> *(2004, p.201)*

This innateness, or necessity to represent and consume sexual representation has been a key driver of innovation in the communication realm, fuelling inventions and applications which have had important cultural and social benefits beyond the zone of sexual representation. This, indeed, is the first and most obvious way in which pornography can be said to have changed the world and made it a better place. Without it, the technologies of media production, reproduction and consumption might not have developed as fast as they have done.

Print culture and the birth of the pornosphere

The tools available to human beings for the production of cultural artefacts have evolved from prehistoric times, in which natural dyes and other materials were used to create rock paintings and engravings of the type found in Germany in July 2011 and estimated to be around 12,000 years old. For the entire prehistory of the pornosphere, sexually explicit representations were like cultural texts in general – made by hand, in editions of one (and if more than one, laboriously copied by hand). In medieval times books and artworks were very expensive, and thus exclusive to the wealthy elites who commissioned them and acted as patrons for their makers.[10] To the extent that these artefacts represented the sexual, they functioned in more or less the same way as modern pornography, although the embryonic pornosphere they made possible was of course much smaller and less complex than the digitised, globalised, networked entity we see in the twenty-first century (Figure 2.1).

The technology of print, when it arrived in Europe in the late fifteenth and early sixteen centuries, revolutionised many aspects of human culture and society.[11] Johann Gutenberg's invention of 1440 made possible the mechanical reproduction of texts, and thus the emergence of journalism and a public sphere. It made possible modernity and the civilising force of the Enlightenment, to which the capacity to write for and be read by multitudes was so fundamental.

Elizabeth Eisenstein's account of *The Printing Revolution in Early Modern Europe* (1983) makes clear the central role of print technology in facilitating the development of cultural capitalism, through its enabling of the cultural commodity in the form of relatively cheap, content-rich objects which could be produced, circulated, bought and sold with ease. The printed book made collective thinking and organisation possible, one might say, by providing the raw material for progressive thought and action to mass audiences, spreading new ideas as and when they emerged from the minds of thinkers like Martin Luther and William Shakespeare.

Others who took advantage were people such as Pietro Aretino, the Italian poet whose bawdy rhymes found, in print culture, a vehicle for transmission to readers all over an emerging European cultural marketplace, illustrated with lithographs that could also be mass reproduced. Aretino's sonnets, as they are known today, became, in the form of the *Postures*, one of the first banned books, prohibited by the Pope in 1529. Then as now, however, being banned merely enhanced the transgressive appeal of Aretino's words and pictures, and transformed them into a means, not just of individual masturbation, but of collective resistance to authority. From Aretino on, notes Barss, 'pornography became a commonly used tool among political agitators, advocates of free speech and critics of government and religious leaders' (2010, p.68).

The sexually explicit texts of early modern Europe were principally literary, of course, and often written with high philosophical and aesthetic ends in mind. The Marquis de Sade's late eighteenth-century works exemplify this characteristic, which is one reason why they have circulated legally even in societies where pornography was tightly controlled. Philip Kaufman's account of de Sade's incarceration, in the film *Quills* (2000), dares to present the writings as deeply arousing to those who encountered them, such as the prison maid Maddy (Kate Winslet). De Sade was a provocateur who used transgressive sexual discourse as a weapon against the elites of Napoleonic France, but in this film the political ramifications of his work are less important than the fact that Maddy finds them a huge turn on, as do those on the outside of the asylum to whom she smuggles the Marquis' handwritten texts.

Even today, and even in the knowledge that subversion of religious and political power were at their heart, works such as *The 120 Days of Sodom* are disturbing to read. And whether or not they can themselves be regarded as pornographic, they present in literary form a model for subsequent pornography, in that they chiefly comprise a catalogue of transgressive acts presented with the minimum of aesthetic adornment.

As in contemporary porn, the episodic sex becomes more extreme and elaborate as the protagonists approach climax. That said, the writings of de Sade descend to levels of cruelty and violence which would not be accepted (or legal) in contemporary visual pornography.

His libertine delight in cruelty and the torture of vulnerable innocents is today most echoed not in pornography but in the 'torture porn' movies of those such as Eli Roth (*Hostel*, 2005; *Hostel II*, 2007) and Tom Six (*The Human Centipede*, 2009; *The Human Centipede II: Full Sequence*, 2011). They are echoed too in Bret Easton Ellis' controversial novel *American Psycho* (1991) which can be read as an adaptation of the

Sadeian worldview and aesthetic to late 1980s America, and its 'greed is good' yuppie culture of entitlement and licensed excess. Patrick Bateman, like the protagonists in de Sade's writings, perceives himself to be morally superior to ordinary humanity, and thus not bound by social conventions and moral constraints. He tortures and kills because he can, and because it is his pleasure that counts above the suffering of others.

Not all sexually explicit writings of early modernity were 'sadistic' in nature, of course. There were many more straightforwardly dirty books, transgressive in their depictions of sexually insatiable nuns and the like, but lacking the cruelty and violence of the Marquis' vision, and clearly intended to deliver sexual pleasure rather than disrupt elite power. There was also political pornography which, if not provocatively violent and amoral in the manner of *120 Days of Sodom*, nevertheless portrayed aristocracy and theocracy as corrupt, decadent forces in early bourgeois society.

In these works explicit sexuality became a means of mockery and ultimately a tool of revolution, stripping bare as they did the pretensions of inherited or divinely ordained power, revealing its holders to be lascivious, carnal beings like the rest of us (Hunt, 1993). Amanda Foreman's biography of Georgiana, Duchess of Devonshire in the late eighteenth century, recounts how the flamboyant and high-profile aristocrat was frequently subjected to this kind of sexually profane satire (1998).

Pornography and mass culture

Returning to our analogy with journalism, we observe that the invention of print created the conditions for the emergence of a bourgeois pornosphere, more accessible and expansive than that which existed in the scribal culture of the pre-Gutenberg age but still exclusive, and limited by access to wealth and education. The sexually explicit works of Aretino, de Sade, and their counterparts in other countries, could be consumed only by the wealthy and the literate, and in the days before public education became a norm of capitalist social organisation that was only a small minority of the population.

As with journalism, the beginnings of a truly mass pornosphere required, in addition to the availability of cheap printed texts the arrival of mass literacy, a process associated with the social reform movements of the nineteenth century. As the lower middle-classes and working classes learnt to read and write in the nineteenth century, popular newspapers developed to service their demand for content. 'Yellow' journalism became the commonly used term for what was later known as tabloid journalism, connoting distasteful, unwholesome content of potential danger to polite society.

Pornography also circulated in the expanding mass medium of print for the first time, amidst sectors of the population previously excluded from its consumption, bringing with it heightened elite anxiety and the determination to police that consumption. Hence the 'secret museums', which housed texts and images deemed dangerous to the extent that they could be accessed by mass readerships. Explicit books such as John Benjamin Brookes' *The Lustful Turk* (1828) circulated widely in the late nineteenth century. And then came photography.

The first 'hard core' photograph is dated to 1846, a few years after Louis Daguerre invented the first commercially viable photographic process.[12] In accordance with the pattern established with the invention of print and all subsequent waves of communication technology, sexually explicit images were among the first applications of photography. Artists used it from the outset to create 'classic' nude studies for paintings, while early pornographers used it to create sexualised images which for the first time fused the representation of sexual activity with its physical reality. Photographs depicted things and people who actually existed, as opposed to being merely invented in the imagination of the artist. They were pornography, in my definition, because they were made with the aim of sexual arousal (which may not have been true of a photograph of a nude woman intended, let's say, to assist an artist in his work).

The pornographic repertoire seen in photography was not substantially different from that seen in the lithographs and engravings of an earlier age, but the involvement of real human beings in their production brought something qualitatively new to the experience of consumption. Because here in the picture, naked and posing, or fucking, was a real person, or persons. This sex had actually happened, as opposed to being conjured up by an author or a visual artist. The scenes were staged for the camera, of course, and thus in an important sense not 'real' or true (in the same way that reality TV is something other than 'real'). But they involved real people, having real sex, and presumably real orgasms as they did so, thus creating the conditions for a much closer connection between voyeur and object.

The human eye reads the photographic image as real in a way that can never be true of a painting or drawing. The illusion of automaticity is overwhelming, the maker of the image invisible. In Courbet's *Origin Of The World* (1866) – sometimes seen as a protoypical pornographic text (see Chapter 8) – we see in full frontal display the vagina and torso of a naked woman, so realistic in its style that the work still has the capacity to provoke shock and censorial outrage, but above all we see the artist, and his individual vision. The painting is a Courbet before it is anything else. The scene may be sexual, but it is no more than a construction of oil and canvas, conceived from the memory and observational powers of the artist. In a photograph, on the other hand, although there is construction and mediation (the image is two dimensional, the colour is chemically processed, the size and scale are not of the actual physical world) it appears to the naked eye that the image has been captured rather than constructed. Someone has pushed a button and recorded a scene. Human subjectivity has been replaced by mechanics.

This new relationship between pornography and its user was heightened further with the invention of moving image photography in 1888, and the subsequent development of film and cinema. The apparent realism of the photograph combines with the illusion of seamless movement as thousands of individual images race through a projector and onto a flat surface. As with print and photography, the technology of film was quickly applied to the production of pornographic texts, such as the early French examples collected in *The Good Old Naughty Days* (Michel

Reilhac, 2002). These 'stag reels', as the short, silent porn film came to be known, were typically viewed in men-only settings such as gentlemen's clubs and brothels. They reflect the fashions of the era in dress, etiquette and body type – lots of beards, pot bellies and pubic hair on display, for example – but otherwise remind us of contemporary porn in the repertoire of activities and practices they depict. As the film's compiler noted in an interview to promote the release, 'the modern porn industry did not invent anything – everything had already been filmed by our great-grandparents'.[13]

The expansion or 'massification' of the pornosphere proceeds in stages from this point, driven by the introduction of the facility for cheap photographic printing, then colour images, glossy magazines and videos. The impact of each phase of development in communication technology was to widen access to the pornographic, simply by making porn texts cheaper and easier to obtain. Magazines such as *Playboy* and its harder successors such as *Hustler* date from the 1950s, while pornographic films began to be shown in 'adult' cinemas from the late 1960s, with the iconic *Deep Throat* released in 1972 (see next chapter). 'Hard core' glossy magazines were circulating widely in the 1970s and 1980s.

In the 1970s video recording technology removed the great limitation of filmic porn – that it required access to tape reels and projectors to be viewed – not inexpensive items even in the late twentieth century. For the vast majority of consumers, viewing moving image pornography before the introduction of the VCR meant going out of the home and into the X-rated cinema, the 'red light zone' of shame and reputational risk. As illustrated by the scene in *Taxi Driver* (Martin Scorsese, 1976) where Travis Bickle (Robert De Niro) takes his naïve young girlfriend Betsy (Cybil Shepherd) to a porn movie in New York, this was not an environment where women were expected to be seen, or were likely to feel comfortable. After the introduction of domestic video technology in the late 1970s and 1980s the consumption of pornographic movies became something which could be done within the privacy of the domestic space, as was already possible with magazines and books. One still had to go out of the home to purchase the material, or have it mailed (which in some jurisdictions involved breaking the law, of course, and risked serious negative consequences), but using it for masturbation became a private, isolated activity which could be undertaken in secret. The production of pornography for one's own use also became a practical possibility for the average person (as opposed to the hobbyist who might have access to the production of home movies in 8mm format, and was able to develop sexually explicit film in safety), a scenario depicted in Paul Schrader's *Autofocus* (2004). This film is based on the true story of US TV star Bob Crane, who in the late 1970s became an early adopter of the first home video cameras and players. Schrader's story documents the birth of the home video era in the United States, and its liberating power in respect of who could produce what, pornographically speaking.

The introduction of cable and satellite distribution systems in many societies around this time enabled the emergence of subscription channels dedicated to pornography, including material accessed from outside a given national jurisdiction and which thus evaded local censorship rules. Now, and with video players adding to the range of possibilities, pornography could for a small outlay be watched on an ordinary TV set. Conveniently, in 1968 the landmark Miller versus California case gave pornography legal protection under the first Amendment on the basis that 'any media that portrays adults engaged in consensual sexual activity would not be considered obscene by community standards based on its popular consumption' (Ferguson and Hartley, 2009, p.324). This decision allowed the emergence of a legal porn industry in the United States, at the same time as the invention of the VCR and the spread of cable enabled the domestication of pornography within the private sphere.

The networked pornosphere

Let us turn now to the single most important influence on the structure of the pornosphere since the invention of photography – the internet. Throughout the 1990s pornography drove the expansion of the internet, allowing (like video and cable, but with even greater ease) access to images which were much more explicit than local censorship regimes allowed. By 2002 it was estimated that around four million Britons were logging on to porn sites each month.[14] Pornography also drove the evolution of technologies for secure and reliable online payment which are now used for the sale and purchase of many goods other than sexually explicit ones, as depicted in the film *Middle Men* (George Gallo, 2010 – see next chapter). Companies such as Adult Check and Cybernet were making up to $320 million annually as of 2001 from paid-for porn services, facilitated by payment services such as Paycom and CCBill.[15]

The impact of the internet on the pornosphere is, once again, analogous to that of the trends seen in the public sphere since 1994 and the establishment of the internet as a mass medium (Bruns, 2008; Burgess, 2009). Pornography, like journalism, has become part of a global digital network (Johnson, 2010) comprising a mix of professional/corporate producers and amateurs, where the producer-consumer boundary is blurred and the power of the state to control the flow of pornographic texts is eroded. The internet respects no barriers of time and space, enabling instantaneous access for billions of people the world over to a vast quantity of information of all kinds, including pornography.

At present (although access to the internet is increasing rapidly all the time, not least in the developing countries of Africa, Asia and Latin America) the globalised pornosphere is limited to those in possession of the necessary technology – a computer and an internet connection. Users do not require a censorship regime liberal enough to permit their access to pornography, although this naturally makes their lives easier, because wherever in the world the internet has penetrated, and regardless of the severity of the penalties imposed by governments for accessing pornography, it *is* accessed online, in Iran, Saudi Arabia, China, albeit at great risk to the consumer (Jacobs, 2011). As a result pornographic consumption (and production) has become, whatever else it is, a gesture of defiance to authoritarian regimes who seek to deprive their subjects of individual freedom and choice (see Chapter 9).

Just as the internet liberated political speech and imagery from the confines of national cultures and customs by introducing the globalised digital network, so it globalised sexual speech, including the pornographic, and expanded its reach across, between, and within countries. One observer has described the digitised pornosphere as a 'capitalist web' within which 'online commercial pornography plays a pivotal role in maintaining the hegemony of both patriarchy and capitalism' (Johnson, 2010, p.152). It would be just as valid, however, to assert that the rise of the blogosphere and Google has had no impact on News Corporation, or that YouTube reinforces the 'hegemony' of the capitalist music industry. New media technologies have not ended capitalism, or patriarchy, but they have qualitatively changed the dynamics of power within these systems and, in the case of patriarchy, contributed to its ongoing transformation, not least in the sphere of sexual representation.

Citizen Porn & the democratisation of the pornosphere

Just as the emergence of the internet has enabled user-generated news content to gain unprecedented access to and visibility in the public sphere, a phenomenon captured in the familiar if misleading concept of citizen journalism,[16] so it has enabled a trend towards what we might call *citizen porn* – pornography made by enthusiastic amateurs armed with digital cameras and the facility to upload their video. Public participation and interactivity are features of digital communication generally, and in the porno-sphere no less. One may search for the category of 'amateur' in porn tubes[17] and find thousands of these videos, shot in grainy digicam, depicting their makers having sex. Kevin Smith's *Zack and Miri Make a Porno* (2009) takes this trend as its premise, in that two friends assemble the equipment and other resources required to produce their own pornographic video, which they hope will go viral on the internet and make them some money. Part of the porno chic movement discussed in the next chapter, Smith's film also illustrates just how mainstream and uncontroversial the idea of do-it-yourself pornography had become by the end of that decade.

As Hodgkinson notes above, the desire for DIY porn is not in itself new. Perhaps the early cave paintings of sexual activity were made with this motivation. In Peter Weir's tale of life in a Soviet prison camp one artistically inclined prisoner survives by drawing naked women for the prison thugs (*The Long Walk*, 2011). Ever since the invention of photography people have been capturing themselves. Polaroid photo-graphy encouraged this trend, by removing the need to send one's photos to a developer. So did VCR and digital video, both of which enabled people to create and view without third party involvement moving images of their sex lives, usually for private consumption. The advent of the internet, however, made the products of these DIY enthusiasts newly available to the global online network, where they could be viewed, shared, copied for the voyeuristic pleasure of others, in the same way that content is increasingly shared around social networking platforms such as Facebook, Twitter and Google+. Noting the trend in 2002, Libby Brooks of the *Guardian* observed that 'the making and misappropriation of intimate videos has regularly proved a compelling creative device' utilised by celebrities and non-celebrities alike, who have 'extended the parameters of what constitutes acceptable-consensual-sexual experimentation'.[18] 'Women are quite heavily involved', she continued, 'subverting the notion that women's erotic power can only be located in their role as paid-for sexual objects, rather than as active sexual subjects'.[19]

> The camcorder is providing people with a safe and satisfying method of reclaiming and recreating public images of sex for their private pleasure. And with that comes a better understanding of the potential of desire – that we might transform ourselves into anyone and anything.

Such understanding does not require that the whole online world be able to access one's private pleasurings, of course. But the existence of the internet makes possible what was perhaps always part of the pleasure of this type of porn – that others could watch and share one's experience, spectators in the process of sexual self-identification and expression. In this sense the explosion of user-generated pornography can be characterised as a democratisation of the pornosphere, in the same way that the use of social networks to share mobile phone footage of police brutality at an Iranian pro-reform demonstration is a democratisation of the public sphere. In both cases, the capacity to produce content and have it accessed by global publics represents an enhancement of popular power, an erosion of the traditional elite hold on the means of intellectual and cultural production. Not all DIY porn is welcome to everyone, and as with pornography in general, one is not required to defend everything the globalised pornosphere makes possible in order to argue that the loss of elite control over sexual discourse is a positive, progressive trend. Citizen porn may be crude and messy (in more ways than one). It may be misogynistic. A lot of what circulates on the internet is distasteful or offensive, such as racist hate speech, religious extremism, online bullying and stalking. But democrats welcome the onset of the digital revolution nonetheless, and for good reason. The benefits for human society of the internet far outweigh the costs of free internet speech.

This calculation applies equally to the realm of sexual speech. Child pornography, for example, is made easier to produce and share with the DIY and networking technologies we have explored in this section. But that is no reason to shut down the net, or to criminalise adult pornography, made for and by consenting adults. As Operation Ore and many other transnational policing initiatives have shown, it is quite easy to identify and close down paedophile porn networks where they exist, and many hundreds of people who have used digital tools to make or access child porn have been convicted.

The de-heterosexualisation of the pornosphere

The evolution of the pornosphere, like that of the public sphere, has been a process shaped by the socio-economic structure of the times and places in which it has occurred. Access to the pornosphere has for most of its history been restricted to the wealthy male elites of capitalist societies, and the pornography circulating in the pornosphere has been made principally for them. The perception that pornography is a heterosexual male preserve, bound up with patriarchy, has not been inaccurate. The same could be said of most other forms of culture, of course, but in the case of pornography the confluence of patriarchal power and heterosexual male pleasure has endowed this form in particular with a much-criticised role in the subordination of women. Like much advertising of a 'sexist' kind, straight male porn came to be indexical of patriarchy in ways that sexist cinema, literature or drama never did.

As the pornosphere has expanded however, and been digitised, there has been a structural transformation in which the range of those sexual communities and groups accessing it, and contributing to it, has also broadened. Put simply, the consumption of mediated sexuality, of pornography, can now be seen as a practice which not only straight men engage in (see Chapter 6). That they largely monopolised access to sexually explicit culture for the first four centuries of the pornosphere reflects, not some essential or biologically-determined maleness, but men's socio-economic domination, and the associated cultural taboos on women participating in sexual consumption (other than as sellers of services, of course – prostitution being the oldest profession). Only with the rise of feminism and its colonisation of mainstream discourse and culture in the late 1980s and into the 1990s could women safely declare themselves to be interested in the pornosphere, not merely as critics and scrutineers, but as willing participants (Moran, 2011). As the political economy of desire was transformed by feminist politics, pornography lost its straight male exclusivity.

New technologies of pornographic production and consumption – the internet especially – have opened up access to the pornosphere to women, allowing desire to be translated into consumption. Accessing sexually explicit material became an activity which could be practised in the privacy and security of the domestic environment, without the requirement to go outside the home and visit an X-rated cinema, or trawl the red light zones of cities in search of magazines or videos to purchase. In short, with the emergence of the internet it became easier to access pornography while escaping the social stigmas which had hitherto been associated with it, even for straight men. The same transformation occurred with respect to homosexuals, and to the variety of paraphilias and fetishes which had always existed within a given human society, but had not hitherto found expression in easily accessible sexual imagery. Writing of the Nordic countries, but with general application, Susanna Paasonen observes that 'as porn distribution increasingly shifted online, the accessability of a virtually endless range of niches, tastes and kinks rendered conventional forms of regulation ineffective and impossible to maintain' (2009, p.591). Katrien Jacobs observes similarly that in recent years 'digital media networks have allowed women and queer groups to develop and distribute their own types of sexually explicit media and to create niche industries' (2011, p.186). She cites the example of *Big Beautiful Women* (BBW), a sub-genre of online porn in which overweight women 'present themselves as privileged objects of desire'.

One can find in the digitised pornosphere, for example, a sub-category of 'alt porn' which depicts women (and men) adorned with tattoos, piercings, scars and other emblems of alternative lifestyles.[20] Susanna Paasonen illustrates the diversity of the contemporary pornosphere with her 2009 essay on 'sneaker porn' – images in which, yes, sneakers are endowed with sexual resonance. Elsewhere she observes that 'the proliferation of alternative, independent, queer, artistic and amateur pornographies on the internet has given subcultural products and tastes unprecedented visibility' (2007, p.161). Overall, 'the body of "mainstream porn" leaks towards niches and paraphilias, incorporates them and becomes transformed in the process' (Ibid., p.163). Katrien Jacobs' study of pornography in China, Taiwan and Hong Kong notes of the latter that 'pornography has moved away from a male-oriented consumer market and has become a medium for other user groups such as women and queers to define sexual selves' (2011, p.19).

There is also a growing body of pornography intended for consumption by older people, disabled people, and other sexually marginalised groups. In 2011 the growing diversity of the pornosphere was illustrated by a news report about Shigeo Tokuda, a 77-year-old Japanese porn star described as 'the unlikely face of a brand of Japanese blue movie that taps into the country's fast changing demographics'.[21] Porn films featuring older actors, went the story, are an expanding sub-sector of the industry in Japan. 'Silver porn' is estimated to account for some 20 per cent of the Japanese porn market as a whole, servicing that fifth of the population now over the age of 65.

The pornosphere had then, by the end of the 2000s, been diversified, democratised, and de-heterosexualised by the power of communication technology on the one hand, and the impact of progressive sexual politics on the other. Gay men have been using pornography for decades of course, and before the gay rights movement made its first advances in the west, sexually explicit material for gay men (and women) was playing an important role in the articulation of sexual identity and the gratification of gay desire (Mowlacobus, 2007) This reminds us of Linda Williams' assertion that 'pornography produced by, and featuring, sexual minorities, could provide a political response to the misogynistic and aggressive pornography of the mainstream market, offering a platform for the discussion of non-oppressive sexual practices and identities' (1990, p.64). This educational, performative function of the pornographic is enhanced in the online era, where 'the consumer can access non-normative pornographies with unparalleled ease and comparatively little investment'. Mowlabocus accepts that 'perhaps it is too much to expect of pornography that it undermine and dismantle the binaries of homo/hetero, male/female and active/passive, but the possibility at least is there, and the internet has made this possibility far more tangible' (2007). Simon Hardy argues similarly that:

> pornography, in its many forms, has always claimed to reflect the truth of human sexuality, and has serviced a desire to see that truth represented. But it has also been claimed that pornography distorts that truth or that it represents only some aspects of sexuality; male, heterosexual, limiting. Now media technologies are making it possible for a far greater range of human sexual experience to be reflected.
>
> *(2009, p.15)*

The globalised pornosphere is a democratised pornosphere, therefore, not just in expanding access to sexual discourse in general, but in the space it provides for previously marginalised or excluded identities and communities to have their sex-ualities represented. It is, like the globalised public sphere, a segmented structure comprising a wide variety of niche tastes and desires. Straight male pornography does still comprise the greatest part of the pornosphere, as Big Media content dominates the global public sphere, but in the digital environment there is room for any number of alternative sub-spheres. The internet is rich with porn for straight women, gay porn for both men and women, porn for all manner of perversions, kinks and fet-ishes. For some this is evidence of cultural degeneration. For those who believe that freedom of expression of sexuality is a human right, or ought to be, even if it has been historically monopolised by heterosexual men in patriarchy, it is significant progress.

It is worth noting at this point that these trends have led to a decline in the sale of traditional forms of straight male pornography. In April 2002 it was being reported that Bob Guccione's General Media International, the company which published *Penthouse* magazine, was on the verge of bankruptcy. Challenged by the rise of the internet on the one hand, with its ease of access to more explicit images than *Penthouse* could provide, and the 'lad mags' on the other (*Loaded*, *Nuts*, and others, with their reshaping of the male style culture ethos), magazines like *Penthouse* were in steep decline. Guccione's company blamed its troubles on 'the change in social climate towards men's magazines, together with certain advances in electronic technology, including the proliferation of retail video outlets and the increased market share of cable television and the internet'.[22] The *Guardian* concluded that *Penthouse*'s troubles were a consequence of 'the proliferation of more explicit images on television, videos and the internet'.[23] Between 1997 and 2001 sales of the magazine fell by one third to 700,000 (from a peak of seven million in the 1970s). When hard core pornography was increasingly easy to access on the internet, consumers, it seemed, were becoming reluctant to pay good money for soft core. In 2003, with circulation now down to 530,000, General Media International filed for bankruptcy in the US. Even lads' mags such as *Loaded*, *Maxim* and *FHM*, which had led the magazine market in the 1990s, began to see their circulations decline. *FHM* dropped from 717,000 to 571,000 sales in the UK in 2001–2. *Loaded*'s circulation fell by 12.1 per cent in the same period.[24] Nostalgia and retro-chic notwithstanding, the decline of good old fashioned sexist culture can be regarded as one of the reasons why pornography has changed the world for the better (see Part II), if indeed the heterosexism of tradi-tional pornography has been a major reason for the condemnation of the form by feminist critics.

Conclusion

By 2005, with the critical praise heaped on *Inside Deep Throat*, a documentary about the notorious 1972 film which produced the first wave of porno chic (see next chapter) it could be observed that an end may be in sight for hardcore porn's 30-year long march from the sticky-floored fleapit to near respectability. Porn is a thriving mainstream industry whose financial returns compare to those of the music and movie industries. The industry itself is never going to be mainstream in the full sense, but its subterranean reach is broad and deep. Porn may still lurk in the shadowy fringes of the mainstream, but *Inside Deep Throat* is more evidence of its slow, steady progress into the light.[25]

McKee *et al.* in their study of pornography in Australia note in passing that:

Today, pornography is downloadable from millions of websites. It has become one of the most successful global media industries ... A growing number of young women consume pornography, often with their partners. More people are making their own porn and sharing it online. There is also far more pornography than ever before in the range of sexual acts and fantasies being catered for ... there is now a far wider range of pornography being made by women for women that is careful not to parody them as mere objects for indiscriminate male pleasure.

(2008, p.21)

As Zoe Williams puts it:

There probably hasn't been a time in history, no pause for breath in the segue from patriarchal consideration of decency to a feminist crusade against objectification, when pornography has been considered as acceptable as it is now.[26]

Companies devoted to the distribution of pornography in hotels and other spaces have benefitted from the increased tolerance of, and demand for pornography. In 2002 one observer noted that:

porn is certainly profitable, but there are signs that it is also becoming respectable, at least as a legitimate investment vehicle. Most of the distributors of pornography are household names, including all the national telecom operators, cable and satellite TV firms, broadband networks and hotel chains. One of the most complete victories in the fight for free expression has also been one of the least heralded: We now live in a world of ubiquitous and infinitely varied pornography. Forty years ago, porn – however defined – was not only relatively tough to find, it was relatively homogenous and restrained in its manifestations.[27]

Not so anymore. As *The Wall Street Journal*'s Business columnist, Holman W. Jenkins Jr., observed in the conservative journal *Policy Review* in 2010 'porn has moved out of a few segregated public spaces, the seedy book shops and triple-X theaters, and become ubiquitous on the web, on cable, in neighborhood video shops.'

Paradoxically, porn is more available than ever, yet less of a public issue … the result might be called John Stuart Mill's wet dream, combining the philosopher's penchant for 'experiments in living' with his defense of a maximized private sphere in which consenting adults are mostly free to do as they please.[28]

The next chapter explores the impact of that transformation on non-pornographic culture.

3

PORNO? CHIC!

I think it's imperative for the good of society that we should all strive to make porn a treat. This has been especially challenging for me as I write this book because, of course, I am at home at my desk, on my lap top, at all times one click away from watching people fuck – and in the most fascinating, shocking ways.

(Sarah Silverman, 2010, p.97)

This chapter explores the colonisation of mainstream culture – its *pornographication* (McNair, 1996, 2002)[1] – by texts in a variety of cultural forms, genres and styles which borrow from, refer to, or pastiche the styles and iconography of the pornographic; which are often referred to under the umbrella term of *porno chic*.

Porno chic is *not* the pornography which fills the pornosphere, nor is it necessarily erotic in form or function. While some forms of porno chic *may* seek to appropriate the eroticism of pornography, and thus to be sexy or arousing to their target audience (and perhaps sexually transgressive in the context of the space where they appear), this is not their defining characteristic or essential *raison d'etre*. Porno chic, as I use the term, is not necessarily celebratory or approving of pornography. On the contrary, there is a sub-category which references porn chiefly for the purposes of condemnation or critique. The UK Channel 4 documentary *Hard Core* (Stephen Walker, 2001),[2] about the US pornographer Max Hardcore, was in this category, as in a more nuanced way was *Pornography: The Musical* (Brian Hill, 2003), also first shown on Channel 4. Both presented on mainstream free-to-air TV what were relatively explicit accounts of the porn industry, but in a context of critical commentary.

Why define such texts as porno chic? Because their existence is a measure of the emergence into mainstream visibility and popular consciousness of pornography. Porno chic need not be pro-porn, in other words (although most examples will be, if not explicitly approving of porn, at least non-judgemental). Porno chic can be characterised as the echo, or shadow, of the low culture form of pornography in non-pornographic cultural spaces, including those of art, pop, journalism, fashion and academia. In porno chic pornography sheds its status as unambiguous trash – as the 'pariah of representational practices' (Ellis, 1992, p.158) – to be associated instead with a variety of other cultural forms such as comedy, news and entertainment, sometimes in the context of sex-political campaigning and protest, not to mention higher education and the scholarly discourse of books such as this one.

Porno chic can aspire to be funny, or trendy (literally, chic), or politically and morally subversive, as well as educational and informative about sexuality and the erotic. Porno chic is, from that perspective, an exemplary form of post-modern culture – one manifestation of the late twentieth century's rise of mass culture and the associated breakdown of high/low culture distinctions associated with modernity.[3]

Porno chic assumes that pornography is familiar to and widely understood by the mainstream audience. Not only that, it assumes, in most of its forms (though not all, as noted) that pornography is no longer a cultural pariah, a taboo mode of representation, stigmatised and shameful in its consumption, but legitimate (or verging on legitimacy, if still edgy enough to be transgressive). It assumes that there is something fascinating about pornography, and attractive to media audiences. In 2005, for example, a musical adaptation of the iconic porn movie *Debbie Does Dallas* toured the world. An Australian observer noted that 'it is not the actresses who are being exploited here, but the very notion of pornography itself, as the show cashes in on the genre's hard-core image without ever delivering the money shot'.[4]

Why is porno chic?

Although, as the previous chapter showed, the pornosphere has expanded dramatically since Aretino's *Postures* and the beginnings of what we today call pornography, the form retains a taboo quality, a paradox which largely explains its 'chic-ness'. To consume pornography is still, despite its enhanced visibility and accessibility, an activity constrained by prevailing societal expectations of what is and is not appropriate sexual behaviour. Masturbation, to state it simply, remains for many a symbol of moral weakness, if no longer outright perversion. If the force of the taboo against masturbation has weakened greatly in recent times, it remains a stigmatised act from childhood up, particularly for females (Kaestle and Allen, 2011; Hogarth and Ingham, 2009).

The film *Middle Men* (George Gallo, 2010), about the early days of the online porn industry, opens with a refreshingly direct statement of this cultural ambivalence. In monologue the main character (played by Luke Baldwin) describes the significance of the porn industry thus:

> The porn industry takes in $57 billion a year worldwide, with no-one ever admitting that they watch. This is going on every second of every day, all over the world. Gone are the days of trips to seedy book stores in the dead of night, or hiding in the adult section of your local video store, or waiting for a plain brown paper-wrapped package to arrive in the mail. Everything you want to

see is there in your home or your office, twenty four hours a day, and it's ready when you are. Discreetly, privately, in whatever flavour you choose.

Not only that:

Every guy, gay or straight, prince or pauper, every last one of them [is] sneaking off somewhere and whacking [masturbating].

And quite a few gals, one might add. While there is substantial evidence to show that a significant minority, if not the majority, of adults in advanced liberal democracies have used or do use pornography – see Chapters 5 and 6 – many of them, if not all, continue to feel that their use is embarrassing or shameful. When in 2009 the British Home Secretary's husband was found to be accessing pornography on cable TV the UK press had a field day of scandalised recrimination. Yes, the cable TV subscription package had been claimed as an expense by the MP in question, which gave the scandal journalistic legitimacy in the context of growing public disquiet around MPs' use of taxpayers' money to support their lifestyles. But the vision of spousal porn use, within the household of the minister responsible for law and order (including the laws governing porn, which at that time were being toughened in controversial ways), gave the story a voyeuristic, moralistic quality that many examples of MPs misusing their expense allowances in much worse ways never acquired.

Perhaps the most interesting element of the Jacqui Smith story lay in the fact that the Labour Home Secretary had hitherto been, like most of her predecessors, a vocal critic of pornography, basing her opposition on familiar anti-porn feminist arguments (see Chapter 4).[5] That her husband, meanwhile, should be accessing, and presumably masturbating to cable porn while she was out of the room seemed to capture the dishonesty and hypocrisy which routinely surrounds the issue – public condemnation, private consumption; say one thing, do another. Porn use is commonplace, even in the Home Secretary's household. Being caught at it is still grounds for moral opprobrium, however. As a consequence, very few people will admit to using pornography unless their anonymity is assured, as in McKee *et al.*'s study of Australian porn use (2008).

The survival of porn's taboo status in liberal democracies can be attributed largely to the power or 'memetic memory' of religion, even as it is recognised that the Christian churches have lost much of their traditional authority. Lapsed Catholics, for example, may still retain a sense of the sinfulness of masturbation, and the images used to facilitate it which defies rationality and logic in modern environmental conditions, but is so deeply ingrained in the culture that it is hard to shake off. The venality of porn, in short, is precisely what makes it attractive in many cases. Even those who do not live in fear of hellfire may derive from deep in their subconscious a thrill at the illicit promise of sexual gratification offered by pornography, a sense that they are challenging a higher power, defying moral authority. As we shall see in Chapter 8 on the aesthetics of sexual transgression, the erotic power of transgression fuels the work of many great artists who have dealt with sex as a subject. That the same force should motivate the masturbation of millions of porn users is hardly surprising.

Apart from the taboo which derives from porn's apparent violation of moral values (however tenuous and contested those values have become in recent decades), the innate intimacy of sexuality must also be regarded as a probable source of porn's continuing marginalisation in the shadow realm of the pornosphere. Sex is often talked about in reality TV, daytime talk shows and other popular media formats (McNair, 2010). Many people use sexual commodities and aids, including pornography, but nonetheless feel inhibition and shyness in publicly addressing these topics with the directness one might apply to discussions of foreign policy or law and order. Those spaces in culture where sex and porn *are* talked about, therefore, retain a quality of transgressivity which is attractive because it is still, and notwithstanding the liberalisation of sexual culture which is one of the pre-conditions of porno chic, boundary-breaking.

The prevalence of porno chic in the late twentieth and early twenty-first century – its evident appeal as a set of cultural forms which in various ways relate to porn, but are not in themselves pornographic – reflects a transitional phase in sexual culture, where pornography is 'out' but not yet proud, still edgy and rebellious. If and when this phase ever ends, and the consumption of pornography becomes so 'normal' that there is no longer any novelty or transgression involved, this will perhaps be when the concept of porno chic ceases to have resonance (and indeed the concept of pornography itself, as it has been understood for centuries).

For now, however, the taboo remains, expressed not as a strictly enforced law but as a shared social expectation, or etiquette. And in that context, still, porno chic appeals as a cultural strategy to artists, as we see below and later in Chapter 8, because art has always been, to a great extent, a site of transgression where boundaries are crossed and taboos violated. Art at its most powerful breaks the rules, almost by definition, creating space for social and cultural evolution. If pornography has been and remains a societal danger-zone – a red-light zone – artists have appropriated its riskiness and capacity for outrage and continue to do so.

Advertisers, on the other hand, have always found that sex sells, and the phrase is one of the most commonplace truisms of our times. The Dunlop corporation fused the Velvet Underground's hymn to sexual fetishism, *Femme Fatale*, with an S&M-themed short film to sell car tyres (McNair, 1996). S&M chic may be regarded as a sub-set of porno chic, referring to a particular sexuality, but one which is familiar to the broader culture and can thus be referred to in confidence that the connotation will be understood. Ads that refer to pornography by simulating its look, as many campaigns have done, therefore play to a cultural knowingness about the marketing appeal of sex in general and, in the era of the expanded pornosphere, of pornography in particular.

Journalists and news editors like porn because it presents an opportunity to talk about sex, perhaps scandalously or disapprovingly, while at the same time showing images of scantily-clad women. In *Mediated Sex* (1996) I showed the rising curve in the number of press articles about pornography in the US and the UK from the late

1980s. I myself subsequently contributed a number of press pieces to newspapers in my home country, Scotland, which explored the phenomenon of porno chic.[6] Editors commissioned these with some enthusiasm, knowing that their readers were fascinated by the subject, if perhaps reluctant to concede to being actual users of porn. With the aid of a photo of Madonna in sexualised performance, or supermodel Sophie Dahl in the nude alongside, even scholarly commentary on sex sold newspapers, and still does.

Academics and scholars are drawn to porn, and contribute to the literature in porn studies (a form of porno chic, as I have defined it) because it is still relatively new terrain, and thus a fertile field for the exploration of culture, sexuality, sexual politics and many other topics. Moreover, it remains a little risky, especially for a man, who may well be accused of harbouring ulterior motives in his interest.[7]

The academic sub-field of porn studies (a branch of cultural studies, gender studies, sociology and media studies) has expanded significantly since the 1990s, with much of the most interesting work coming from women who, like the pop-culture figures discussed later in Chapter 6, self-identify as feminist but reject the anti-porn feminist orthodoxy which dominated research and writing on the subject for decades (Williams, ed., 2004).

For female scholars there is evident appeal in remaking an established field, characterised by a conservative consensus, with a new set of arguments about the nature of female sexuality and its relationship to the pornographic – arguments which the very achievements of feminism have for the first time made credible in the context of mainstream, public debate. Feona Attwood, Clarissa Smith, Susanna Paasonen, Lauren Rosewarne and many others typify this movement, and one sees in their writing an energy and intellectual excitement which perhaps derives from the fact that they are breaking boundaries which have been, and still are in some quarters, fiercely policed.

They too are transgressors, although they represent a growing proportion of the female scholarly community, and are rapidly becoming mainstream with their assumption that women are interested in sex as much, and in many of the same ways, as men, and that this interest includes the pornographic representation of sexual activity for the purpose of arousal and masturbation. These writers have decisively broken with the reflex anti-porn feminism which had dominated study of the form since the late 1970s, and insist on the right to consider its forms and functions without the obligation to denounce its effects.[8]

If the reasons for porno being chic are not difficult to understand, then, let's now consider the nature of this cultural category in more detail: the dual meanings of the term, and some key moments in the brief history of the form.

What is porno chic? Part I

The term *porno chic* dates from 1973, and has had two meanings, associated with two distinct waves in the sexualisation of western culture.

The first, covering a few brief years in the late 1960s and early to mid-1970s, and thus best read as a by-product of the sexual revolution, refers to the infiltration or migration of *actual* pornography into mainstream American culture, with the release of the film *Deep Throat* (Gerard Damiano, 1972). This was the event that led to the coining of the term 'porno chic' in a 1973 article by journalist Ralph Blumenthal in *The New York Times*.[9] Blumenthal drew attention to the growing visibility of pornography outside the adult or red-light zones of X-rated cinemas where it had hitherto resided, and the apparent acceptance of the sexually explicit *Deep Throat* by a mainstream, otherwise 'normal' audience of cinema-goers including courting couples, men and women of the cloth, and senior citizens eager to find out for themselves what the fuss being generated by this Linda Lovelace and the movie in which she starred was all about.

Deep Throat, let's be clear, *was* pornography, in the fully unexpurgated sense – scripted and intentionally comic, but sexually explicit, full of vaginal, anal and oral penetration, and come or 'money' shots in which nothing was hidden from the viewer. In this context, the first iteration of the *porno chic* concept is a literal reference – *porno* had suddenly become *chic*, and publicly accessible, in that 1970s New York nightclub sense captured by the disco band Chic later in the decade.

That porno could be chic was news in 1973, because pornography had never been fashionable or tolerated in mainstream culture before. Suddenly it was, for reasons linked to the sexual revolution of the 1960s in America. From the 1950s onwards, through the emergence of teen culture and sexualised icons such as Elvis Presley, the launch of *Playboy* and other sexually explicit publications aimed at the ordinary guy rather than the stereotypically perverse porn hound, sexual culture in the western world as a whole was steadily liberalised, culminating in the phenomenon of *Deep Throat* and the broad popular interest it provoked.

Deep Throat's mainstream cinema distribution in American cities was particularly significant because it was *hard core* pornography as defined by Linda Williams (1990), more explicit than the soft core *Playboy*, which had been in circulation since 1953, and the more explicit if still not fully 'hard core' *Hustler* published by Larry Flynt as a provocation to Hugh Hefner's sanitised (as Flynt saw it) and hypocritically tame magazine.[10] The film was no less explicit than the stag reels to be found in adult theatres and peep shows of the time. While the latter were fenced off and restricted to the red-light zones, *Deep Throat* found a place in mainstream cinema culture – novel in its explicitness, but far from a cultural pariah. This normalisation was assisted by the perception of *Deep Throat* as a 'serious' film: one with scripts and a plot and professional production values, as opposed to the unadorned sexual activity of the short stag-reel format.

Deep Throat was not the first 'serious' porn movie of the type to which Paul Thomas Anderson pays homage in *Boogie Nights* (1997), his tale of the 1970s LA porn industry and the people who worked in it. There were others, less famous, before and after, such as *Mona* (Michael Benvenisite, Howard Ziehm, 1970) – described by one commentator as 'the blue print for 70s porn chic'[11] in that it was feature-length, and combined explicit sexual content with 'artistic' flourishes such as worked out dialogue and cinematography. Richard Corliss identifies *Pornography in Denmark* (Phyliss and Eberhard Kronhausen, 1969) as a significant moment in the pornographication of mainstream culture, representative as it was of a sub-genre of film presented as 'educational' while permitting explicit sexual images to be shown. But *Deep Throat* was the *first* film to be described as 'porno chic', becoming the symbol of a new cultural environment within which pornography could be accessed in public spaces without attracting automatic stigmatisation or moral outrage.[12]

In the following months and years other hard core films such as *Behind The Green Door* (Mitchell Brothers, 1972) were similarly accessible, and the plot of *Boogie Nights* focuses on this era of 'respectable' pornography, when directors and writers sought to make dirty movies that were at the same time credible as dramatic works. With hindsight they are rarely worth watching as drama, or comedy, although attempts have been made to treat them, and the soft core variants made later in the UK and elsewhere, as culturally significant works (Hunt, 1998; Williams, 2008). *Boogie Nights* itself treats this era of porn production with respect and affection, while making clear the futility of their makers' aesthetic pretensions. One can say that at least they were sincere, and notwithstanding Linda Lovelace's subsequent disowning of her work in *Deep Throat*, well-intentioned.[13] Given that the film industry as a whole has more than its share of bullies, tyrants and megalomaniacal directors, that there were some like that in the porn industry is hardly surprising. There were also many like the character played by Burt Reynolds in *Boogie Nights* – directors who saw themselves as artists and genuinely cared for the welfare of their employees.

As has been described in the extensive literature around the 'sex wars', a combination of anti-porn feminism and moral conservatism had, by the late 1970s, brought this first wave of porno chic to an end, and consigned pornography once again to the margins of mainstream culture. Pornography was defined by radical feminism of the Dworkin-MacKinnon school as the cultural essence of the patriarchal oppression of women, as propaganda for rape, and by moral conservatives as degenerate and obscene in its celebration of sexual promiscuity and experimentation. Not until the late 1980s, and the fragmentation of the feminist movement into pro- and anti-porn, and pro- and anti-censorship strands, did pornography again emerge from its status as cultural pariah. To this day it has never returned to mainstream channels of film distribution in the US or comparative countries. Hard core pornography of the *Deep Throat* type is still not to be found in mainstream cinemas, nor broadcast on free-to-air linear TV channels.

It *has* been available for decades on the adult zones of subscription cable and satellite TV channels, and on video, and now of course on the internet, as the previous chapter described, but not in the city-centre multiplexes of New York, London, Sydney or Tokyo. After *Deep Throat* and those few years of liberal indulgence of the truly pornographic, the form returned to the clearly designated 'Red Light' zones of cultural consumption, where it remains. At the same time, however, beginning in the late 1980s, pornography became 'chic' in another way – as a source of inspiration and commentary across a broad spectrum of cultural forms. That it did so, and has remained so for more than two decades, can be understood as one expression of sexual liberalisation in general, and an apparent desire amongst media consumers to talk about sex, and have sex talked about, in ways which were not possible before the maturation of the sex-political processes associated with feminism, gay rights and the sexual revolution. The rise of the second wave of porno chic reflects the evolution of societies becoming ever more comfortable with the public display and discussion of sex, and steadily more tolerant of diverse sexualities, nearly all of whom have had some use for and interest in porn which cannot be reduced to the 'propaganda of rape' paradigm.

What is porno chic? Part II

I have described the second wave of porno chic in some detail in previous work (McNair, 1996, 2002). Here I summarise and update those accounts to cover the period since 2002, and group the range of forms within this more recent meaning of porno chic into three categories, which I will characterise as: (a) the *playful*; (b) the *pedagogic* or *didactic*; and (c) the *metaphorical*.

Playing with the pornographic

First, and most recognisably, the second wave of porno chic includes all those cultural artefacts which are overtly inspired by and may aspire to look like pornography, even to the point of impersonating its sexually graphic, explicit qualities. These are works of homage to, or celebration of, the pornographic, which by their existence demonstrate the chic-ness and cultural fascination with pornography as a form with a distinct style and presence within the parent culture. Often they work with the language of pastiche, parody and humour, a strategy seen most commonly in advertising.

Where in the past advertisers often made crude use of the female body to sell all kinds of products which had nothing to do with sex as such – and were criticised for their objectification of women by feminist commentators – today they play to a postmodern culture where it is accepted that porn is part of the lives of millions of people, men and women, that it is both transgressive and absurd, funny and sexy, naughty and nice. Advertising styles and fashion movements which refer to porno-graphic dress and style codes, including those known by the related term of *S&M chic*, have included a 2000 TV advertisement for Grolsch lager, made with the cheesy *mise en scène* of the 1970s *Colour Climax*-style stag reel.[14] In the ad a moustachioed plumber comes to a suburban door, which is opened by a scantily clad housewife.

In 2005 the American Apparel clothing company produced a series of advertise-ments referring in their look to 1970s soft core pornography of the type found in magazines such as *Penthouse*, *Men Only* and *Playboy*. Not only that, they featured a real-life porn-star, Lauren Phoenix. In 2007 the Tom Ford fashion and perfume company produced a series of ads which were so sexually explicit that they provoked complaints to the UK's Advertising Standards Agency (the complaints were not upheld).

The logic of playful subversion utilised in advertising porno chic also applies to the comedy of those such as Sarah Silverman (and that of a long trail of male comedians who in the 1990s broke with the convention that one's porn use could not be mentioned in public, and certainly not on prime-time TV). In the quote from her 2010 autobiography which heads this chapter she calls for porn to be considered 'a treat', making it the basis of a joke, and pretending to be shocked by its excesses. Porn, for Silverman, is funny as well as arousing.

Madonna's *Sex* book made extensive use of humour, as in the X-rated comic book insert titled 'Dita in The Chelsea Girl'. There is an acknowledgement in such work that porn, and maybe sex too, although erotic, are also funny. Other sections of the book, with their shaved heads, brandishing of sharp instruments and simulated rapes – convey the same erotic charge or menace as some pornography, although distancing that eroticism within the frame of Art (or in Madonna's case, Pop), and fantasy. Madonna is *playing* with the repertoire and conventions of pornography in these images.

Another artist who has pioneered the playful appropriation of pornography, in the process becoming both notorious and revered in his own country, as well as a global cult figure with celebrity fans such as Björk (who commissioned him to photograph her for her 1996 album *Telegram*), is the Japanese photographer Nobuyoshi Araki. I will say more about Araki in Chapter 8 on the aesthetics of sexual transgression. He belongs in this chapter, however, as an artist who plays exuberantly with the pornographic, in the form of explicit, often sado-masochistic photographs of Japanese women (and sometimes couples).

Araki has also made 'straight' pornography, producing hundreds of photosets of heterosexual couples having sex, and also of himself in the act. These images have often been produced in the style of, and sold as, cheap pornography in the Japanese porn market. They are described by Jeffreys as 'auteur pornography' (2005, p.258), and Araki has never sought to distance himself from that characterisation of his work. On the contrary, as documentaries about his life and artistic process make clear, he revels in a hyperactive sexuality which is as 'naughty' and teasing as it is the foundation for a unique body of art. His 'bondage' pictures have been controversial, as one would expect, but they also have a playful quality. They are often commissioned, by women who clearly wish to expose themselves to Araki and the world in this way. He has, largely as a result of his sexually explicit work, become a pop-culture celebrity in Japan, where wealthy, sophisticated women queue to be the subjects of his work. Incongruously, these scenes tend to be shot to the accompaniment of much bawdy laughter, crude schoolboy-ish jokes, and an air of mischief rather than menace.

Araki creates his own original works, unmediated, where other artists have used found pornographic images, as in Marco Brambilla's *Sync* short film in the anthology *Destricted* (Abramovich *et al.*, 2006), a two-minute long piece assembled from still and moving images of hundreds of pornographic films. Digital artist Thomas Ruff manipulates explicit images sourced from online porn sites, typically creating fuzzy, if still graphic scenes. Like Brambilla's work, or Richard Prince's *House Calls* (also from *Destricted*) these artists take actual pornography and filter it through an artistic lens until it emerges as something other (see Chapter 8).

Chicks chucking brown eyes, and other porno-art provocations

One often sees in these more playful strands of artistic porno chic a critique, implicit or explicit, of the pornographic mind set, especially its patriarchal and heterosexist themes. Work of this type, while tapping into our cultural fascination with the form, also seeks to make the viewer look afresh at the pornographic gaze, and sometimes to find fault. Work of this kind differs from that of, say, Araki, in that, while simulating or pastiching porn in various ways, it may also be disapproving. In September 2001, for example, *The Australian* reported on an exhibition by photographer Lee-Anne Richards at the gallery Photo Technica in Sydney. Titled *Arseholes*, Richards had photographed the anuses of a number of female models. The images were described by the reporter as 'a series of chicks chucking what can only be described as brown-eyes'.[15] The artist herself explained her intentions with the work thus:

> I wanted to challenge the idea of the male gaze in pornography. What is unsettling about the photos is the fact that they follow porn conventions up to a point and then fall short, or perhaps go a little too far in some direction. The effect is a bit unnerving.

This approach to pornography is provocative, certainly, but also humorous, like that of the 2002 Turner prize-nominated Fiona Banner's *Arsewoman In Wonderland*.[16] This work is a representation of Banner's own description of a pornographic film, captured in text so dense on the large billboard that it is said to be nearly impossible to read in the normal way (since I have not seen the original I can't say if this is true).[17] The point of such a presentation was, for Banner, to invite reflection on the teasing nature of the pornographic, which always promises more, but delivers less, compelling the viewer to close the gap with his or her own imagination. *Arsewoman in Wonderland* both titillates (because we know it to be a sexually explicit account of a pornographic film) and alienates (because it cannot be read in comfort, nor used to masturbate, which is an essential characteristic of actual porn). For the *Guardian*'s Emma Brockes, 'Banner uses pornographic film to explore sexuality and the extreme limits of human communication'.[18]

During this second wave of porno chic, pornography also became a theme in sitcoms such as *Friends* and *The Simpsons* (Boyle, 2010). In the former, and an episode entitled *The One With the Free Porn*, we are invited to regard Joey and Chandler's accidental accessing of free cable pornography as funny, rather than depraved or sinister.

As more and more artists, musicians, and advertisers worked with the codes of pornography, the second wave of porno chic gathered steam. In earlier work I cited as an example the UK Channel 4's forty-eight-programme series on transgressive sexual culture, *The Red Light Zone*, which included several documentaries on pornography (McNair, 1996). More documentaries followed, and then narrative feature films such as *Boogie Nights* and the Oscar-winning *The People Versus Larry Flynt* (Milos Forman, 1997). The difference between these and earlier films about porn such as Paul Schrader's *Hardcore* (1979) lay in their refusal to demonise and caricature the form or those involved in making it, including the performers. In Schrader's vision pornographic film actors were portrayed as pathetic victims, the producers and directors as degenerate. In *Boogie Nights* and *Larry Flynt* pornography was represented as a space in which human beings lived and worked, where the centrality of sexuality to human experience was acknowledged and serviced, where refuge and sanctuary and empathy could be found. In these films the world beyond porn was crueller and more dangerous than anything to be found within the porn industry.

In the period since these releases there have been many more examples of porno chic in cinema, many of them playful. *Zack and Miri Make A Porno* (Kevin Smith, 2008), for example, is akin to *Boogie Nights* in its treatment of the subject, although straightforwardly comedic and without the former's depth and ambition. The premise of Smith's film is simple: two friends need to make some money fast. In the modern world, where pornography is available and in-demand, making a porno movie has become a realistic option for a 'normal', 'respectable' person, though still transgressive enough to be the foundation for edgy comedy. YouPorn.com is full of such material, produced by amateurs, as the principals note before embarking on their own porno production.

So Zack and Miri embark on what is a quite conventional comedy of the type which dominated multiplexes in the 2000s. Making pornography is not in this world a demonic or evil occupation. It does not indicate depravity or the desire to rape and murder innocents. It is, if any judgement is to be made, banal, boring, embarrassing, and devoid of authentic erotic charge. This was the dominant tone of second-wave porno chic: non-judgementalism and respect, if not an outright celebration of pornography as a cultural form; sometimes bemused tolerance rather than outraged condemnation. In the US films mentioned above, the production and consumption of pornography is cast as a question of individual freedom and personal choice. You may be sad if you're into porn, but not really bad.

A similarly non-judgemental, even playful tone underpins *The Notorious Bettie Page* (Mary Harron, 2005). This biopic of the iconic 1950s porn-star who specialised in sadomasochistic imagery also peered beneath the veil of notoriety to examine her life and motivations. Bettie's normalness is stressed, as is that of the people who view her pictures and films. As with *Boogie Nights* and its representation of the 1970s/1980s LA porn industry, in Bettie Page 'the world of fetish producers comes across as a haven of support and camaraderie'.[19] Harron is a feminist director previously best-known for *I Shot Andy Warhol* (1996) and here, as with her study of Valerie Solanas in that film, seeks to expose the humanity and the humour of her subject, as well as the darker elements of her make up (Page is shown to have been raped as a young woman, for example, with the implication that this has helped shape her adult sexuality).

The commercially successful teen comedy *The Girl Next Door* (Luke Greenfield, 2004) plays into teen fantasies (male, at least) of proximity and access to a porn-star, having one move in next door to its central character. The dramatic tension and humour in the story arises from the clash of two worlds. It is the porn-star who is portrayed as being the most rounded and interesting character, whose role in the narrative is to loosen up the uptight college boy.

In *The Moguls* (Michael Traeger, 2005), the residents of a small US town decide to make a porn movie as a way of putting their community back on the map. The film was not well reviewed and failed at the box office. For our purposes, it fits into the 'playful' category of porno chic in documenting a moment in US culture when the idea of 'ordinary' people – i.e., people who are not depraved or damaged – making pornography was still unusual and transgressive enough to be funny, although entirely believable.

Pedagogic and didactic porno chic – talking about the pornographic

Porno chic includes works of narrative film and literature which are not intended to look like pornography, but are *about* pornography, such as Chuck Palahniuk's *Snuff* (2008) and Irvine Welsh's *Porno* (2002), PT Anderson's *Boogie Nights* (1997), Lukas Moodysson's *A Hole In My Heart* (2004) and George Gallo's *Middle Men* (2010). The latter is described by one critic as '*Boogie Nights* versus *Goodfellas*'[20] and was released straight-to-DVD in the UK and other markets, having failed at the US box office. As this book went to press two films about the life of Linda Lovelace were in production in the US, and one each about Russ Meyer and Hugh Hefner. The *Sunday Times* noted in a report that 'films about the $10-billion-a-year pornography industry, which is garrisoned just a few miles from Hollywood in the San Fernando Valley, have become their own subgenre'.[21]

This sub-category of porno chic also includes the many film and TV documentaries which have been made about porn, and quasi-journalistic photography which documents it, as well as seeks to comment upon it. Timothy Greenfield-Sanders' book *XXX* (2004), for example, comprises thirty diptychs of porn-stars, clothed and naked, including Jenna Jameson and Nina Hartley. Author Martin Amis wrote the text for a book of photographs by Stefano De Luigi depicting the making of pornography, and the performers involved, called *Pornoland* (2004). As is typical of this type of porno chic, the treatment is largely sympathetic and curious, rather than condemnatory. Who are these people who make their livings by having sex in front of cameras? What drives them?

Lukas Moodysson's *A Hole In My Heart*, although gruelling at times in its unrelenting realism, portrays those who make porn in Sweden as sympathetic characters deserving of our understanding rather than disapproval. In contrast to Kevin Smith's comedy, Moodysson's film does not airbrush or sanitise the pornographic production process. The film includes scenes where the characters produce extreme porn, including vomiting and simulated rape, and avoids eroticisation. But the viewer is invited to feel sympathy – or empathy – for the characters, and permitted to know why they have arrived at this place in their lives, making grainy porn in a Swedish housing estate.

The story follows Tess, Geko, Richard and Erik. Richard is making a cheap porn film starring Tess, with the support of Geko, while Erik sulks in his bedroom, emerging only to humiliate and abuse his father, Richard. Richard's wife has died and he has a history of childhood sexual abuse, which may explain his anger and dysfunction. Indeed, all the characters share a history of some kind of abuse, which brings them together and elevates them to the status of a family. Tess has been rejected for the Swedish version of *Big Brother*, and all are 'losers', by their own estimation. But they have each other. As with *Boogie Nights*, although the *mise en scène* and mood are very different, Moodysson's film is ultimately about family, dysfunctionality, damaged relationships, and people's need to belong to something. His characters are not evil, just flawed. For them, casual sex and the making of porn are ways of coping with loss. They have been abused in various ways, and are survivors. As the director explains it:

> The film is an attack [on pornography], and it is also a defence. And it is not just the story of four damaged people. It is the story of four wonderful people. It defends pornography, and it defends the people working in pornography.[22]

The defence of pornography is not just in the humanity of the characters, but in their articulation of the universality of what they do. Tess says: 'Some people say that what we're doing is fucking dirty and ugly. But if that's the case, the whole of mankind has a problem. We're just giving people what they want.' Moodysson himself has stated:

> I wanted to talk about the sexualisation of public spaces, like commercials, and the way porn seeps into everybody's living room, but I didn't want to be part of it. Then after a while I realised I couldn't draw that line, so the film becomes part of what it's talking about. It's a symptom, not a diagnosis.[23]

The work *is* porno chic, then, as well as commentary upon it. Beyond this formal ambition, Moodysson wishes us to feel empathy for the people who 'perform' the porn scenes recreated in his film. Like *Boogie Nights*, he constructs the porn business – even at this low-fi end – as a surrogate family for people who have no other.

> They [performers] are stigmatised by both sides – the feminists and the moral majority. But they have a good reason to be in porno. I think that there are strong links between people who have been abused in the past, and a kindness between hurt, broken people. They take care of each other.[24]

In the sphere of literature, two novels by best-selling writers have adopted the same approach, viewing the pornosphere as a kind of community where the abused and

damaged find protection and dignity, doing what they are good at. Chuck Palahniuk's
Snuff (2009) tells the story of a porn-star undertaking a marathon 'gang bang' involving sex with some 600 men. Will the stunt kill her, and is death perhaps what she
wants? Palahniuk's story asks these questions, and the narrative focuses on why its
characters might have reached a stage where they prefer death to life. But he also
portrays a certain dignity in the lives of the performers.

Irvine Welsh's *Porno* is a sequel of sorts to his best-selling *Trainspotting*, and catches
up with some of the earlier book's characters after they have become involved in the
porn industry. Welsh is reflecting the fact that by 2002 porn is indeed 'chic'. Again,
we see represented in porn a world that is legitimate within its own logic and rules,
where people live their lives and have problems not so different from everybody else.

A minor sub-genre of porno chic in cinema – that involving real-life performers –
is represented by *The Girlfriend Experience* (Stephen Soderbergh, 2010). It stars
'extreme' porn actress Sasha Grey[25] – her presence a feature of the production which
was prominent in the marketing. The film signals a mainstream movie industry curious about, and perhaps even comfortable with, the idea that a young woman should
become a star through her capacity for extreme and exotic pornography. Grey plays
Chelsea, who is not in the story a porn performer but a 'sophisticated escort' – a
woman who is a sexual commodity, but with a measure of control over her work
and conditions. In the opening scene she is 'reviewed' by a man who promises her
wealth and success if only she will give him a 'taste'. The review he gives her, we
later discover, is cruel and negative, highlighting Chelsea's powerlessness. She also has
a boyfriend, Chris, who is supportive and affirming. In a scene where Chelsea
describes how she is feeling threatened by some competition from 'a new girl', he
tells her:

> Listen to me … Honestly, can I tell you something? You are the best at
> everything you do. There's always gonna be new girls that come on the scene,
> but nobody does what you do, okay? I know you're competitive, and you
> always want to be the best, but you are the best.

Chelsea's work as a prostitute is here coded as legitimate, respectable, worthy of
examination – qualities which might be thought to extend to her real-life occupation
as a porn-star. In this film she does not 'do' porn, but prostitution. Her presence in the
film is itself, however, a direct consequence of porn's contemporary chic-ness.[26]

Sasha Grey is not the first porn-star to cross over into non-pornographic movie
production (Traci Lords featured in John Waters' *Cry-Baby* (1990); Catherine Breillat's
Anatomy Of Hell (2004) stars Italian male porn-star Rocco Siffredi). But Soderbergh's
employment of a real porn-star playing a prostitute occurs in a context where the
assumption is of female power, albeit power constrained not only by her own needs
but by the sexual needs, frailties and impositions of men. The final scene depicts
Chelsea meeting a client, who climaxes merely by touching her. The neediness of
men is displayed, and the need of Chelsea to look after her clients is framed as noble
rather than submissive.

Pornography as metaphor

Porno chic, as I employ the term, also includes work which uses explicit sex, represented in such a manner as to deliberately suggest or reference the style of pornography, which then functions as a metaphor or allegory for something bad, evil or negative. Such texts are not pornography in so far as they rarely have the intention to arouse, but they may be equally transgressive and graphic. Neither do they display any sympathy with the notion of pornography as a positive cultural force. Rather, porn in these contexts is premised as a dark, demonic form – a destroyer of individual and public morality, a theatre of cruelty.

One thinks here of *Baise-Moi* (Virginie Despentes, Coralie Trinh Thi, 2000) and *A Serbian Film* (Srdjan Spasojevic, 2010), both films which attracted the kind of critical attention, indeed opprobrium, usually reserved for pornography, but which were devoid of erotic appeal (at least to this viewer), and intended by their makers not to arouse but to shock. Texts of this kind may present an impression of pornography as horrifying or evil – playing on the varying levels of porno fear which have accompanied sexualisation and pornographication since the 1960s, while intending to subvert some set of values or beliefs.

A Serbian Film gained global notoriety in 2010 with its explicit depiction of the making of a violent and abusive pornographic film, including scenes where a newborn baby is raped, a woman decapitated, and a man penetrated by another man through his eye socket. The production crew who film these outrages are dressed in Serbian military uniforms, which indicate the aim of the work – in the words of the director, to use pornography as a metaphor for the violation and exploitation of the Serbian people (and those non-Serbians whom the Serbs also abused) during the regime of Slobodan Milosevic. According to director Srdjan Spasojevic, 'pornography was the only possible metaphor for "almost indescribably and exploitative chaos" that had defined his life'.[27]

Indeed, it is difficult to characterise the film as erotic in the sense that pornography aspires to be. The film is a confrontational provocation, designed to attract attention precisely by breaking taboos – notably those surrounding children and sex, but also those associated with sex and death. My own viewing brought to mind those clumsy art-shock horrors of the Dadaists in 1920s Paris, and the innumerable avant-garde excesses of young artists down the ages as they seek to upset the parent culture. The film begins with a voiceover reference to the main character's status as an 'artist of the fuck', thus referring us to the long history of attempts to fuse Art and Porn within a single text. The trajectory of the narrative strongly suggests, however, that the effort is doomed, and immoral to begin with. Those who declare the aesthetic value of porn are those, we soon see, who will rape and kill to produce their effects. These are not characters to be admired.

I will not seek to justify every taboo-breaking scene in *A Serbian Film* in terms of the inviolability of artistic expression, because I do not think freedom has no limits. But even the most transgressive images are in no sense realistic, and even less erotic. The viewer is in the same relationship to the material as he or she would be to a

Brecht play – aware of its artifice and intention, and thus distanced from its surface horror. Aware, at least, that it had an intention, other than that of eroticising sexual violence and depravity for their own sake. The film is not, therefore, pornography as I and most others define it, but a statement about authoritarianism, excess and corruption which utilises what is perhaps the key transgressive language of our time – the pornographic – to critique those things from within the director's own culture and society.

A Serbian Film also contains a critique of the destructive impact of pornography on the family. The porn-star's family are corrupted by his involvement in the porn business, even to the point where the young son watches old videos of his father's work. In one taboo-breaking moment the son is himself raped by the father, a scene signalling the depths of the depravity to which the film-makers bring him, and us. The protagonist's once healthy sexuality has been distorted and damaged by his work in porn. Not only that, his family are destroyed too.

It may or may not be significant that post-dictatorship Serbia has produced at least one other 'porno-allegory' devoted to social critique, *The Life and Death of a Porno Gang* (Mladen Djordjevic, 2009). In this, also satirical work, a gang of porn producers seek revenge on 'rural' Serbia, expressing their political message through the medium of porn. One sees here the strategy of subversive artists going back to the Marquis, applied now to the real-life horrors of the late twentieth and early twenty-first centuries, which are of course much greater than any pornography, or any art, could possibly capture.

One finds in these works, regardless of judgements about their aesthetic quality, a reassertion of the subversive politics of the pornographic text, as practiced by the Marquis de Sade and many others following him. Sex is the instrument of social satire, directed at the powerful and/or the complacent – in these Serbian examples, perhaps, those who are deemed complicit in the rise of dictatorship and the horrors that followed. In a society which gave the world the massacres and concentration camps of Srebrenica, can even the most extreme pornography begin to capture the extent and embeddedness of real, as opposed to representational, evil?

Porno chic and the liberalisation of sexual culture

As porno chic was consolidated, the impact of the internet was steadily undermining traditional censorship regimes. In the UK, hitherto one of the most conservative countries in respect of sexual culture, the turn of the century saw an unprecedented liberalisation of the pornography market, and also of the non-pornographic film scene's treatment of sexuality. The British Board of Film Classification, under its director Andreas Whittam-Smith, began to permit for general release films such as *Baise-Moi*, *Irreversible* (Gaspar Noe, 2002), *9 Songs* (Michael Winterbottom, 2004) and *Shortbus* (John Cameron Mitchell, 2006). Under Whittam-Smith's leadership the BBFC decided that 'explicit sexuality was no less generally shocking – and less likely to disrupt society through imitation – than graphic violence'.[28] It recognised, too, that the rise of the internet meant that 'any banned visual material was rapidly distributed without control and so it was preferable to have a controlled official release'.

Patrice Chereau's *Intimacy*, released in 2001, was one of the first films to benefit from the new liberalism. Starring Kerry Fox, the film contained what one review described as '35 minutes of explicit screen sex, including the first brief shot of a serious actor [Fox] fellating her co-star' (*Sight & Sound*, 2011). Other directors engaged with explicit sex, including Michael Winterbottom, whose *9 Songs* (2004) took the form of a series of sexual encounters between one couple, following their relationship from beginning to end. For Cosmo Landesman in *The Sunday Times*, 'if a film like *9 Songs* can be granted an 18 certificate, then the line between art and porn is dead'.[29]

The return of porno fear

Porno fear, as I have characterised it (McNair, 2009a), did not go away during this period. Joel Schumacher remade Schrader's 1979 polemic against the Los Angeles porn industry, *Hard Core*,[30] in the form of *8mm* (1998). Martin Amis – whose 1984 novel *Money* employed the pornographic as a metaphor for his view of the commercialised decay of 1980s Britain[31] – wrote of the degradation experienced by women working for the gonzo pornographer Max Hardcore, at the same time as a documentary of that name was broadcast on Channel 4 television in the UK. Schrader's 2004 film *AutoFocus* linked pornography to the downfall of American TV sitcom star Bob Crane (*Hogan's Heroes*). These, *pornosfearic* texts are also part of the second-wave of porno chic. They were not typical of the pornographication of the mainstream in the 1990s and 2000s, but they reflect the fact that growing public tolerance, acceptance of and fascination with pornography were not without their critics. In the next chapter I consider the arguments made by those critics.

4

PORNO FEAR

Pornography is what the end of the world will look like if we don't reverse the pathological course that we are on in patriarchal, white-supremacist, predatory corporate-capitalist societies.

(Robert Jensen, 2010, p.105)

Glasgow, December 13, 2010. The BBC's peak-time radio news and current-affairs show *PM*, presented by Eddie Mair, is reporting on the high number of viewers' complaints received by the broadcast regulator Ofcom about the previous weekend's *X Factor* final, when pop stars Christina Aguilera and Rihanna delivered guest performances modelled on Aguilera's then-current starring role in the film *Burlesque* (Steve Antin, 2010). According to Mair there had been 'horror' amongst parents who, while watching the popular talent-cum-reality show with their children at a pre-watershed hour, were subjected to Aguilera dressed in fishnet stockings and 'gyrating with a chair'. Rihanna had performed her song *What's My Name* in a bikini-type outfit described by one critic cited on the programme as 'like underwear'.[1]

The director of the online Mumsnet organisation, Justine Roberts, came on the programme to argue that 'it was a bit cringy [watching with her seven-year-olds] … an example of the creeping into the culture of sexualisation'. She linked this to her organisation's campaign – Let Go Of the Girls – which, she explained, worked to persuade commercial organisations not to sell products which are inappropriate for young girls.[2] 'We are sleep walking into a pole-dancing culture', she added, referring to the vogue for women to buy kits which allow them to learn basic pole-dancing as an exercise tool or a sex aid within a relationship.[3] In one notorious case of allegedly inappropriate sexualisation, reported by *The Sun* newspaper in June 2010, club owner Sarah Burge 'is teaching her seven-year-old to pole dance'. As *The Sun* reported, 'parenting experts and child abuse campaigners warned she is sexualising Poppy far too young'.[4]

As it happened, I had began drafting this book that very day, and the item thus seemed fortuitously timed to sum up the environment of current anxieties around cultural sexualisation which is my starting point for this chapter.

Defining sexualisation

As Feona Attwood defines it, a sexualised culture is one in which there is

> a preoccupation with sexual values, practices and identities; the proliferation of sexual texts; the emergence of new forms of sexual experience; the apparent breakdown of rules, categories and regulations designed to keep the obscene at bay; a fondness for scandals, controversies and panics around sex.
>
> *(2004, p.79)*

This definition certainly fits the UK and comparable societies in the 2000s. Of the UK in particular, the *PM* item described above exemplifies the phenomenon. On the one hand we have a successful Hollywood feature film, *Burlesque*, which fits quite well into the category of porno chic which gives this book its title (see Chapter 3).[5] We have a popular TV programme going out at prime time in the UK, which refers to the film and translates it into a short music and dance routine for a mainstream audience including children. The critical response from some viewers – parents in particular – then connects this to a broader trend of cultural sexualisation, and the sexualisation of young people, which needs to be addressed with action.

The BBC radio item also included comments by Ben Walters, Cabaret editor of *Time Out*, in defence of burlesque as a form which, in contrast to the passive female sexuality said to be present in so much of popular culture, invites women to experiment with their bodies and sexualities in ways which are empowering and thus positive.

> Burlesque at its best, and it's a very contentious form, should be about a very individual form of expression, physical performance, sexuality, but in a very individual, non-clichéd way. Burlesque deals with issues like sexuality, in ways which wouldn't be appropriate for a tea-time audience, but it's very much about female performers enjoying their own bodies and their own sexualities.[6]

The contrasting views contained in this item embody the key trends and issues I want to explore in this chapter. In it we see the expression of public anxiety about inappropriate sexualisation, triggered by popular cultural displays which are very much part of the pornographication of the mainstream, or *striptease culture*, and which are linked by their critics to the sexual coarsening or degradation of society in some way, and to harms caused to vulnerable groups, and young girls in particular. Against that, we hear a plea for the progressive, feminist power of the allegedly offending form to be acknowledged.[7]

Associated with anxiety about cultural sexualisation is the more specific phenomenon of *porno fear*, focused as the term suggests on the increased visibility and perceived extremism of pornographic images. While clearly connected to the broader issue of sexualisation, I use the concept of *porno fear* as a shorthand for the range of critical responses to the expansion of the pornosphere, including a distinct set of concerns about the social (and moral) impact of the increased accessibility of pornography, and the limits of censorship, regulation and control of sexual imagery in contemporary culture.

Another example, from my home country of Scotland, will illustrate. In July 2009 the feminist campaigning organisation Scottish Women's Aid was reported to have rejected a donation of £600 from a group of women who had produced a calendar depicting themselves in the traditionally discrete state of undress (the original Calendar Girls phenomenon remained popular more than a decade after it made headlines and inspired a movie starring some of Britain's grandest *dames de théâtre*).[8] According to SWA representative Jacquie Kelly, 'we are opposed to the sex industry and we have an issue with women removing their clothes'.[9] Journalist Gillian Bowditch, who reported the story for *The Sunday Times*, objected to the 'humourously dogmatic' equation of these women's choice to pose nude for charity with the pornography industry, and drew a more general conclusion:

> All too often these groups take a crude, blanket approach to the problems they are charged with alleviating. Distorted through a feminist prism, all nudity becomes pornography irrespective of context. All men are viewed as potential rapists and all women as potential victims. If we cannot tell the difference between nudity and pornography, between a charity calendar and the sex industry or a well-meaning fundraiser and a stripper, then we are in an ideological cul de sac from which there is no escape.[10]

Not all feminists would object to the calendar, of course. A key aspect of current anxieties around sexualisation is that they have split the feminist movement as much as they unite it against the patriarchy. To be a feminist today is not necessarily to be either anti- or pro-porn, pro- or anti-cultural sexualisation. There is no single feminism, or feminist 'dogma' about porn and its cultural offshoots to which any but a small minority adhere. Rather, we see a spectrum of views and readings which reflect differences within feminism as to the nature of female sexuality and the appropriate limits of feminine sexual agency. As this example shows, one woman's charitable disrobing can be another's dabbling with the sex industry.

A more recent example of this division can be seen in the coverage of an anti-porn protest which occurred in London in September 2011, at a 'summit' of adult-entertainment industry executives.[11] Coverage of the protest quoted *Pornland* author and anti-porn campaigner Gail Dines stating that 'you cannot have a massive industry built on the sexual torture and dehumanisation and debasement of women'. This report also pointed out that:

Not all feminists agree, however. Catherine Stephens, an activist for the International Union of Sex Workers, said opposing pornography as a whole did not make sense as there were so many different kinds.

In her introduction to a special edition of the *Sexualities* journal exploring the pedagogy of porn studies, Feona Attwood observes that

> pornography has come to signify men's brutalisation, women's exploitation and the dangerous power of the media – and more recently, commodification, individualism, neoliberalism and a backlash against feminism. Pornography, seemingly so marginal a genre, has somehow emerged as central to understanding the dynamics of culture itself.
>
> *(2009, p.548)*

How, then, did we get there – to this state of renewed anxiety, of panic and porno fear, emanating from a variety of sources and perspectives – from the environment of porno chic described in the previous chapter?

The return of porno fear

Sometime around 2003 commentators began to identify cultural sexualisation as a major social problem. In *The Sunday Times* in April of that year Bryan Appleyard wrote, in response to the London production of a sexually explicit Spanish play called *XXX*, that 'we are now coated in sex to the point where we hardly notice that, daily, we swim in an ocean of erotica'. Notwithstanding the sensual tone of his prose, matched elsewhere by copious references to 'floods' of sex, Appleyard did not regard this as a good thing.[12] A year later Cosmo Landesman referred to Winterbottom's *9 Songs*, and to Larry Flynt's opening of a branch of his ill-fated *Hustler* club in London, to complain that where sexuality used to be underground, held in check by shame, now it was out in the open. 'Sex has undergone a kind of moral and aesthetic surgery – it has had all its ugly bits removed: the sleaze, the dirt, the aura of deviance and, most importantly, the embarrassment.'[13]

Also in 2004, following controversy over Janet Jackson's 'wardrobe mishap' at the Superbowl final in which she briefly flashed a breast while in performance with Justin Timberlake, it was reported that 'the American media are redrawing the boundaries of public taste and decency'.[14] The long-term trend towards liberalisation 'has now been thrown sharply into reverse'. Duits and van Zoonen noted in 2011 that 'not since the feminist pornography debates of the 1980s has there been such an outburst of discussion, research and publications about sexualised images of women and girls' (p.491).

The sexualisation of culture is real, although it is hardly new. Journalist Hadley Freeman writes of how, as a 12-year-old in 1989, she fell in love with Madonna's *Like A Prayer* album, and went to see the *Blonde Ambition* show. Both featured highly sexualised content, which got Madonna into trouble with the Pope and Pepsi Cola among others. Freeman experienced 1989-era Madonna as a revelation, however. I quote her account here at length because it challenges so directly many of the assertions of anti-porn feminists about the harmful effects of cultural sexualisation. Ms Freeman appears not to have been damaged by Madonna's shameless cavorting, going on to achieve professional distinction as a *Guardian* journalist. She writes of *Like A Prayer*:

> Not being Catholic, there was no rebellious appeal in the album to me, and my parents apparently had no problem with their Jewish daughter watching – if not quite understanding – a music video that featured a woman named Madonna apparently giving a blow job to a black Jesus. I've spent my entire life too busy dancing around and singing the lyrics ... I like songs that make me dance and make me happy and it just so happens that a song about blowing Jesus has been making me happy for the last two decades. Although *Like a Prayer* was not my first album, Madonna was my first music concert. For my 12th birthday I proved my coolness by going with my babysitter to the *Blonde Ambition* tour and repeatedly expressed bafflement at why people weren't sitting down as I really would have been able to see better. I saw enough. To all parents out there, there is no better way to open your little girl's eyes than packing her off to watch a woman masturbate on stage.
>
> Unlike many of my friends, I do not have any hangover idolisation of Madonna herself. She personally peaked for me when she humiliated Warren Beatty in *In Bed With Madonna*. But no matter what she's done to her face, her body and the world of cinema since, she will always be the woman who introduced me to MTV, pale denim and masturbation. And for that, I thank her.[15]

The key issue in debates around sexualisation, as the above perspectives illustrate, is one of meaning and interpretation. How do we read a cultural environment in which not only is sexual representation more explicit and pervasive than ever before in the history of media, but women such as Madonna have been at the forefront of the processes whereby that has happened?

Feminists have divided around the meanings to be drawn from sexual culture since at least the early 1980s, when Carol Vance published the *Pleasure and Danger* (1984) collection of essays by women who objected to what they saw as the enforced anti-porn consensus of the movement up until that point. Many authors, including this one, have documented the ensuing 'porn wars', and I will note here only that by the early 2000s liberal capitalist societies had become relaxed about pornography and sexual culture in general, while women's and gay rights had advanced steadily.

Even in Britain, that stalwart of sexual censorship through much of the twentieth century, the year 2000 had seen a New Labour government permit a significantly more liberal censorship regime for cinema, allowing films like *Baise-Moi, 9 Songs*, and *Irreversible* to be released in mainstream movie houses around the country. Women, including feminists, appeared to be more comfortable than they had ever been with forms of sexual culture previously dismissed by radical feminist ideology as patriarchal propaganda. As pornography become so embedded in culture as to be unremarkable, feminism became what some called post-feminism. The frequency and intensity of debate about sexual culture declined from the heights of the 1990s.

The turn away from porno chic and towards porno fear and the emergence of current anxieties became apparent mid-decade, however, first in the form of journalistic commentaries around the theme of what Ariel Levy called in an influential *New Yorker* article 'raunch culture'.[16] These pieces were reactions to the perceived submission of young women in America (and everywhere, by extension, that American trends in sexual liberalisation were adopted) to resurgent sexist stereotypes and impositions. In *The Sunday Times* in late 2005, Maureen Dowd complained of the continuing tyranny of oppressive stereotypes of female beauty.[17]

Ariel Levy's 2005 book *Female Chauvinist Pigs* developed this argument at length. Based on her *New Yorker* article, the book identified 'raunch culture' as 'an example of the strange way people are ignoring the contradictions of the past, pretending they never existed, and putting various, conflicting ideologies together to form one incoherent brand of raunch feminism' (2005, p.74). For Levy, female performances of the type exemplified by Madonna, or Aguilera, or the other post-feminist icons of the time were not progressive statements, but commercially driven surrenderings to the male gaze. 'The conception of raunch culture as a path to liberation rather than oppression is a convenient (and lucrative) fantasy with nothing to back it up' (2005, p.82). In Australia, *The Sydney Morning Herald* columnist Miranda Devine echoed this critique with her observation that pornographication and cultural sexualisation has 'normalised [women's] self-destructive slutty behaviour'.[18]

Many more examples of this turn in feminist cultural criticism could be cited, much of it consistent with the premise of anti-porn ideology that women were not naturally predisposed to sexual self-display or self-objectification. Surprisingly, perhaps, given her history as a critic of anti-porn feminism, Camille Paglia's essay on Lady Gaga for *The Sunday Times* in 2010 echoed these critical readings in judging her to be 'a manufactured personality, without a trace of spontaneity', and 'a figure so calculated and clinical' that she represents 'the exhausted end of the sexual revolution'.[19] Paglia unfavourably compared Gaga to Madonna, forgetting perhaps the torrent of criticism that rained down on Madonna at her transgressive peak. For Paglia, Gaga was a phoney, lacking the authentic sex appeal of her idol. Others, such as Alex Needham in the *Guardian*, defended Gaga precisely because she was more than just a sex object, and had 'never presented herself' as such.[20]

> She sells weirdness and eye-popping spectacle, not sex. She isn't posing in a meat bikini to woo *Nuts'* one-handed readers, and why should she? Though Paglia's tome *Sexual Personae* posits sex as the prime mover behind all culture, you'd still think that as a feminist she'd applaud the fact that there's a massive female pop star whose appeal doesn't depend on how many men she manages to arouse.[21]

As with Madonna, so with Gaga – a culture in contention about the meaning and significance of a female sexual performance. The great Gaga debate was merely one example of the fact that following a period of around two decades after Madonna's *Sex* book scandalised the mainstream, but in which cultural sexualisation was not widely viewed as a problem in the liberal capitalist world, there had been a resurgence of the issue, and a sharpening of the divisions underpinning the various positions. It also sheds light on what porno fear is, and thus what the critique of cultural sexualisation is really about. Gaga, like Madonna before her, makes parents uncomfortable. The anti-cultural sexualisation movement is, from this perspective, another iteration of the generation gap, in which the older generation sees the younger as possessing loose morals, behaving badly in the sexual sense, and being victims of a corrupting and immoral mass media.

Others linked the raunch culture thesis to a revival of traditional anti-porn feminism. Catharine MacKinnon, for example, in her 2006 book *Are Women Human?* restated her longstanding belief that 'pornography promotes rape myths and desensitises people to violence against women so that you need more violence to become sexually aroused if you're a pornography consumer. This is very well documented.'[22] She added, though without evidence or substantiation, that 'women and children are being *increasingly* violated to make [pornography] and *more and more* of them are being abused through its use' (my emphasis). In a piece linking the backlash against raunch culture to the reappearance of anti-porn feminism Sarah Baxter in *The Sunday Times* noted that for Mackinnon, 'post-feminism is really a return to pre-feminism'.[23]

By early 2007, a revival of organised anti-porn feminism was evident, linked to pornographication. The *Guardian* reported that, as a result of 'mainstreaming of porn-type images ... [and] the mainstreaming of the porn and sex industries', there had been an upsurge in anti-porn feminist organisations in English universities, such as Sheffield Fems, Resisters, Mind The Gap, and the Warwick Anti-Sexist Society. These groups were dedicated to rolling back porno chic and to 'raising awareness about misogyny in lads' mags and the extent of porn sold in WH Smith'.[24] For one of the campaigners, blogger Charliegrrl:

> Porn used to be men perving in their bedrooms, something hush-hush. Lads mags and the attendant lad culture are normalising not just our objectification, but our harassment. The normalisation of porn, and sexual violence ... are connected.

India Knight in *The Sunday Times* articulated a common theme in the resurgence of anti-porn arguments, that it was popularising a 'ludicrous and alarming new kind of machismo' through its 'contempt and hatred' for the women who appear in them. Pornography was disseminating a toxic masculinity. 'Any internet trawl reveals, within seconds, that a disproportionately large number of porn sites specialise in brutality toward women.'[25] Knight linked this to an ongoing crisis of masculinity identified by myself and others in the 1990s: 'it is as though [men] feel so emasculated by contemporary culture that they need to exaggerate their masculinity to cartoonish proportions'. In 2011 the UK-based anti-porn campaigning group Feminista organised a screening in London of the 2001 TV documentary *Hardcore*, arguing that 'it depicts the true face of the oft-glamorised pornography industry'.[26]

At the beginning of 2010, British writer Natasha Walters published her *Living Dolls* book – a sustained attack on pornographication and cultural sexualisation, and their effect on female sexuality. In *The Sunday Times* Walters argued for a public debate on the effects of pornography.[27] In similar vein, Charlotte Raven in the *Guardian* described contemporary culture as 'a sorry place for feminism',[28] because it led to a situation where 'we are hyperconfident, hypersexual and hypercandid about our readiness to do whatever it takes to secure top billing'. Raven then asserted the baleful influence of Madonna in contemporary cultural sexualisation:

> The Madonna-ised woman [sic] views femininity as a tool for getting what she wants, whatever that may be. Madonna-ised woman believes she should have everything, with everything defined as every possible dress and sexual permutation.

This argument – that women in the first decade of the twenty-first century had let the side down by embracing forms of sexuality and identity that were in effect a betrayal of feminism and authentic femininity – continued to feature prominently in journalism and scholarly writing for the rest of that decade. The evidence of widespread female participation in sexual culture was made sense of as a function of delusional femininity at best and at worst of women desperate for male approval.

Connecting pornographication to cultural sexualisation

Alongside these developments – a growing concern about how young women were using their new sexual freedoms, and anxieties about the normalisation of pornography – came what seemed to be a transnational effort to persuade publics of the harmful effects of cultural sexualisation, on children especially. Chuck Kleinhans in 2004, for example, wrote of 'the continuous expansion of sexualised images of children and the controversies these cause' (p.71). There has been a longstanding, recurring concern about protecting children and young people from the media which goes back to the days of the early comic books. Now, however, traditional moral panic has fused with the perception of accelerating pornographication to generate a more sustained anxiety.

First up to bat was the Australia Institute, a 'left-leaning' think tank, and its report on *Corporate Paedophilia*, authored by Emma Rush and Andrea La Nauze in 2006. The title of the report was explained as 'a metaphor used to describe advertising and marketing that sexualises children ... such advertising and marketing is an abuse both of children and of public morality' (2006, p.6). Examples of corporate paedophilia included the fact that in the media:

> sexualised girl models almost always have long hair.

(p.7)

girls are sometimes pictured with adult-looking handbags.

(p.11)

children are dressed in clothing and posed in ways designed to draw attention to adult sexual features that the children do not yet possess.

(p.13)

Ads in which girls and boys adopted adult poses were identified as 'implicitly pae-dophiliac'. Although the report conceded that 'a direct causal link between the sex-ualisation of children and their vulnerability to paedophilia has not been proven' (p.39), it proceeded on the basis that proof wasn't necessary, because the link was self-evident.

Corporate Paedophilia fed into a growing anxiety about the sexualisation of children in Australia (McKee *et al.*, 2008), and prompted an Australian Senate inquiry, as well as a lawsuit from the large Australian department-store chain David Jones, which had been prominent among those companies implicated in the 'corporate paedophilia' allegations. The subsequent Australian debate was lively, with some websites such as Mamamia and Online Opinion opposing the anti-sexualisation argument, and others such as Quadrant supporting the critics of sexualisation and pornographication. In a piece published in April 2010 Mamamia founder and editor Mia Freedman observed that

> emotive labels like 'child sexualisation' are being used as a Trojan horse by extremely religious or conservative groups whose true intentions are to turn back the clock on all sorts of other things ... like sex education, access to contraception, information about sexual health and reproduction.[29]

Albury and Lumby have pointed out – in their submission to the above mentioned Senate Inquiry and an article for the *Media International Australia* journal – that, contrary to the tone of anti-sexualisation advocates, women and girls were just as sexualised in earlier decades, perhaps even more so.

> Young Australian girls have been dressed in apparel that acknowledges adult fashion trends for at least three decades. For example, the late 1960s and early 1970s saw young Australian girls dressed in 'hotpants', flared jeans, 'boob' tubes, ponchos, mini skirts and bikinis.
>
> *(2010b, p.143)*

In their Inquiry submission they point out that, however one evaluates the trends in cultural sexualisation, women's (and girls') status in Australian society has improved hugely over time, while teenage pregnancy rates have fallen by nearly 400 per cent. In short, if contemporary cultural sexualisation is deemed inappro-priate, there is no evidence that it has caused the harms often attributed to it by critics.

In Australia, the age of consent was ten in the 19th century, and twelve in the early part of the 20th century. It was common for much of the 20th century for girls to marry as young as sixteen. The teenage fertility rate significantly decreased over the last three decades from 55.5 births per 100,000 in 1971 compared to 16 births per 100,000 in 2005.[30]

Notwithstanding such attempts to historicise and contextualise the debate, the concept of 'corporate paedophilia' has continued to have currency in Australia. In March 2011 columnist Phillip Adams opined in *The Australian* that

> sexual [sic] pornography seems comparatively harmless ... For really damaging sexual pornography, look at the kiddie porn produced by major advertisers ... Instead of picking people their own size, many of our biggest businesses attack childhood itself, seeking to sexualise kids at an ever earlier stage – while turning them into a profitable 'demographic'. Compared to this cynicism, much internet porn seems almost innocent.[31]

The United States

Following hard on the *Corporate Paedophilia* report was the American Psychological Association (APA), whose *Task Force On the Sexualisation of Girls* published its findings in 2007.[32] This study was framed by the APA as a 'response to public concern' about the sexualisation of American culture, and of girls in particular. This, asserted the APA, was a 'broad and increasing problem ... harmful to girls' (2007, p.2).

The APA document embodies the characteristic features of anti-sexualisation reports as they have emerged elsewhere in the world in recent years: (1) it assumed – in the absence of evidence beyond the anecdotal – that there was growing *public anxiety* about (2) an increased level of something called *sexualisation* which (3) was assumed to be *harming* a vulnerable group (usually, though not only, girls and young women); and (4) on the basis of the first three stages of the argument, the call was made for *control* of the harmful images.

There is one feature of the APA report which recurs in other studies: its appropriation of social-scientific discourse and packaging to convey the impression of rigour and systematicity in its preparation. The APA is an impressive label, conferring instant credibility upon anything to which it is attached. However, close reading of the report quickly reveals a lack of the conceptual clarity, empirical depth and analytical sophistication which would be necessary to make it a persuasively evidence-based indictment of the sexualisation trend. On the contrary, the study incorporates a number of assumptions which are, at best, subjective. Not necessarily wrong, I hasten to add. In value debates of this kind let us accept that there is often no 'right' and 'wrong' separate from the ideological or moral framework within which the judgement is made; but they are certainly contestable.

For example, at the core of the study is the concept of sexualisation, defined as the reduction, by the media, of a person's value to his or her sex appeal only, as measured on purely physical criteria: what is sometimes called body fascism, as in the pressure on young girls to be thin; or, in other terms, *sexual objectification*. The report takes as its starting point what is true for some people but not all: that sexualisation and objectification are unwelcome impositions of a patriarchal culture, something which is *done to us* by the media, rather than something we might choose to embrace as part of a 'healthy' and well-adjusted individuality. That women (or men, for that matter) might desire to be looked at and might invite the sexualised gaze by dressing and looking 'good', that in fact they do so much of the time as a matter of routine for all kinds of reasons ranging from the desire to boost self-esteem to the deliberate manipulation of cultural codes on sex and gender for career advancement, is not acknowledged in the report. Sexualisation is simply assumed to be a *bad thing*, and the media its agents.

Sexualisation is said to be getting worse, and too prevalent in many forms of American popular culture. A crude form of content analysis is used to assert, for example, that American sitcoms contain 3.3 incidents of 'sexual harassment' per episode. As any first-year media student knows, however, without any analysis of the context of this harassment, one cannot assess its meaning within the text. Perhaps it is being used in a way that sheds a critical light on male harassment of women, or to mock masculinity. With regard to pop videos, '57 percent featured a woman portrayed exclusively as a decorative sexual object' (APA, 2007, p.7).

Assertions of impact are made so loosely as to be meaningless. Decorative women in pop videos, for example, '*likely* drive home the point that being a successful sex object is the way to be perceived as mature and successful in the music industry' (Ibid., my emphasis). The fact that young men are also usually decorative in pop videos, and that sex is just as central to the selling of their music as it is to that of female performers, is not mentioned.

In TV cartoons, meanwhile, 'there is anecdotal evidence that they *may* contain sexualised images of girls and women' (p.8, my emphasis). In movies, there is asserted to be a 'near-absence of female characters in top-grossing motion pictures', while the 'sexily-clad Bratz dolls' have the '*potential* power' to influence girls (Ibid., my emphasis).

The case of Bratz makes an interesting example of how contemporary sexualised commodities are often contrasted with earlier, more 'innocent' commodities aimed at young females, such as the globally iconic Barbie doll. This rationale falters under close examination, however. Barbie, who was derived from an adult sex toy manu-factured in Germany in the late 1950s and 1960s,[33] was submissive, subordinate and safe, reflecting attitudes to women in the 1950s when she was invented, and retaining an iconic blonde innocence right up to her starring role in *Toy Story 3*, when she finally found some righteous feminist anger. Bratz, on the other hand, are the pro-ducts of forty years of second-wave feminism, hip-hop and 'post-feminism'. These girls don't take no shit, we might suggest, because forty years after the birth of second-wave feminism their young female consumers wouldn't either. The market loves them, and has made them internationally iconic, just as it has given us the 'Porn star' t-shirt and the domestic pole-dancing kit.

The APA continue:

> Frequent exposure to media images that sexualise girls and women *may* affect
> how girls conceptualise femininity and sexuality ... The sexualisation and
> objectification of women in the media *appear to* teach girls that as women, all
> they have to offer is their body and face, and that they should expend all their
> efforts on physical appearance.
>
> *(p.28, my emphasis)*

'May', 'potential', 'likely', 'appear to' – these qualifying terms reveal the flimsiness of
the report's arguments and render it limited as evidence. Instead, it reads as a plea for
action from one clearly distressed sector of the parental generation as they seek to
address a perceived moral decline affecting America's young women, their daughters.
The report routinely generalises from research on adult women and media to girls
and young women. Acknowledging the lack of research on mediated sexuality and
young people (a valid point, and one which continues to be true) the APA simply
assume that what applies to adults also applies to young girls and children. The
following statement is typical of the report:

> There is massive exposure to portrayals that sexualise women and girls and
> teach girls that women are sexual objects.
>
> *(p.15)*

In one memorable sentence, the APA report observes that 'young women in swim-
suits performed significantly worse on maths problems than did those wearing
sweaters'. Boys, too, were said to be affected adversely by cultural sexualisation. 'Even
viewing a single episode of an objectifying TV program such as *Charlie's Angels* lead
men to rate real women as less physically attractive' (p.29).

The main conclusions of the APA report found their way into subsequent articles
and book-length writings on pornographication. Sarracino's and Scott's *The Porning of
America* (2008), published under the auspices of the Unitarian Universalist Association
of Congregations (a liberal church commendably welcoming to gays, bisexual and
transgender worshippers within its ranks) states in its introduction:

> We identify sexualisation – which is rampant in our culture – as the root pro-
> blem underlying the damaging and dangerous practice of turning individuals,
> especially girls and young women, into sexual objects. Through sexualisation
> individuals are seen as having no value beyond their sexuality.
>
> *(2008, p.xix)*

'By the 1990s', they argue, 'not only had children become thoroughly sexualised in
movies, advertisements, and marketing, but something more general had begun to
occur: the sexualisation of just about everyone, regardless of age or status in society'
(p.29). These authors are unusual, for those approaching the issue from a religious

standpoint, in acknowledging the universality of sexual culture, including its explicit and transgressive forms.

> Porn has always existed in some form in America, and it can be found in all the cultures of the world, ancient and modern. If nothing else, the universality of porn forces us to acknowledge a fundamental reality: men and women are, in fact, sexual creatures.
>
> *(p.xii)*

They also highlight the lack of evidence for a key strand of the anti-porn argument, that consumption of pornography leads to sexual violence. They cite recent statistics to show that despite the expansion of pornography in American society, 'rates of rape and sexual assault dropped 68 per cent between 1993 and 2005' (p.163).

These concessions granted, the authors focus their critical attention on sexualisation, that more nebulous process leading to objectification and reduction of self-value to a calculation of the physical attributes of the body. As in the original APA report, it is this sense of something being wrong with, inappropriate about, female sexuality in twenty-first-century America that motivates the book. Given the moral premises of the authors, it cannot be allowed that 'raunch' culture and the forms of cultural sexualisation found objectionable are expressions of what women are becoming in late patriarchy, because feminism has created the space for them to do so; rather, they must be viewed as the negative effect of a dysfunctional media system which disseminates harmful messages. Harmful because?

> Girls evaluate and control their own bodies more in terms of their sexual desirability to others than in terms of their own desires, health, wellness, achievements or competence ... Perhaps the most insidious consequence of self-objectification is that it fragments consciousness. Chronic attention to physical appearance leaves fewer cognitive resources available for other mental and physical activities. Thinking about the body and comparing it to sexualised cultural ideals disrupts mental capacity.
>
> *(p.27)*

The United Kingdom

In the United Kingdom too, anxieties around cultural sexualisation built as the decade progressed. A 2003 study by Buckingham and Bragg had found that 'two thirds of children are getting their information about sex and relationships from soap opera and adult chat shows'.[34] Media coverage of this work tended to emphasise the fact that 'the media play an important role in shaping children's development, moral framework and understanding'. One press report noted that 'the subject of the power that the media exert over children is rising rapidly up the agenda'.[35] As indeed it continued to do through the decade, with a particular focus on the power of the media to sexualise children and young people.

Against this background, psychologist Linda Papadopoulos produced a report on *The Sexualisation of Young People* which set out to explore 'how hyper-sexualisation and objectification of girls on the one hand, and hyper-masculinisation of boys on the other, perpetuate and reinforce each other' (2010, p.3). The study was premised on 'popular perceptions' that inappropriate sexualisation was happening, and proceeded to present a series of assertions which could neither be proved nor disproved (a feature the report held in common with the Australian and US documents). An example, and typical of the style of the report, was the observation that:

> a dominant theme in magazines *seems to be* the need for girls to present themselves as sexually desirable in order to attract male attention.
>
> *(p.7, my emphasis)*

'Seems to be' is a subjective assessment, and in any event young women have been under pressure to look attractive to men since the days of Adam and Eve. If this pressure *is* real, in other words, it isn't new. The report's conclusions are repeatedly qualified by get-out clauses: 'some', 'may be', 'suggests that', and so on. Papadopoulos' report adds to the criticism of Bratz dolls, noting for example that 'most dolls in the range are heavily made-up, some are dressed in miniskirts and fishnet stockings' (p.38). Which may well be true, but then again, wasn't Barbie dressed to impress in the 1960s? In her report Papadopoulos includes references to the research evidence showing that 'high pornography use is not in itself an indicator of high risk for sexual aggression' (p.12) and the Buckingham and Bragg finding that 'some children and young people are highly media-savvy and well able to negotiate media content' (p.28). In short, the connections between media content, behaviour and attitudes, so blithely assumed elsewhere in this and the other reports discussed above, are conceded to be rather weak.[36]

Papadopoulos' approach, like that of the Australian and US variants, is to identify a range of cultural phenomena which 'we' – the great, anonymous public called forth to justify the investment of time in the cultural sexualisation problem – do not like or approve of, which are then linked to allegedly negative trends in sexual culture and behaviour, especially impacting on the young and the vulnerable. The evidential base for the argument is consistently weak to non-existent, there is no historical context to the analysis, and for every 'negative' trend identified there is, as we will explore in more detail in Part II, a competing positive reading.

Responding to the extensive media coverage which accompanied Papadopoulos' report, and following on from campaign commitments by the Conservative Party before it won office in 2010, in February 2011 the new UK government announced a review 'looking at the pressures on children to grow up too quickly',[37] or 'the commercialisation and sexualisation of children'. Chairing the review, which reported in May 2011, was Reg Bailey, chief executive of the Mothers' Union. *Letting Children Be Children* was expressly intended to respond to public anxieties around cultural sexualisation, and to make parents in particular feel that they were being listened to on the issue. As Bailey explained, 'sexualised and gender-stereotyped clothing, products and services for children are the biggest areas of concern for parents' (p.9). He called on the regulators and the media companies to 'play [their] part in putting the brakes on the unthinking drift towards an increasingly commercialised and sexualised world for children' (p.12).

Interestingly, however, Bailey acknowledged that this concern was being 'fanned by a sometimes prurient press' (p.9), perhaps of the kind that would juxtapose a report on the murder of Milly Dowler with a 'page three' photograph of a topless 17-year-old girl in a red top tabloid such as *The Sun* or the *Star*. And the report itself held back from making recommendations that would seriously restrict the freedom of the media in Britain. On the contrary, his suggestions sought to define more clearly the distinctions between the adult 'Red Light Zones' and those in which parents and children could reliably expect not to be confronted with inappropriate images and advertising messages. They included: reducing the visibility of sexualised images in public spaces; policing the TV watershed (9pm in the UK), and introducing a ratings system for pop videos; enhancing the scope for parental control of their children's access to the internet; preventing the sale of age-inappropriate goods and services; and improved media literacy for parents and children. All of this made sense in the context of an increasingly deregulated and uncensorable media environment, and was not in itself incompatible with the liberalisation of sexual culture I have suggested to be a positive trend in itself.

Of course parents should be able to control what their children watch on TV or other media platforms. There *should* be boundaries between the public sphere and the pornosphere, and watersheds to manage the spaces in the culture where those boundaries are blurred, such as in the promotional videos of Gaga or Rihanna. The Bailey report, contrary to expectations, steered a cautious course in negotiating these issues, favouring a self-regulatory, consensual approach over legislation (although leaving open the prospect of legal interventions at a later date).

The resurgence of anti-porn feminism

Accompanying the various reports and journalistic responses to reports which have driven public policy in the area of sexual culture since 2002 were a number of interventions by anti-porn feminist scholars. Karen Boyle's *Everyday Pornography* collection, for example, set out to challenge the assertion of Linda Williams and other adherents to the 'new paradigm' that porn studies no longer requires 'agonising over sexual politics' (Boyle, 2010, p.1). For Boyle and the authors she assembled in her collection, the diversification and democratisation of the pornosphere was less important than the fact that pornography remained a predominantly male, heterosexual interest. Her first chapter, an account of a round-table discussion based on Gail Dines' anti-porn slideshow, took as its starting point that 'pornography is a form of violence against women'.[38]

The volume also contained some less overtly condemnatory essays, such as Ana Bridges' piece on content analytical methodology as applied to porn, which began from the premise that 'pornography serves as a teacher — a way to instruct youth about appropriate and expected behaviours in sexual situations' (2010, p.35). Sarah Neely wrote about the representation of sex in the Second Life virtual world, discussing among other topics debates amongst users about the ethics of virtual rape and other scenarios (2010). Susanna Paasonen, whose work is exemplary in its respect for evidence and women's experience (including her own), contributed to the volume, arguing for a more nuanced feminist approach to the meanings inherent in pornography. She noted, for example, that 'pornography can just as well ridicule or exaggerate relations of power to the level of the absurd as support or justify them' (2010, p.75). Paasonen's essay was entitled 'Repetition and hyperbole', and

> argues for the need to resist literal readings of [pornography's] meaning … The chapter suggests that feminist analyses [of porn] should push beyond readings that are either literal (as in reading relations of control displayed in pornography as exemplary of power relations, one-to-one) or symbolic (as in interpreting pornography as symptomatic of an ideology).
>
> *(2010, p.63)*

With these exceptions, however, *Everyday Pornography* was characteristic of a resurgence of anti-porn writing which tended to blur the boundaries between research, commentary and campaigning polemic. Reist and Bray's edited volume on *Big Porn Inc* (2011), for example, contained mainly short commentaries which would have sat equally well in a newspaper or online opinion site.[39] In *Big Porn Inc* Julia Long noted 'a remarkable resurgence' of anti-porn feminist activism in the UK since the mid-2000s (2011). In December 2011 Long and Gail Dines wrote in the *Guardian* that their revival of anti-porn discourse was not a 'moral panic', but a legitimate response to 'the corporate-controlled media industry that produces these images'. They disputed that their anti-porn campaigns have had anything in common with 'right wing attempts to police sexual behaviour'.[40]

> Feminists who organise against pornification are not arguing that sexualised images of women cause moral decay; rather that they perpetuate myths of women's unconditional sexual availability and object status, and thus undermine women's rights to sexual autonomy, physical safety and economic and social equality. The harm done to women is not a moral harm but a political one, and any analysis must be grounded in a critique of the corporate control of our visual landscape.

This they tied to a broader, and older, left-wing tradition of fighting capitalist control of the media,[41] and to an array of perceived problems such as 'women's self-loathing' (described as 'big business' which 'supports a global capitalist system'; a growth in cosmetic surgery amongst women; 'hypersexualisation'; low pay for women in industry; and more). Connections between these phenomena – and their extent can be questioned (for example, if sexualisation causes eating disorders and anorexia by promoting thinness, as is often claimed, why is obesity amongst both women and men the advanced capitalist world's most urgent emerging health problem?) – were not substantiated anywhere.

Anti-porn arguments have, then, been framed in qualifying, hesitant terms that shed their rigour when scrutinised. For example, in an article published by the *Guardian* newspaper on 'The Men who Believe Porn is Wrong' Dr Andrew Durham, a 'social worker', is quoted thus:

> Pornography reinforces the wider media-led messages about the roles of men and women, and can also reinforce a particular attitude towards sex, an attitude that is devoid of trust, caring, and in the worst cases, consent.[42]

For the first statement there is no evidence provided, nor any clarity on what 'media-led messages' about men's and women's roles are. In the second, there is not even a claim, merely a theoretical possibility asserted. One might just as well say, the Bible *can* reinforce a particular attitude about how to deal with blasphemers and unbelievers. Whether it drives behaviour, for the great majority of Christians, is doubtful. Kira Cochrane, the author of the article, states that porn 'might shift' the way men respond to women in the real world. Then again, it might not. Cochrane notes 'the terrible way in which women are sometimes treated in the industry'. And yes, women are sometimes treated terribly in the porn business, as in every other business. As are men.[43] As are we all, sometimes, in every walk of life.

According to Mary Eberstadt, a contributor to *The Social Costs Of Pornography* (Stoner and Hughes, 2010),

> studies have shown that porn abounds with degradation and violence, particularly towards women, and that consumers of these sexual messages are more likely to try such acts themselves. Studies also show that contemporary pornography broadcasts grossly distorted messages about women – chiefly that they enjoy anything at all being done to them, no matter how degrading or painful.[44]

Gail Dines asserts that 'we are bringing up a generation of boys on cruel, violent porn, and given what we know about how images affect people, this is going to have a profound effect on their sexuality, behaviour and attitudes towards women'.[45]

These claims are without empirical foundation, as even many anti-porn commentators acknowledge. Pamela Paul's *Pornified* contains, amidst its wealth of alarming assertions about what porn is doing to men and women in America, the acknowledgement that 'social science has had a difficult time scientifically proving that pornography affects men either positively or negatively' (2005, p.73).[46] We know, in fact, very little about the effects of the media on individual behaviour, and even less about the impact of porn consumption on sexual attitudes. Dines continues nonetheless:

> I have found that the earlier men use porn, the more likely they are to have trouble developing close, intimate relationships with real people ...

The more porn images filter into mainstream culture, the more girls and women are stripped of full human status and reduced to sex objects. This has a terrible effect on girls' sexual identity because it robs them of their own sexual desire ...

Pornography is the perfect propaganda piece for patriarchy. In nothing else is their [men] hatred of us [women] quite as clear.[47]

Dines also states that pornography 'normalises and legitimises sexually abusive behaviour'.[48]

Some of these arguments have been in circulation for decades, while others, such as the addiction thesis examined below, are more recent. Hundreds, if not thousands of research projects have sought to prove the various kinds of harmful effects hypothesised in the anti-porn literature. Despite the confident assertion of Karen Kinnick that 'more than thirty years of empirical evidence ... overwhelmingly support the case for harmful effects [of pornography] to both individuals and society' (2007, p.17), none have produced reliable scientific evidence that the consumption of pornography causes sexual violence, or makes it more likely by affecting the attitudes of the user, for example by making him (and these studies almost always assume that the user of porn is a he, and heterosexual at that) more 'callous' towards women.

Many anti-pornography commentators accept that point, and qualify assertions about harms caused with the frequent use of terms such as 'may', 'some', 'perhaps', 'it seems' and so on. These terms act as escape clauses, allowing anti-porn campaigners to avoid the issue of what constitutes convincing evidence in the substantiation of a cause-and-effect relationship between pornography and behaviour and to rely instead, along with a news media which breathlessly reports every twist and turn in the sexualisation debate (with suitably revealing pictorial illustrations),[49] on anecdote, supposition and assumption, all of which are sufficient to reinforce the views of the already-converted but have no empirical validity. Where research *has* been done on the content of the pornosphere in recent years, there is no evidence of an increase in violent or misogynistic material as a proportion of the whole (McKee *et al.*, 2008).

The evidential basis for much of the anti-porn discourse is typified by a report on the work of Princeton psychologist Susan Fisher, who 'showed, using MRI scans, that when men viewed pornography, and then real women, their brains processed the images of real women as objects rather than human beings – in other words, pornography did affect the way men viewed real women'.[50] One may ask: What does it mean to view someone as an 'object' rather than 'a human being'? Are human beings not objects? Is 'objectification', far from being a patriarchal imposition, not an inevitable consequence of perception, which carries no ethical connotation unless one wishes to see it? Here we are in the realm of metaphysics rather than hard science, which is fine as long as the two are not confused.

Men and porn

Part of the porno-fear wave was a resurgence of the men's movement politics of the 1970s and 1980s, in which male authors declared their disgust for and opposition to pornography. Prominent amongst these was Robert Jensen, whose *Getting Off* (2007) asserted that the dominant masculinity in the US was 'the masculinity of a mob, ready to rape' (p.1). American men were 'toxic', and pornography was to blame. 'We live in a rape culture', he went on, 'a world that hates women and children.' Pornography is 'a mirror of the way this culture hates women and children' (p.50). Jensen confessed to shedding tears at the horror of it all. In a later edited collection he wrote an essay with the title 'Pornography is what the end of the world looks like' (2010). By this he was not harbouring 'apocalyptic delusions', but merely meant that pornography

> is what the end will look like if we don't reverse the pathological course that we are on in patriarchal, white-supremacist, predatory corporate-capitalist societies.
>
> *(p.25)*

As we shall see in Chapter 5, women and children were treated with much greater cruelty in the past than in the twenty-first century, and today are treated with much greater cruelty in societies where pornography is illegal or strictly controlled. There is evil in the world, we can agree, but pornography is rarely the cause of it. It is, indeed, far less implicated in the commission of evil acts such as rape, genocide and child abuse than the holy books of the world's great religions. As for the fact that porn users include women, gay men, and many other groups who are not associated with 'toxic masculinity', Jensen doesn't mention it.

In 2010 men's consumption of porn was even being blamed in some quarters for the global financial crisis, albeit in a certain tongue-in-cheek manner. According to *The Wall Street Journal*:

> Ever since the dawn of the culture wars, when widespread obscenity seemed to symbolise all that was going wrong with America, no subject has furnished more demagogue gold than pornography ... Take for example the current outrage at the Securities and Exchange Commission, where, according to an inspector-general's report that was made public last week, employees spent a great deal of time and used up prodigious amounts of computer resources gazing at Internet pornography. What's more, their porn habits date back to 2007 and 2008, when the need for an attentive SEC was at its greatest.[51]

Other male authors declaring themselves in opposition to pornographication and cultural sexualisation in this period included Michael Kimmel, Michael Flood and Clive Hamilton, the latter working with the Australia Institute in a sustained lament about the commercialisation of sexuality which echoed that of D.H. Lawrence.

Porn addiction

In 2003 Edward Marriott in the *Guardian* wrote that 'pornography, like drugs and drink, is an addictive substance'.[52] Another *Guardian* piece written eight years later reflected the changing nature of pornography consumption when it examined the issue of porn addiction amongst women. While many anti-porn campaigners were still disputing that women could really like porn, this author took that fact for granted, focusing on female porn users such as Caroline, 21, who 'has just finished seeing a sex addiction therapist to help get her porn habit under control'.[53] The article reported that one third of clients treated by the UK-based Quit Porn Addiction counselling service are women, that 60 per cent of women view porn online, and that nearly one third of female porn-users described themselves in a 2006 survey as 'addicted'. The article continued that women, like men, go through a cycle of exposure, addiction and desensitisation. The appeal, for women as for men?

> Orgasm releases a dopamine-oxytocin high that has been compared to a heroin hit, and many regular users of internet porn report experiencing an almost trance-like effect that not only makes them feel oblivious to the world, but also gives them a sense of power. As porn becomes more pervasive, women are using it as a quick way to have sex without emotional investment, just as men traditionally have.

Wendy Maltz notes that 'up to half of all regular pornography users report some type of negative consequence or concern about their use' (2010, p.12). She agrees that porn stimulates the reward and pleasure centres in the brain, instantly and dramatically increasing the production of dopamine, a neurotransmitter associated with both sexual arousal and drug highs. In addition, using porn for sexual stimulation

> has been shown to increase production of other 'feel-good' chemicals, such as adrenaline, endorphins, testosterone and serotonin; with sexual climax, it releases powerful hormones related to falling in love and bonding, such as oxytocin and vasopren.
>
> *(p.16)*

For these reasons, the logic follows, 'a person becomes addicted to a set of behaviours that, in turn, powerfully alter brain chemistry'. Thus, 'pornography is moving from an individual and complex problem, to a public health problem, capable of deeply harming the emotional, sexual and relationship well being of millions of men, women and children' (Ibid.). Researchers Sithartan and Sithartan, on the other hand, are sceptical of the addiction model, if it is applied too literally. 'In our view', they write, 'engaging in any "excessive" behaviour is a learned habit and can be unlearned.'[54]

Conclusion

At the core of porno fear is a set of tastes and judgements about what is appropriate in the realms of sexual identity and fantasy, a literal reading of the images found in porn, and corresponding rejection of any conception of their status as transgressive fantasy, and a determination to see all porn as synonymous with the worst, most misogynistic porn (of which there is certainly a lot around, just like there is a lot of misogynistic advertising, hip hop music, stand up comedy, 'torture porn' movies, and so on). We see in much of this commentary a campaigning, sometimes openly emotional mindset, in which consideration of the evidence matters less than a subjective belief or gut feeling about the appropriateness of what others choose to do with their lives, in and out of the bedroom, the night club, and the burlesque show. Part II will present a range of alternative readings of the pornographic.

PART II

How pornography changed the world and made it a better place

PREFACE TO PART II

It would be wrong to suggest that all or even the bulk of writing and commentary on pornographication and cultural sexualisation, which has been produced since the resurgence of porno fear in 2004/05, has been fearful, critical or condemnatory. I, for example, have contributed to print, broadcast and online media, such as the Melbourne-based online publication *The Conversation*, where I enlisted Lady Gaga in order to interpret cultural sexualisation as evidence not of patriarchy's resilience but of feminism's advance.[1]

The piece joined others by Australian academics Lauren Rosewarne and Kath Albury who, in their scholarly work, have engaged with the anti-porn arguments in Australia.[2] Albury wrote about the Australian Feminist Porn Awards (which according to the website 'have been celebrating feminist smut for five sexy years').[3] The *Online Opinion* journal published a series of articles by Jennifer Wilson, including on September 5, 2011 a piece entitled 'How to incite a moral panic about sex', critiquing a University of Buffalo report on sexualisation which was, Wilson noted, based entirely on images found in *Rolling Stone* magazine.[4]

The scholarly literature, meanwhile, has been reflective of the new porn studies paradigm shift identified by Feona Attwood, engaging constructively with the emergence of female (and gay or non-heteronormative) sexualities which have, in their deviation from both patriarchal and radical feminist stereotypes of femininity, been made possible by sex-political progress.

That said, porno fear is real, and anti-porn commentary has tended to attract more attention in the popular media than the work of Smith, Paasonen and others. In Part II, therefore, I will set out the various ways in which, in my view, pornography has indeed been good, for individuals and for societies in general, and for the positions of women and men, gay and straight within them. Porn producer Anna Arrowsmith observed in a newspaper article published in October 2011 that:

Since Andrea Dworkin wrote about pornography as being anti-women in the early 1980s, we have become acclimatised to the idea that porn is bad for us, and must only be tolerated due to reasons of democracy and liberalism. In the past 30 years this idea has largely gone unchallenged outside academia and, in the process, feminism has been conflated with the anti-porn position. We have effectively been neuro-linguistically programmed to equate porn with harm. Not only is there no good evidence to support this view, but there is a fair amount of evidence to support the opposite.[5]

The following chapters summarise that evidence.

5

WHAT HAS PORNOGRAPHY EVER DONE FOR US?

The argument from evidence

The previous chapter showed how, given the lack of evidence on behavioural effects, the focus of critical commentary has moved away from pornography itself towards the broader range of phenomena associated with cultural sexualisation, and the harms allegedly caused by this trend to girls' self-esteem, boys' perspectives on girls, and other attitudinal features. These claims are, however, even more difficult to prove than the various theses which have circulated around porn's harmful effects on behaviour.

So we are not talking about hard science here, but as in so many areas of the humanities and the social sciences, complex matters of judgement and interpretation as studied with the aid of methods reasonably described as contentious. By their nature, the kinds of psychological experiments traditionally employed over many years to measure the effects of porn have been limited by their inescapable artificiality.

Do subjects in a laboratory environment respond to pornography, and the questions put to them about their sexual attitudes before and after viewing sexually explicit content, in ways which have a bearing on their actual behaviour in real social situations, where there exist a complex array of social conventions and constraints intended precisely to inhibit certain kinds of behaviours and reward others? The subjects of studies on males have often been American college students, in the grip of early manhood and peer pressure. How might that, and the knowledge that they are participating in an experiment, shape their responses to questions about porn use, sex and attitudes to girls?

This is not to dispute that such research can be of value in understanding how, in some circumstances, some people respond to sexual culture. Nor is it to dispute that there are associations and correlations to be observed between some porn users and some pathological behaviours. Pornography *is* used by paedophiles to groom children for sexual abuse. The making of child pornography, like all porn, has become much easier with digital technology, as has its distribution and consumption. Such images are illegal in most jurisdictions, and many producers and users have been successfully prosecuted. Sex with children, because it cannot be consensual under the law, is by definition a criminal act, and pornography the record of that crime. The illegality of child pornography is not, however, a consequence of the fact that it has been shown to *cause* child abuse (as opposed to accompanying such abuse, or grooming victims of it). Such images *are* child abuse.

Such activity was endemic in human societies long before pornography emerged. Child abuse happens, regrettably, in every society, in every era, with or without the involvement of pornography, and is usually perpetrated by trusted carers such as parents, family friends and priests. Incidents of sexual abuse or assault committed by adults on children to whom they are not related or otherwise connected are the exception to a much more depressing rule – that the majority of child abusers are, and have always been, trusted individuals in positions of access to children, who have not required the stimulus of pornography in order to carry out their abusive acts.

The still-unfolding global epidemic of paedophile priests is deeply rooted in a church which bitterly opposes pornography and cultural sexualisation (as well as homosexuality, divorce, contraception and so on). As this book was nearing completion in early 2012 a child-abuse scandal involving Benedictine monks who ran a number of Catholic boys' schools in England was being widely reported in the British media. No one asserts that pornography is to blame for the hundreds of thousands of children sexually abused by Catholic clergy over the decades (and, indeed, centuries). Neither can the Bible, or Jesus Christ be blamed. The truth about priestly paedophilia is much more complex than the attribution of blame to any image or category of text which may have 'made' them do it. So too is the truth about sexual violence in general, and the relationship of pornography to it. To repeat – it is not necessary to deny *any* connection between pornography and sexual violence or abuse for us to be entitled to say, on the basis of the evidence, that there is no proven *causal* connection.

Pornography is used by some men to groom their female (adult) partners into participating in activities to which they might not otherwise consent. Pornography can in this sense 'script' sexual activity, and may be utilised in a manner that could be judged to be coercive or intimidatory. It is certainly used by couples in a manner which is neither of those things (see Chapter 7). The same is true of alcohol and other substances used as tools of seduction, and there have been many trials involving alcohol in which the line between consent and coercion has been at the heart of the case (the 2010 Swedish allegations of rape and sexual assault against Wikileaks founder Julian Assange provide an example of how contentious such debates can be).

Some notorious sex offenders, such as Graham Coutts, whose murder of Jane Longhurst in 2003 provoked the campaign which led eventually to the introduction of the 2010 Extreme Pornography legislation in the UK (Attwood and Smith, 2010), have used pornography which anticipates their crimes – that is to say, represents in the form of pornography acts which the offender has, or is alleged to have, carried out on a victim without her consent. In late 2011 the conviction of Vincent Tabak for the murder of Joanna Yeates in the UK was accompanied by media reports that violent pornography, including scenes of choking, had been found on his computer (he had choked his victim to death). Around the same time British paedophile and serial killer Robert Black was reported to have been a user of child pornography during the years when he was active. The 2002 case of the German 'cannibal' who ate the penis of another man he met online (with the man's consent, apparently) and made a video recording the entire episode for his and other's private sexual arousal, is well known.[1]

To make these connections between representation and reality is relevant to the discussion of porn's impacts on sexual behaviour, although they do not prove a cause and effect relationship. Did porn cause the aberrant behaviours of, for example, Graham Coutts and Vincent Tabak, or did the predisposition to aberrant behaviour lead the perpetrators in these cases to seek out pornography which reflected their violent sexual fantasies and desires? Would they not have committed their crimes had they not used pornography at some point in their pasts? Did they access pornography in the hours or minutes before the murders, and did this exposure push them into enacting transgressive fantasies which led to the murders of two women?

The answers to these questions are rarely known, in the absence of the convicted men's explanation of their motives and the role played by pornography in triggering the crime. Even if they or their defence lawyers do claim a cause and effect connection, as did the serial killer Ted Bundy in relation to his crimes in the 1980s, would the claims be reliable, given the obvious self-interest which attaches to the denial of personal responsibility for criminal behaviour, and the blaming of some other factor than individual choice?

What if the answers to all of the above questions were 'yes', however, and we could prove beyond doubt that crime A was caused by exposure to pornographic image B; if we could prove that this image, or set of images, led to criminal acts which would not have occurred otherwise? Would this be sufficient evidence to justify the conclusions of anti-pornography campaigners, and laws such as the UK's 2010 Extreme Pornography Act which are intended precisely to limit or even prohibit the consumption of images such as those favoured by Tabak and Coutts?

In my view, no. It is a commonplace to remark that porn can no more be blamed for the crimes of Fred and Rosemary West than the 'voice of God' can be blamed for the attacks in the 1970s and 1980s on prostitutes by Peter Sutcliffe, the 'Yorkshire Ripper'.[2] We cannot 'prove', one way or the other, that this piece of media content caused that deviant act, nor can we legislate against the possibility that someone who at some time uses pornography will commit a sex crime inspired by the image.

Banning religion would not end sectarian hate crime, nor would it be fair to the hundreds of millions of people who follow religion but do no harm to others. Banning pornography would not end misogyny and male sexualised violence, nor would it be fair to the hundreds of millions of people who use it without causing harm to others. Sadomasochistic porn, for example – which includes some of the categories of 'extreme' material prohibited by the Extreme Pornography Act – is regularly used in consensual relationships by people who engage in BDSM activities as a lifestyle. For them, the violence or coercion depicted in the content is a representation of the kinds of role play which they enjoy in their private lives.[3] Clarissa Smith explains the process of pornographic reading thus:

> In coming to a sexually explicit publication, readers bring expectations – pornography has social meaning before any instance of use of it – and they measure the material in front of them in light of those expectations ... People don't interpret pornography, they respond to it and in and through those responses accord it a significance in their understanding of themselves, their pleasures, the sexual pleasures of others, the social, economic, medical and cultural place of sexuality.
>
> *(2007, p.227)*

If we assume that the figures for pornography consumption are even approximately correct (and they underestimate the reality, because of lingering social stigma around porn use), we might conclude that in a society such as the United Kingdom, more than half of all adults have used pornography at some point in their lives. We might agree that this number has increased as the pornosphere has expanded, and that this pattern is replicated all over the world. And yet, as we shall see in a moment, the incidence of sexual violence has declined significantly over that same period in the UK, as it has elsewhere.

Consider the example of knives. In the United Kingdom, and this author's home country of Scotland in particular, knives are a major cause of criminal injury and death, often fuelled by the disinhibitor alcohol. It would be entirely inappropriate, however, to ban their use, or the consumption of alcohol, on the grounds that of the many millions who use them responsibly and for the purposes intended by their manufacturers, a few hundred transformed them into dangerous weapons which they then used against their fellow citizens. One can say that a knife caused a death in a particular instance, but not that knives 'cause' violence. Violence has its evolutionary, psychological and emotional causes, its contexts and meanings in specific times and places, and there are many ways of inflicting it. If not knives, then human beings will use guns, or broken bottles, or hammers, or potentially any object with the capacity to wound another human body.

Sexual violence also has its causes, complex and deep-rooted, and those predisposed to it can easily find forms of pornography which reflect or even endorse misogynistic and sexually violent behaviour. McKee *et al.* note that 'like other media forms, pornography depicts the range of social attitudes towards female sexuality. In some cases it celebrates sexual expression; in others it links sexuality with humiliation and violence' (2008, p.183). Some may interpret pornographic images as calls to action of some kind, as others may interpret the Bible as a call to kill prostitutes, or the Koran to kill 'infidels'. In none of these cases is a ban justified.

The documented connections between pornography consumption and pathological, sociopathic sexual behaviour are real, however, with real consequences for those on the receiving end of sexual violence. This is a truth that all who support the liberalisation of sexual culture must acknowledge (as those who support freedom of media must acknowledge that the uses to which it is put may not always be progressive or humanitarian).

It is the flipside of the fact that many, including many women, find forms of sex-ualised violence such as sadomasochism and BDSM sexy, and engage in it con-sensually with male or female partners. Many users of extreme pornography would never dream of enacting those scenes on a partner, even as it arouses them in the privacy of their own imaginations. Neither truth supports a cause–effect model for making sense of pornography's relationship to sexual violence, because such a model cannot possibly capture the complexity of human sexuality, and the nature of the interaction between fantasy, representation and behavioural reality.

Human behaviour can be explained and made intelligible only in the environ-mental context within which it is shaped and influenced. That context cannot be reduced to one stimulus or trigger, even if it might appear so in some situations when viewed in isolation. Heterosexual men have sex with other heterosexual men in prisons where they have no access to women. This does not mean they are homo-sexual. Some women indulge in submission and rape fantasies. This does not mean they wish to be tied up and raped in real life (Kipnis, 1996).

On the one hand, there are so many potential influences on a given individual's thinking and behaviour that isolating the precise role of one is practically impossible. On the other, no one stimulus has exactly the same meaning or significance for any two people. Meanings vary, reflecting each individual's infinitely variable make-up. The 'voice of God' he says he heard in his head made Peter Sutcliffe murder women he judged to have sinned against God's law. Others – the vast majority of religious believers – will regard the word of their God as a guide to living lives of charity and kindness to others. The same logic applies to pornography, the users of which are to the same extent as the population in general good, decent, kind-hearted people.

These debates are rehearsed endlessly in a vast wealth of research literature, never to a conclusion accepted by all sides. So, rather than seek to solve the unsolvable problem of what came first – the deviant chicken or the pornographic egg – I wish in the remainder of this chapter, and in the next two, to explore three indices of socio-sexual relationships as they have developed over a period of decades. This period coincides with the pornographication of mainstream culture on the one hand, and major advances in the political and socio-economic rights of women and homosexuals on the other. It is a period in which patriarchy has been substantially transformed, and heterosexist hegemony replaced by an environment in which homosexuality, bisexuality, transsexuality and other types of sexual identity, once suppressed, mar-ginalised or simply ignored, have become visible and accepted by a large proportion of public opinion. Against that background I will consider, in turn, trends in:

- The incidence of sexual violence against women;
- The socio-economic status of women; and
- The incidence of child abuse.

I will ask, not 'Does pornography cause sexual violence?' but:

- Why, if pornography is so harmful in sexual terms to women and children, has the incidence of sexual violence declined in those countries where pornography has expanded the most, and is today most commonplace?
- Why are attitudes to homosexuality and other sexual minorities more tolerant in societies where pornography circulates with relative freedom?
- Why, if pornography is a cause of such damaging beliefs on the part of men, were attitudes to women and gays so much more backward and hostile in the age before porn became mainstream?
- Why, if porn is so harmful to women, and reinforces the misogynistic attitudes which fuel rape and other crimes, are women as a group treated so much worse in societies where even the mildest forms of pornography are banned?

Pornography and sexual violence – a comparative transcultural analysis

Steven Pinker's study of trends in human violence notes that there has been a dramatic decline in its incidence over the period of recorded human history (2011).[4] We live, he concludes from a careful consideration of the statistical evidence, in the most non-violent era in human history. Pinker cites statistics which show steep declines in violence in the US and western European countries from the 1950s to the late 1960s, then a rise associated with demographic and cultural trends until the late 1980s, followed by another steep decline to the present.[5]

The decline includes the violent crimes of rape, sexual assault and domestic violence, as well as various forms of child abuse, including sexual abuse. Although we may, in large part because of the ubiquity and intensity of contemporary news culture, perceive that we live in a world of unprecedented conflict and horror, to the extent that we may experience what has been called with some justification 'compassion fatigue' (Moeller, 1999), the incidence of actual violence has fallen steadily on a number of measures since human societies began their long march towards what we may call 'civilisation'.

Moreover, the most developed societies – the advanced liberal democracies of the capitalist world, and societies more broadly where government is established and consensual – are those in which violence has declined the most, and the values of compassion and empathy progressed furthest. Wars are still fought by the advanced capitalist powers, murders still committed by citizens of those societies, but their scale and frequency are hugely reduced in comparison to earlier periods in history, such as the Mongol invasion of Europe and the 100 Years War.

Public attitudes to violence have also changed for the better, as Pinker's marshalling of the evidence makes clear. Where public executions and elaborately sadistic state-sanctioned torture were once commonplace (and still are in some societies),[6] advanced capitalist societies have evolved much more humane modes of punishment and civil control. The Abu Ghraib atrocities of 2004 in Iraq were horrifying, but also exceptional. The controversy around waterboarding – regarding whether it is torture or robust interrogation – stemmed from the very fact that, even in war time, even when civilians are threatened by suicide terror attacks capable of killing thousands, physical means of obtaining information from suspects are deemed unacceptable by the vast majority of citizens, as well as their elected representatives. States and their representatives may violate these behavioural norms, and be embarrassed when caught out, as the US was by exposure of the Abu Ghraib atrocity photography in 2004, and by Wikileaks' release of the Collateral Murder video in 2010. But the expectations are real, and they do matter.

Pinker is not the first to make the point about declining levels of violence in human societies over time. Media studies scholars have long drawn attention to the paradox that, while Hollywood films and video games are regularly condemned for becoming more violent, on the grounds that this causes or encourages violence in society, the actual incidence of recorded violence has gone down steadily. But Pinker's analysis of the evidence over such an extended period reminds us of just how much *has* changed for the better in the way we live and are governed, and the value of taking an historical perspective on issues which concern us in the present.

Can the same then be argued of sexual violence, and what we might think of as the governance of sexual relationships and identities? As public anxiety around cultural sexualisation and pornographication has intensified, is there any evidence whatsoever to support the assertion that the cultural trends alleged to be negative have harmed women, children, or any other group of victims? The short answer to this fundamental question is no. There is no evidence other than the anecdotal that cultural sexualisation, or pornographication, has damaged or is damaging women and other groups. Catherine MacKinnon asserts that '*certainly* the level of threat and damage to women's status and treatment and to equality of the sexes *worsens* as pornography has gone mainstream and is seen as more legitimate' (2011, p.11, my emphasis). Robert Jensen states that 'we live in a pornography-saturated culture in which women are routinely targets of sexual violence and intrusion' (2011, p.25).

Both assertions are unfounded, and the linkage of the two phenomena – pornography saturation and 'routine' violence on women – misleading. The situation Jensen describes is in fact the opposite of what we see in officially compiled statistics of violence against women and children in societies where pornography and cultural sexualisation have proceeded furthest. Research generated by the US Commission on Obscenity and Pornography (1970) found no evidence of a causal link between pornography and rape. Kutchinsky (1991) examines and discusses the findings of subsequent research, noting that a number of laboratory experiments have been conducted akin to the types of experiments developed by those researching the effects of nonsexual media violence. As in the latter, a certain degree of increased 'aggressiveness' (itself a methodologically problematic term) has been found under certain circumstances, but in the main:

> Studies of rapists' and nonrapists' immediate sexual reactions to presentations of pornography showed generally greater arousal to non-violent scenes, and no

difference can be found in this regard between convicted rapists, nonsexual criminals and noncriminal males.

(p.47)

Kutchinsky's review also sought to test the necessary precondition for a substantial causal relationship between the availability of pornography and the incidence of rape – namely, that increased availability of such material was followed by an increase in cases of reported rape. The incidence of rape and attempted rape during the period 1964–84 was studied in four countries: the US, Denmark, Sweden and West Germany. In each there was a significant expansion in the availability of pornography over these two decades, while the incidence of reported sexual violence stayed the same or fell. Thus, writes Kutchinsky:

> The aggregate data on rape and other violent or sexual offences from four countries where pornography has become widely and easily available during the period we have dealt with would seem to exclude, beyond any reasonable doubt, that this availability has had any detrimental effects in the form of increased sexual violence.
>
> *(p.62)[7]*

A summary of more recent research by Ferguson and Hartley finds similarly:

> The available data about pornography consumption and rape rates in the United States seem to rule out a causal relationship, at least with respect to pornography availability causing an increase in the incidence of rape. One could even argue that the available research and self-reported and official statistics might provide evidence for the reverse effect; the increasing availability of pornography appears to be associated with a decline in rape.
>
> *(2009, p.328)*

In the US, note these authors, the recorded incidence of rape declined steadily in the 1990s, at the same time as pornography was expanding, a pattern which continued into the 2000s until, by 2009, the incidence of rape in the US was at its lowest level for 50 years. This is consistent with the conclusion that 'pornography consumption may actually reduce rape and other sex offending' (p.326). They observe that:

> most industrial nations are currently experiencing a significant decline in rape and sexual assault rates despite the increasing availability of pornography.
>
> *(p.323)*

Pinker's historical study of violence includes a substantial discussion on the decline of rape, other forms of violence against women such as domestic violence, and the rise of women's rights (which he asserts are linked trends, associated with changing attitudes and moral frameworks).

On rape, having reminded his readers of how extensive this crime has been throughout human history, and in every culture for which records exist (a 'universal' of human society which he and others attribute to evolutionary drivers associated with genetic reproduction) Pinker notes that since the early 1970s and the flowering of second-wave feminism with books such as Susan Brownmiller's *Against Our Will* (1975), both public tolerance and the recorded incidence of rape have declined sharply, despite suggestions to the contrary from some of what he calls 'advocacy groups'.[8] In the United States, according to Bureau of Justice Statistics cited by Pinker, between 1973 and 2008 the recorded incidence of rape fell by 80 per cent, from 250 per 100,000 to 50 per 100,000. This corresponds to studies of university students showing that in the US over a 25 year period (1970–95) attitudes to women have become 'steadily more progressive' (2011, p.651). For example, public tolerance of domestic violence in marriage fell from more than half who believed it to be acceptable in some circumstances as recently as 1987, to less than 14 per cent in 1997.

With respect to the UK, data allows comparisons to be made from 1981 to 1995, when sexual offences peaked, then up to 2008, when their incidence had reached an historic low. Although the UK Home Office does not present data on trends on rape, Pinker observes that the recorded decline in domestic violence in Britain is similar to that in the US, and that rape can also be assumed to have declined over this period. In short, although there is room for debate and difference of interpretation around statistical trends in the US, the UK and comparable countries, the overall trend is downwards when it comes to all forms of violence against women.

If we accept that pornography has not increased rape, but are reluctant to say that it has reduced it, what else might explain the fall in rape rates? For Ferguson and Hartley, 'if rape is about domination and control of females by males, can the advanced integration of females into more economically and politically powerful positions explain the decline in rape rates irrespective of increases in the availability and consumption of pornography?' (2009, p.327). Yes, we can answer, although the two explanations are not incompatible. Pornography may permit the expression of sexual desires that would otherwise be dangerously suppressed, at the same time as women are making socio-economic and political progress and thus becoming less vulnerable to assault by men.

Women *are* of course targets of sexual violence, and do experience what Robert Jensen calls 'intrusion'. They always have been, and no text is more violent and gleefully gory in its descriptions of violence against women (and children, and men) than the Holy Bible. Regrettable though this is – and the reasons for male violence against women are much debated by evolutionary psychologists – men are much more likely to be the victims of violence in general than women.

Those most likely to be the victims of random violence in a country such as the UK and a city such as Glasgow are young, single men out on the town of an evening. In the UK the British Crime survey 2009 (Walker *et al.*, 2009) found that all violent crime had fallen by 49 per cent since 1995, and that in the same period 'there have been large falls in domestic and stranger violence' (p.6). Sexual offences comprised one per cent of all recorded crime, and men were twice as likely as women to be victims of violence (with 16–24-year-old men at the greatest risk). Sexual offences in 2008–9 in England were at the lowest level since the introduction of the National Crime Records System. Serious sexual crimes fell by two per cent year-on-year in 2008–9, and some offences, such as prostitution, by as much as 11 per cent.

It is true that rape and other crimes of sexualised violence are more likely to happen to women, which reflects the power relations of patriarchy as much as the physical variations of male and female. However, the incidence of sexualised violence has fallen dramatically in recent times, as has societal tolerance of it in the sexually liberal countries. Forty years ago in the UK or the US, domestic violence was regarded as 'routine', probably because not long before that women had been viewed by the law, and by patriarchal custom, as the property of the men they married. Men could beat women with impunity in many countries until quite late in the twentieth century (as parents could beat their children). Like child abuse, even after the legal climate changed, domestic violence was an invisible crime, an unrecognised assault on human dignity, and discussion of its incidence and cures subject to taboo. Now these forms of violence are widely condemned by the public and punished by the law in countries such as Australia, the US and the UK (if not always sufficiently, some may think).

In relation to child sexual abuse, there has also been a decline in reported incidence, although the picture here is complicated by the fact that, until quite recently, this particular crime was subject to a societal taboo and therefore hugely under-recorded.

Until the 1980s child sex abuse was hardly ever talked about in the main-stream media, or addressed as a social problem, but kept invisible by a conspiracy of silence. Then there was a period of moral panic around 'satanic sex abuse', with high-profile cases in the UK and elsewhere receiving substantial media attention for some years. These proved in the main to be bogus allegations inspired by social workers and religious extremists in search of the devil's work and finding it in the most innocuous places, although they nonetheless increased public awareness of the subject.

Since the early 1980s, notwithstanding occasional lurches into 'paedophile panic' of the kind satirised by Chris Morris' spoof current-affairs programme Brass Eye in 2001,[9] it is a welcome fact that the reality of the sexual abuse problem has been recognised, and that the protection of children against sexual and other forms of abuse has become a recognised function of the liberal state. One abused child is of course one too many, but it is important to note that the incidence of child sexual abuse over the last two decades has not increased. On the contrary, where long-itudinal data is available, this particular form of sexualised violence appears to have decreased. In the US for example, between 1990 and 2006 the incidence of reported sexual abuse of children fell by 33 per cent.

As with many forms of sexualised violence, the sexual abuse of children is common in tribal societies and developing countries. As Steven Pinker's sobering book notes, the physical and sexual abuse of children, even their murder, are universals of human culture, and were routine in Western societies until quite recently.

The global child-abuse scandal which has overrun the Catholic Church often relates to incidents which occurred decades ago and were successfully covered up, until the heightened public awareness of sex abuse encouraged victims to come forward. And as noted above, the majority of child sexual abuse has happened within the family (Finkelhorn, 1994), or in other contexts where children have been entrusted to carers, such as their local church (in 70 to 90 per cent of child sex abuse cases in north America as of 1994 the perpetrator was known to the victim; half of all abuse cases involving girls took place within the family). Later studies by Finkelhorn and Jones confirm this pattern, as well as the significant downward trend in the incidence of recorded sexual abuse over the period 1990–2006. McKee (2010) cites data showing that sexual abuse of children has decreased in Australia, and that in the US 55 per cent of perpetrators are family members.

The decline of violence in general is what Steven Pinker calls 'a fractal phenomenon', seen at all time scales from millennia to decades (2011).[10] The decline of sexualised violence, as a sub-set of the larger trend, matches this pattern. Moreover, the declines have been greatest in societies where pornography is more freely available. That is to say, there is a positive correlation between the availability of pornography and lower rates of sexualised violence. To repeat, this does not mean that the availability of pornography is a causal factor in the reduction of sexualised violence – merely that there is no substance to the view that we live in a society which is more sexually violent, more abusive to women and children, more disrespectful of the human rights of these sections of the population, and nor therefore to the argument that the expansion of pornography is to blame. The negative phenomena attributed to pornography by some of its critics simply do not exist, other than in the minds of anti-pornography advocates. Where sexual abuses *do* exist – where women, children, homosexuals and other sexually defined minorities are at real risk of imprisonment, violence or death, often at the hands of the state, are precisely those societies in which pornography and sexual culture are prohibited. Producer of porn for women, Anna Arrowsmith, has observed that:

> Women's rights are far stronger in societies with liberal attitudes to sex – think of conservative countries such as Afghanistan, Yemen or China, and the place of women there. And yet, anti-porn campaigners neglect such issues entirely. A recent study by the US department of justice compared the four states that had highest broadband access and found there was a 27 per cent decrease in rape and attempted rape, and the four with the lowest had a 53 per cent increase over the same period.[11]

Attitudes to sex

If sexual violence can be shown to be in decline, so too are the attitudes which underpin it. *The British Social Attitudes Survey, 1994–2008* shows that recorded levels of liberalism and tolerance in sexual matters have increased in the UK since 1994. For example, 42 per cent thought same-sex sex was acceptable in 2008, compared to only 22 per cent in 1994. In 2008 30 per cent approved of civil union or 'gay marriage'. The significance of these shifts in public attitudes can hardly be overstated, considering the centuries-long history of homophobia which preceded them.

In this survey 60 per cent thought abortion should be legal, and 71 per cent that sex before marriage was acceptable. Interestingly, and as evidence that sexual liberalism does not imply a lack of personal ethics, 63 per cent of people surveyed in 2008 believed that divorce could be a positive step towards a new life, while 84 per cent believed that adultery is wrong.

In relation to the feminist political agenda, 58 per cent disagreed (27 per cent strongly) with the sexual division of labour in which men work outside the home, women inside – up from 44 per cent in 1994. In short, this key tenet of feminist ideology had become a majority view. And despite the positive changes in attitude recorded by the survey, 76 per cent thought that more should be done to promote sexual equality. Only 18 per cent thought that change in the sex-political arena had gone too far. If the period since my research for *Mediated Sex* has been one of increased cultural sexualisation and pornographication, therefore, it has also been one of increasing social tolerance in relation to sexuality and progressive sexual politics.

Conclusion

Many of the assertions commonly and prominently made about the harms of pornography cannot be reconciled with the evidence of what has happened at the macro level of relations between men and women, gay and straight, in those societies where pornographication and cultural sexualisation have proceeded furthest and fastest.

While individual relationships and experiences vary widely, and will in some cases include experience of pornographic abuse, the relevant trends in social and sexual attitudes have all moved in what must be regarded as a progressive direction.

There is less sexual violence in advanced capitalist societies than there was four decades ago; less, in fact, than there has ever been, in any human society for which we have records. Women in advanced capitalism are more equal on all measures than they were four decades ago. They are perceived by most men with much less hostility and prejudice than they were four decades ago. In terms of sex and gender, capitalism has become a gentler, kinder, more egalitarian social system, at the same time as the culture has been subject to unprecedented processes of pornographication and sexualisation.

6

GAGA-ING FOR IT

The feminisation of pornography and sexual culture

In the twenty-first century, we don't need to march against size-zero models, risible pornography, lap-dancing clubs and Botox. We don't need to riot, or go on hunger strike. There's no need to throw ourselves under a horse, or even a donkey. We just need to look it in the eye, squarely, for a minute, and then start laughing at it. We look hot when we laugh. People fancy us when they observe us giving out relaxed, earthy chuckles.

(Caitlin Moran)

The last chapter discussed the evidence that the pornographication of mainstream culture has not been detrimental to women and children, if we are to judge the issue on measures such as recorded levels of sexual violence, child abuse, attitudinal change around gender roles in the home, and so on. I want to argue in this chapter that the trend has indeed been positive, insofar as women who wish to participate in the sexualised culture which has emerged since the 1970s can now do so, if not necessarily as yet to the extent that they would like.

Caitlin Moran's 2011 memoir of *How To Be A Woman*, quoted above, speaks to this frustration when she appeals for a more interesting, authentically female pornography than the male heterosexual 'monoculture' she sees on the web at present. Moran argues similarly that 'it's not pornography that's the problem' (p.35).

The idea that pornography is intrinsically exploitative and sexist is bizarre: pornography is just some 'fucking', after all. The act of having sex isn't sexist, so there's no way pornography can be, in itself, inherently misogynistic. So no. Pornography isn't the problem. It's the porn industry that's the problem. What we [women] need to do is effect a 100 per cent increase in the variety of pornography available to us.

(Ibid.)

As we have seen, a more heterogeneous and diverse pornosphere has emerged in recent decades, in which women's desires and needs are more represented than ever before, but it is clearly not yet diverse enough.

The demand for more and better porn for women can be viewed as an *achievement* of feminism rather than its betrayal, in that it is both a consequence and a reflection of enhanced women's rights. These rights – which include rights of sexual citizenship – did not exist in the liberal capitalist countries until very recently, and still do not in most theocratic and authoritarian societies, where pornography and cultural sexualisation are suppressed as a matter of course.

Like abortion and divorce rights, or the right to serve in front-line military roles, a woman's right, and then choice to participate in contemporary sexual culture represents a diminution of patriarchal power and an extension of control over what they do with their own bodies. In a 2012 interview Annie Lennox, herself a pioneer of feminised cultural sexualisation in the 1980s, expresses some unease with the performance styles of Rihanna and other female stars of the current era, but acknowledges that this is a matter for them, as women.[1]

As we have seen, however, the exercise of these choices has been greeted by many commentators, including some feminists, not with celebration and approval, but condemnation. US scholar Kate Kinnick writes that

> the mainstreaming of pornography is about the inundating of the American public with media content that is borderline pornographic, but not explicit enough to be ruled obscene. In this collage of media images, sex is distorted and commodified, and women are trivialised and objectified.
>
> *(2007, p.26)*

Dines and Long identify an epidemic of female 'self-loathing' sparked by capitalist media.[2]

How, we might ask, do men in patriarchy – the higher echelons of capitalist media management in particular – engineer a situation where apparently intelligent women, among them college students and young professionals, choose to expose their bodies on TV shows such as MTV's *Girls Gone Wild* (Harvey and Robinson, 2007, p.64), or to perform pole-dancing routines for their partners in the bedroom?

Beyond anecdote and speculation about what women in universities and other environments feel 'pressured' to do in order to please their men, who are presumed to be driven by what they see in pornography (as in the trend for depilation, which is often attributed to increased exposure to pornography (Cokal, 2007)) the question remains unanswered. The fact that women should choose to perform their sexualities in such ways is deemed sufficient evidence *in itself* to make the case that they are betraying the feminist cause (or are duped into betrayal).

Harvey and Robinson's essay on the dress codes of female students at a liberal arts college in the US asserts that

> porn chic is not feminism, though it is sometimes taken up as such. Porn chic reinforces both the power and the predominance of the male gaze over

women's bodies by framing individual pieces of women's bodies – the belly, the booty, the (lack of) muffin top – in much the same way that Laura Mulvey describes women on film as 'framed, distilled, and fragmented erotic objects'.

(2007, pp. 72–3)

This is a different kind of backlash, then, than was identified by Susan Faludi in her influential 1991 book. Not imposed by patriarchal men but self-inflicted by deluded, misguided, eager-to-please women. It is a backlash nonetheless, against cultural trends alleged to be just as dangerous for women as Paul Verhoeven and *Basic Instinct* ever were (one of Faludi's targets in her earlier version of the thesis (McNair, 1996)).[3]

Stevenson and Wolfers, in their study of 'declining female happiness' (2009), observe that women have made huge progress on key equality indicators such as pay and conditions in the workplace. Their work asks the question why, when these advances have been made, women appear to be no more 'happy' than they were in the bad old days of unreconstructed patriarchy. Similar studies have been done of the population as a whole, which show that greater affluence does not lead to increases in recorded levels of individual happiness. So women are no different from men in this respect, it may be argued.

On the other hand, measures of 'happiness' are problematic, like the concept itself. What does it mean to be 'happy'? Can something called 'happiness' ever be more than an aspiration? The significance of Stevenson and Wolfers' work, for our purposes here, is not what it says about women's states of mind in the early twenty-first century, but the clear evidence it presents of the substantial advance in female status and power within a declining patriarchy: more women working, in better jobs with more authority and better pay; more women at university, with higher GPAs and better prospects than any preceding generation. Not only are rates of violence against women in decline, as we saw in the last chapter; the socio-economic position of women in liberal capitalist societies has been transformed, as has their access to and control over political and cultural capital.

The source and significance of women's 'unhappiness', if such it is, can be debated, speculated on and written about (see Jeannette Winterson's 2011 memoir, for example – *Why Be Happy When You Could Be Normal?*).[4] But that the material circumstances of women's lives have improved hugely, on average, in those societies where cultural sexualisation has gone furthest and fastest, is beyond dispute. While women have been behaving badly in respect of culture, and often been criticised for it, they have at the same time been advancing on the criteria traditionally used to measure female equality. At the beginning of 2004 Sarah Baxter noted in *The Sunday Times* that

women are reaching senior positions faster and younger than ever before; taking time off to have children for anything from a few months to a few years or more, working from home, working part-time or flexitime, and still managing to earn decent money and have a rewarding home life. Men who aren't jealous should be.[5]

This was an overstatement of the pleasures of late patriarchy for women, no doubt. Elsewhere women were complaining of the pressures of combining paid work with child rearing. The point to note, though, is that the growing visibility of women as producers and consumers of sexual culture was paralleled by growing power and agency in the worlds of work, business and politics. This transformation is key to understanding the feminisation of pornography and sexual culture in general. The *context* and therefore the *meaning* of sexual performance, and of sexual representation including pornography, are transformed at the point of consumption by the *control* exercised by women over the environment within which they occur and are disseminated. Where women have no control (or very little) over their bodies, as has been the case for much of the history of patriarchal societies across the globe, their sexualities are subordinated to those of men, which are imposed upon them with greater or lesser force.

Whatever women in Victorian society or in medieval Europe might have desired, however much they shared the sexual appetites of men, they had little choice but to submit to male power, and patriarchal definitions of what female sexuality was and should be. In this context, the contemporary backlash against 'raunch' culture, 'living dolls' and 'female chauvinist pigs' is a misreading, which understates the intelligence and autonomy of women as they make choices about the performance of their sexuality in conditions where they have access to unprecedented political and socio-economic capital.

Misreading raunch culture

The fear of pornography and 'raunch culture' developed in the context of a countervailing feminisation of sexual culture and the pornosphere, as exemplified by the rise of organisations such as the New York-based *Cake* in 2008–9, a social network for women who wanted to 'celebrate' their sexuality. The Cake mantra, or manifesto as they characterised it, had eight points, which the network's founders expressed thus:

- Women like to initiate sex;
- We get turned on every day of the week;
- We are visual (in appreciation of the sexual);
- We fantasise;
- We get ourselves off;
- We like sex;
- We know how our bodies work; and
- Sex isn't over until we orgasm.

Declaring themselves to be committed feminists, the founders of Cake claimed the territory of the sexual as their own, organising events such as lap-dancing parties and porn screenings for their female clients, in overt opposition to the anti-porn, anti-lap-dancing views of other strands of feminism. 'We are talking about women's sexual equality', they declared. 'Telling a woman that by exposing herself she is a victim to male sexual pleasure doesn't talk to our generation, because we own more of the public space than we used to.'[6] Enjoyment of sexuality is linked here to the new possibilities opened up by the acquisition of power and ownership over public space which feminism has produced. In early twenty-first century capitalism the articulation of female sexual identity and desire increasingly originates with women themselves. *They* decide what they want to do, not the men whom they may or may not set out to please and satisfy with their performances.

Not all women have this control over their sexuality, of course, even in the most liberal of capitalist societies, where patriarchal resistance to the new social-sexual structures remains. There are many, many women who continue to be intimidated, coerced and brutalised by their men, whom they may be unable to defy even if they wished to.

Some women choose not to exercise their new power, although they could. That in itself is a choice, and an exercise of gender autonomy that should be respected. Not all women wish to be part of the feminisation of sexual culture I am describing in this chapter. But those who do, and they include some of the most successful female performers in contemporary art and pop culture, do so in a sex-political context which did not come into being as if by magic, but is the product of feminist struggle and advance over a period of decades.

Here we enter the realm of 'post' or 'third wave' feminism, where the meanings of words and images once clearly understood as functional for the reproduction of sexist social relations – identified and denounced as symbols of patriarchal, hetero-sexist, misogynistic ideology – are transformed through subversive appropriation to become tools not of oppression but liberation. Melanie Klein defines this shift as incorporating:

> A postmodern emphasis on contradiction and duality, as well as a conviction that S-M, pornography, the words *cunt* and *queer* and *pussy* and *girl* – are all things to be re-examined or reclaimed … We want not to get rid of the trappings of traditional femininity and sexuality so much as to pair them with demonstrations of strength and power.
>
> *(quoted in Mumford, 2009, p.189)*

'Girlie' feminism, to use another term meaning roughly the same thing (inspired perhaps by Madonna's 1993 *Girlie* tour, where she performed music from the *Erotica* and *Bedtime Stories* albums), recuperates 'traditional' femininity – dismissed by femin-ists as an ideological apparatus of patriarchy for decades – and subverts it, just as black rappers reclaimed the N-word in their lyrics, and gay activists the Q-word. As Susanna Paasonen puts it, 'girlie', pro-porn, 'bad girl' feminists tend to be 'repre-sentative of a feminism that emphasises active female sexual agency, pleasure and experimentation and is naturally irreverent towards established norms of "good sex"' (2009, p.599). For Klein:

> Girlie feminism is positioned not only as a recuperation of 'girl' as a margin-
> alised subjectivity within mainstream, patriarchal culture, but also as a reclaim-
> ing of a version of traditional femininity 'rubbished' by an earlier generation of
> feminists.
>
> *(quoted in Mumford, 2009, p.189)*

Just as queer culture rejected the politically correct presumptions of some sex-
political activists around what was and was not appropriate for gay men and women –
rejected, indeed, the binary of straight and gay altogether, in favour of a more fluid
notion of sexuality as a continuum or spectrum of preferences and identities which
may overlap – this third wave, post-feminism, incorporated and transformed the
language and rules of the oppressor (patriarchy), preserving those elements which
women decided they wanted, such as *femininity*, and sexual performance, and being
looked at, appraised and objectified. No longer was the aspiration to look 'pretty', or
beautiful in a conventionally feminine way, mocked by feminists as the unwelcome
imposition of a predatory male gaze. Now it was a choice freely entered into, made
by empowered women reaping the benefits of the cultural space won for them by
their feminist sisters, mothers and grandmothers from the late 1960s onwards.

In a dramatic demonstration of this shift, in 2011 a movement of women seeking
to seize the agenda back from the critics of cultural sexualisation launched a series of
'slut walks', which went viral and spread all over the world. The aim of the movement was expressed by Laura Penny in the *Guardian*: 'today's feminists must preserve
a clear distinction between the ongoing struggle to protect women and girls from
abuse, and the misogynist impulse to control and police female sexuality as soon as it
develops'.[7]

Objectify me!

That something called 'objectification' exists and always has, and has become more
visible in mainstream culture in the period we are considering in this book, is not in
dispute. The sexualisation of culture, and the expansion of the pornosphere, are
trends which necessarily involve sexualised bodily display: the reduction of the
human body to its sexual dimension, or the highlighting of the sexual over other
personal and physical qualities, at least momentarily.

This perceived increase in sexual objectification is, as noted above, one of the most
criticised features of cultural sexualisation, being read as something which men do to
women against their will. But women, and men, have dressed (and undressed) to
impress for millennia, in their search for pleasurable sex and productive partnerships.
Sexual display is common in mammal species, and a natural product of evolution, a
mechanism for the selection of the optimal genes in terms of environmental fitness
(Dawkins, 1989).

We humans have, in the course of our particular evolutionary trajectory, overlaid
our equivalent of the instinctive fanning of feathers of the peacock with complex
emotional and psychological layers, and we may not be conscious that when we dress

and wear make-up to look appealing to those whom we may wish to impress on the dance floor, we are enacting a deep biological imperative shared with many other species – that we are biologically programmed to behave this way in order to maximise the chances of successful transmission of our genes. To objectify ourselves is natural, therefore, and one might say necessary, even essential, if genetic reproduction is a goal. Sexual display is part of the human lifecycle.

In patriarchy, however – a social rather than biological structure – objectification happens within a context of unequal power relations, and can seem to have the quality of an exploitative transaction. Where men rule the roost, women objectify themselves in order to secure the best specimens (richest, most handsome, physically strongest) of the socio-economically superior male. As a general rule, the latter are in the dominant position within patriarchy, with their privileged access to financial and other resources. Women are the subordinate sellers in such a market, reduced to the value they can extract from the sexualised display of their bodies. Objectification, in this context, is not a choice but a requirement of survival.

Writers such as Camille Paglia (1993), and more recently Catherine Hakim (2011), challenge the assumption that women were ever as subordinate and powerless as second-wave feminists suggested in their founding texts, preferring to see femininity and the projection of female sexuality through display as merely a different kind of power mechanism to that embodied in physical force, and in the political and economic capital disproportionately wielded by men in patriarchy. Women have always been more powerful in the family and social structure than has been assumed by the feminist critique of patriarchy, goes the argument. In contemporary post-feminist conditions, however, the notion that sexual objectification is necessarily synonymous with patriarchal oppression is much more obviously contentious.

Catherine Hakim's theory of erotic capital identifies the enhanced role of women as sexual actors in a sexualised culture, and appraises this not as a corruption or abuse of femininity, but a consequence of the action of the laws of supply and demand. 'The sexualisation of culture', she observes, 'affects public as well as private life. Beauty, sex appeal, social skills and the arts of self-presentation have increasing value everywhere, helping to sell ideas, products and policies' (2010, p.1).[8]

Women see their erotic capital enhanced in such an environment, although both patriarchal ideology and traditional feminism participate in the 'construction of "moral" ideologies that inhibit women from exploiting their erotic capital to achieve economic and social benefits' (Ibid.). Hakim criticises the tendency to devalue female sexual display and performance in a culture where sexuality does indeed confer power on those who wield it. Echoing Camille Paglia's assertion of the power of female sexuality when strategically deployed, she adds:

> Feminist theory erects a false dichotomy: either a woman is valued for her human capital (her brains, education, work experience, and dedication to her career) or she is valued for her erotic capital (her beauty, elegant figure, dress style, sexuality, grace and charm). Women with brains and beauty are not allowed to use both.
>
> *(p.13)*

Although, of course, they increasingly are, and do. And as Hakim observes, women who *have* used both their beauty and their brains to achieve success, such as Madonna and Gaga, have been attacked both by defenders of the patriarchy and by feminist critics of cultural sexualisation for their excessive self-objectification.

It *may* be a sign of female weakness or 'neediness', still, to focus on male pleasure, but it can also be the choice of women fully aware of the meanings of their sexual displays, and the power they wield in highlighting their sexualities. As Ros Gill has observed,

> the notion of objectification no longer has the analytic purchase to understand many contemporary constructions of femininity ... Increasingly, young women are presented not as sex objects but as active, desiring sexual subjects, who seem to participate enthusiastically in practices and forms of self-representation that earlier generations of feminists regarded as connected to subordination.
>
> *(2009, p.97)*

The point is not that object and subject are irreconcilable opposites, but that these young women choose, as sexual subjects with free will, to be sex objects, from time to time and in certain circumstances; to play the game of socio-sexual interaction using the language and the symbols provided to them in the surrounding culture. These tools – femininity for example – no longer have the same meanings and connotations as they did in the 1950s, 1960s or 1970s. They no longer signify submissiveness or passivity. *Guardian* journalist Zoe Williams has written that:

> The rhetoric of objectification relies on the idea that it's one-way traffic, that only men objectify, and only women are objectified. Before you even consider where that leaves homosexuality, you can only accept this model if you take as a starting point that women have no physical imperative.[9]

The suggestion that women – even 'feminine', conventionally pretty women – might have desires and capacities that are not so different from those of men, has been a key element in the development of this argument. Women like sex as much as men. They like it down and dirty, like men. They enjoy the explicit representation of sex – pornography – just like men, and the only thing preventing widespread public acknowledgement of these facts before the era of so-called 'raunch culture' has been patriarchy's insistence that they did not – could not – because they were women, and thus feminine. In patriarchy, femininity was a disciplinary construct deployed to help ensure that women thought and behaved in certain ways. Those women, bad girls who did not play by the rules – and they have always existed – were branded as 'tom boys', as deviants and weirdos, as figures of fun.

In contemporary post-feminist conditions, femininity becomes a site for the performance of *optional* gender roles which can be subverted and played around with, as well as combined with roles traditionally seen as masculine. Writing in defence of cinematic representations of female killers, such as Uma Thurman's character in

Tarantino's *Kill Bill* movies, critic Molly Haskell has argued that 'if feminism is about anything it's about the right – the obligation, even – to explore, critically and creatively, a whole range of emotional and physical possibilities that have been throttled by restrictive taboos'.[10]

For Haskell, and those of a similar view, the growing visibility of women as protagonists in action movies and other 'male' genres is part of the extension of femininity to include hitherto predominantly masculine behaviours. The redefinition of sexualisation of culture and of objectification, which generated the 'raunch culture' critique, is recognised within this framework not as a negative but a positive trend, expanding as it does the range of contexts in which women can be sexual, and the range of feminine sexualities available to them.

An example of this trend is the video game *Hey Baby*, launched in June 2010 to some controversy because it featured a female protagonist who reacts with extreme violence to the various abusive male figures she encounters on her journey through a virtual landscape. The men harass and otherwise seek to harm her, and the female star guns them down. This was a similar concept to many other games in which male characters perform the violence (*Grand Theft Auto*, for example).

Hey Baby was controversial chiefly because the gender roles were reversed in a format which treated sexual harassment as an offence worthy of death. One critic (female) wondered what the world was coming to when it was deemed 'totally appropriate for a woman to annihilate a man because he dares to speak admiringly to her in the street', a perspective also applied to the broader trend towards 'super-violent – and often very young – female heroines'.[11] This writer would have had in mind a film such as *Sucker Punch* (Zack Snyder, 2011), in which Australian actress Emily Browning takes on and defeats with some force a group of male abusers.

The equation of objectification with sexism was accepted, broadly, across the various strands of feminist thinking at a time when women were systemically subordinate to men, severely lacking in control over their bodies and their sexualities, and when sex and its representation were thus more likely to be viewed, with good reason, as an imposition or violation of the female by the more powerful male. The feminist critique of objectification, and of pornography (like that of advertising, which developed in tandem), makes sense when men are pulling the strings and women expected to dance to the tune. When feminist politics sets women free, however, or at least makes them freer, with unprecedentedly high and steadily growing levels of access to political, economic and cultural resources, they desire and demand access also to sexual pleasure, and to the social rituals which surround it.

Empowerment is key here, invoked not as a new-age buzzword or a utopian aspiration, but a description of the changed context within which sexual culture is lived by women in the twenty-first century. Objectification is still about sexual display, and the reduction of personality to its sexual dimension, even if only for that moment on a Friday night when the girls go out on the pull, or to impress the other girls. But the practice of objectification is no longer merely reactive, driven only by the perceived demands of the male for eye candy which conforms to the latest fashion for body shape or hair colour. In post-feminist conditions it is *proactive*, adopted as a competitive strategy by women who know full well what they are doing, and why, and are making calculations and choices based on that knowledge.

Moreover, the significant gaze in the act of looking at the body reduced to a sex object is no longer that of the powerful male alone. Now the female also has a gaze, which she will exercise in relation to herself, to other women, and also to men. An oft-observed feature of recent decades has been the extent to which men have chosen to objectify themselves: building their bodies in gyms; dieting with the zeal and rigour of the most body-conscious female; making themselves up with expensive lotions and perfumes; taking exquisite care with dress and grooming. Research reported in January 2012 found that 80 per cent of men surveyed – a higher proportion than woman surveyed in the same study – were anxious about their body shape and appearance.[12]

The real man/new man binary is still highly visible in cultural discourse, but the increasing self-awareness of men with respect to their status as sex objects, alongside the emergence of the 'metrosexual' male as a familiar marketing type, reflects an aspect of what was termed 'the crisis of masculinity' in the 1990s (McNair, 2002). At a time when some men were perceived to be reeling under the impact of female advances in education, employment, politics and culture, others were embracing the new possibilities for a gentler, kinder masculinity, one premised not on domination of females but constructive engagement and co-existence with them as equal, if biologically different partners. Gay men had long been recognised as having a sexually-motivated concern with appearance, and popular TV shows such as *Queer Eye For The Straight Guy* illustrate how this interest translated quite smoothly into the construction of heterosexual masculinity in the early part of the 2000s (see Chapter 7). The success of shows of this kind reflected the fact that by the early twenty-first century many straight men were embracing self-objectification as a normal, natural part of their public image.

Post-porn feminists, from Madonna to Gaga

Objectification and all that goes with it can no longer be understood solely as a patriarchal weapon of control over women. In contemporary conditions it becomes part of the repertoire of sexual practice for empowered, feminised women, inspired by the examples of leading female figures in popular culture (and reinforced by the later generations of those women who, if they did not originate the trend, work within a cultural marketplace where female audiences have very different expectations and demands from their heroines). Sarracino and Scott identify Madonna as 'the single most evocative, and provocative figure in the porning of America'. She it was who 'made it her purpose to bring the images and themes of pornography into the mainstream' (2008, p.92).

Following the global media storm which accompanied the publication of the *Sex* book and *Erotica* CD in 1992, Madonna moved away from the very explicit imagery of those texts, both in her music and visual performances. The photographs accompanying her 1995 *Bedtime Stories* album were still overtly sexualised, but depicted her in 1920s and 1930s dress and hair styles. In these images she was not nude, or engaged in transgressive acts of the type depicted in the *Sex* book.

Here, and thereafter through the 1990s and into the 2000s Madonna's public image projected a softer, rounder, more maternal persona (she was by then the mother of two children). Having played the sexualised bad girl in her twenties and early thirties, and found global success in doing so, she moved towards a less provocative posture, confirmed in subsequent albums up to and including *MDNA* (2012).

She has retained her status as the world's leading pop star, partly by virtue of the high quality of her music over an unprecedentedly long period (nearly three decades as this book went to press), but principally (I would argue) because of the influence of her iconic 1980s and early 1990s work, which hugely influenced an entire generation of young female performers, post-feminist artists and pop cultural icons who have embraced the possibilities for sexual expression made possible by Madonna from the late 1980s onwards.

In *How To Be A Woman* journalist Caitlin Moran observes that from her feminist perspective, and reflecting on her influences growing up in working-class England, 'pop is the cultural bellwether of social change. Because of its immediacy, reach and power, any thought or feeling that begins to ferment in the collective unconscious can be Number One in the charts two months later' (2011, p.254). And those thoughts and feelings have in large part been Madonna's and the female performers she has inspired.

Porno chic was not a male-driven trend, in other words – or not exclusively. Indeed, many of the most controversial and contested images associated with pornographication or cultural sexualisation have been made by women. They include Rihanna, Christina Aguilera, Lana Del Rey, and of course Lady Gaga, whose borrowing from, and homages to, Madonna are the most direct.

Gaga's *Born This Way* (2011) was accused of plagiarising Madonna's *Express Yourself* (1988), and to any listener familiar with both the similarities are obvious. But Gaga has openly declared her artistic debts, not just to Madonna but also to David Bowie, the glam-rock bands, Queen and many others. Gaga is the consummate child of the postmodern digital age, steeped in the music her parents listened to, and building on that legacy with music which though allusive to earlier periods, is still distinctive and fresh, and overlaid with an overt declaration of support for feminism. Gaga has stated that:

> I am [a feminist] ... I find that men get away with saying a lot in this business, and that women get away with saying very little. In my opinion women need and want someone to look up to that they feel has the full sense of who they are, and says, 'I'm great'.[13]

Gaga is closest to Madonna, though, not just in her musical style but in her transgressive sexual aesthetic. Moran writes of Gaga that her 'take on sexual mores is to examine female dysfunction, alienation and sexual neuroses' (2011, p.257).

Both Madonna and Gaga have made particularly provocative use of music video, objectifying themselves with abandon, and often clothed in transgressive, avant-garde styles. As observed by Railton and Watson: 'music videos are a site where women's bodies are sexualised and eroticised, that is to say, explicitly positioned within an economy of sexual desire' (2007, p.115). In fact, 'the display of the sexualised body as an object of desire is crucial to music video's economies of both pleasure and profit'. Moreover, 'music video can be a site for the subversion of sexed and gendered roles' (p.116).

Madonna's *Justify My Love* exemplified this point in 1990 (McNair, 1996), and there have been many other examples since. Gaga's *Telephone* and *Born This Way* videos are exuberant exercises in the self-objectification of the artist, combined with confident assertions of sexual autonomy and control. Gaga is a sexualised prisoner in *Telephone*, stripped down to her underwear in the key dance-sequence. But she is also a fighter, a killer, a smoker, possibly a lesbian (in the scenes with Beyoncé), and much else. In *Judas* (2011) she reprises Madonna's *Like A Prayer*, which portrayed the star in controversial, possibly blasphemous, union with a black Jesus and contributed greatly to her global fame and notoriety. Gaga's *Judas* combines biblical imagery and religious references with sexualised imagery.

Female US hip-hop star Khia's *My Neck My Back* is a celebration of female sexual desire, and of cunnilingus and analingus in particular. It is also the kind of text implicated in the sexualisation trend, and thus viewed as a problem rather than any form of progress. In 2012 rising female hip-hop star Azelia Banks attracted attention (and criticism) for her song *212* – a homage to oral sex which included the phrase 'cunt gettin' eaten'.[14] Railton and Watson note that:

> Whether one chooses, on the one hand, to denounce this apparent pornification of the everyday and ordinary as patriarchy passed off as postmodernism or, on the other, to write it off as part of a more general liberalisation of culture, turns precisely on the question of authorship. In other words, the degree to which these images of women's bodies are politically problematic is indexed to the degree to which agency is seen to be removed from the women whose bodies are on display.
>
> *(2007, p.125)*

The meaning of an image is determined not by the extent to which it 'objectifies' its subject, then, but by the extent to which power, agency and control reside with the person, or subject, who is objectified.

Women and striptease culture

The same point can be made of the growing popularity of various forms of sexualised performance by women who are not professional porn-stars, striptease artists, or lap dancers, but who nonetheless enjoy exposing their bodies before audiences which may include partners, friends or strangers. The rapid rise of neo-burlesque in the

UK, the US, Australia and many other countries, signals that striptease culture has lost much of its stigma and shame for women. Now, rebranded as burlesque, it becomes a hobby, an interest, an expression of retro chic in which a self-respecting feminist may safely participate. In 2010, reflecting the popularity of the form, two major feature films were released on the subject. *Burlesque* (Steve Antin, 2010) featured Cher alongside Christina Aguilera[15] and took $100m at the global box office. The French production *On Tour* (Mathieu Amalric, 2010) followed a troupe of American neo-burlesque dancers as they move around France.[16]

Again, we see in the debate sparked by the popularity of burlesque the division within feminism as to the meanings to be drawn from sexualised female performance. The *Guardian*'s Laura Penny has protested that 'burlesque stripping, like lap-dancing, is about performing – rather than owning – your sexuality. It's about posing provocatively for applause. The transaction is one way; you give, they receive. You pout, they clap.' Burlesque, for this observer, is 'a misogynist sham, part and parcel of the packaging of female desire, a process by which young women trade in their sexuality and their selfhood for whatever fleeting power they can grasp'.[17] Again we hear the lament for young women acting against their own interests (as defined by the wiser and usually older observer); of deluded, stupid females (because how else could they be so easily fooled?) being made powerless, rather than powerful, by their decision to perform their sexuality in a burlesque show.

For burlesque performer Starla Haze, on the other hand, this form of display is a skilled art form requiring hard work and deserving of respect: 'sexuality is always performative', she notes, 'even when conducted in private'.[18] Burlesque, in particular, 'is an art form' which incorporates

> striptease, which is still used by many performers to parody sexuality, politics and social values. In burlesque the gaze goes both ways, and this is precisely what I find subversive about it. Burlesque has created a context in which women can be creative, performative and sexually expressive in a way determined solely by themselves, irrespective of their age, shape, size or proportions.[19]

In 2010, reflecting the rise of burlesque as a fashionable and popular recreational pursuit for women, the *Guardian* published the following account of 'What I'm really thinking: the burlesque dancer':

> When I'm dancing, I am very aware of my body as it becomes disrobed. I'll be concentrating on my routine and facial expression, but thinking, 'Now everybody's looking at my arse.' It makes me want to laugh. I try to keep a straight face, to stay in character, but inside I'm laughing. I was really nervous the first time I did it, five years ago. I'd done a singing cabaret act, so I was used to performing, but this was different. I got drunk before I went on, but in the end I found it exhilarating. It feels very decadent and liberating.

I think audiences would be surprised by how much most burlesque dancers enjoy it. A lot of people think it's just a job, that it becomes routine, but it's always exciting. Another common misconception is that we do it to turn men on. It should be sexy, but it's not only for one sex. You don't get many men going to burlesque nights for titillation. Women take them because they think it's a bit naughty, a bit Moulin Rouge. Most men aren't into that old-fashioned sexiness. The best audiences are gay men: they see it as exciting and different – they don't just want you to be pretty and recreate some 50s pin-up nonsense. Drunken straight men can be difficult, but disapproving women are the worst, very cold and hostile. I've always been considered a bit of an exhibitionist, because I've never been bothered about nudity. Burlesque is just a way of being allowed to run around naked and be silly.[20]

In a similar vein, one woman defended her decision to be a lap dancer thus: 'It's a performance like any other. I've never once felt abused or exploited or taken advantage of. Stripping is a laugh, it keeps me amused and it makes me money. It's as simple as that.'[21]

Broadening the argument to other forms of bodily display and self-objectification which have become mainstream in the current phase of cultural sexualisation, Ruth Barcan has argued that 'some forms of striptease have become able to signify sexual liberation, economic freedom and even a "victory for feminism"' (2004, p.242). Holland and Attwood write in their essay on pole dancing that 'sexualised images can now connote strength, independence and the expression of a confident self' (2009, p.167). They go on to say that:

Pole-dancing classes can be understood as a kind of post-feminist homosocial space because of their focus on constructing the self as sexy and pleasure-seeking, and because they are women-only spaces which foreground identification with other women through the pursuit of femininity and fun.

(p.179)

Feminist stripper and author of *Strip City* (2002) Lily Burana argues, in defence of a woman's right to undress in public if she so wishes, that

if feminism's basic tenet is that biology is not destiny, then we must also be mature and accept that aesthetic does not equal agenda. Just because a girl has bleached blonde hair and high heels doesn't mean that she's going to sell the female gender down the river.[22]

Catherine Roach's study of *Stripping, Sex and Popular Culture* (2007) takes a similarly non-judgemental approach, noting that the work of the stripper – and in the US she estimates that there are 250,000 dancers working in 4,000 clubs, contributing to the generation of $15 billion in revenue – is 'hard, hard work, but as the dancers also point out, it can be creative pleasure and sensual play as well' (p.45).

Roach's study focuses on the women themselves, and allows them to define the pleasures as well as the pains of striptease. One interviewee, 'Marie', insists that 'the choice to be girlie has to be acceptable to feminists. It's sour grapes to demand choice for women and then not like what some of us choose' (p.39). Roach allows that stripping, and the requirements it places on women to 'embody a hypersexualised, hyperfeminised ideal image of the female … can lead to body image issues and feelings of inadequacy'. But:

> They can also be a source of power and delight … They come at a cost, but they can pay off to the tune of hundreds of dollars a night, and they can help one feel exotic, sexy, and more self-confident. It all depends on the strength of the sense of self that a dancer starts out with, the goals and boundaries that she brings to her work, the particular environment she experiences at her club, and the support that she receives both there and outside work.
>
> *(p.45)*

Basic health and safety, in other words, and the points made here about stripping would apply equally to shop workers and other categories of service staff who have to face the public regularly. The challenges facing the stripper are more intense and visceral, perhaps, given the intimacy of the bodily display they are required to deliver, but women (and men) in all walks of life experience pressures to perform, to look 'good', to compete with others, to please their customers. Many of them, moreover, earn a lot less than a professional stripper in a well-run club. In 2002, as the UK-based lap-dancing nightclub chain Spearmint Rhino was expanding to sixteen branches across the country one observer noted of the Glasgow outlet that its ethos was not sleazy but celebratory. 'It is an audience in which the erotic is proudly recreational, an alternative reality where nobody minds you looking because the consensus prides itself on being ahead of the mainstream.'[23]

Associated with these trends is the growth in women's consumption, solo or with partners, of accessories hitherto seen as emblems of patriarchy, such as pole dancing kits, sexy lingerie of the type used in striptease, and sex toys. These are sold in stores such as the Babeland and Smitten Kitten chains in the US, and Ann Summers in the UK, as 'safe, liberating alternatives to adult stores', marketed to women who may well be feminists (Heineken, 2007). These companies, often run by women, present the consumption of sex products as 'a way for women to enact feminist politics' and 'a way to practice resistance against older, male-dominated expressions of sexuality' (Ibid., p.123).

The feminisation of the pornosphere

Pornography, writes Feona Attwood, 'has traditionally been emphatically marked as a male genre, and has been the subject of a highly visible critique that represents it as an activity hostile to women' (2005, p.395). More than that, pornography had, until the second wave of porno chic began in the late 1980s, been characterised as the very embodiment of predatory male sexuality. Jane Juffer noted in a 2004 essay that 'much government discourse in the twentieth century tried to establish pornography as a threat to the home in order to fix women in their proper roles as wives and mothers in need of patriarchal protection' (2004, p.47).

While the critics of cultural sexualisation and pornographication often make the same kinds of arguments, fewer and fewer people, including women, are listening. Cosmo Landesman observed with some regret in the *The Sunday Times* in 2004 that 'pornography, once condemned by women as exploitative and degrading, is now seen as empowering and progressive'[24] (although this was before the resurgence of porno fear described in Chapter 4). Women have come to view pornography as less threatening than early anti-porn feminists argued. One could cite many female writers on this point, but Helen Walsh in the *Guardian* exemplifies what we might call the pro-porn feminist perspective:

> The sheer variety and proliferation of pornography makes this a huge, controversial and sophisticated debate. Almost every household in the UK has access to the internet now, which makes all of us – men, women and young adults – potential participants in porn's interactive dialogue ... [for feminists] the concept of woman as consumer is a difficult pill to swallow. Even more difficult is the idea of woman as auteur. But like it or not, women are no longer merely porn's grasping, spread-eagled victims but willing players in the dance, entering the arena not just for economic gain but for the sheer thrill of getting their rocks off.[25]

Pornography, she asserts, 'can be as empowering and fascinating as it can be destructive and injurious'.[26] Just as 'bad girl' artists have, since the 1970s, claimed the territory of the pornographic to make feminist art (see Chapter 8, and McNair, 1996, 2002), ordinary women have adopted and adapted it to the pursuit of their everyday lives (Smith, 2007, Juffer, 2004).

As we saw in Chapter 2, porn for women has grown as a proportion of the pornosphere, and women have become more important as producers and consumers of pornographic material in general. Producers of porn for women include Femme Productions and Feminists For Free Expression. UK porn-producer Anna Span (described in one press report as 'the UK's first female porn director') worked for 12 years in the porn industry before moving into politics as Anna Arrowsmith.[27] She became the Liberal Democrat parliamentary candidate for the constituency of Gravesend in March 2010, and at that time explained her motives for working in the industry in directly feminist terms, declaring access to pornography to be a political issue:

> I have fought long and hard for women's right to sexual expression and consumption, as well as for freedom of speech. I have long since felt vindicated about my choices back at college and know my pro-sex feminist argument is based on sound principles and logic.[28]

US porn-star Sasha Grey explained, in an interview to promote her role in Stephen Soderbergh's *The Girlfriend Experience* (see Chapter 3), that 'only a handful of adult stars continue to push the boundaries of what women are supposed to be, or be like, in bed' and asserts that she, unlike the majority of her peers, is 'determined and ready to be a commodity that fulfils everyone's fantasies'.[29] The lack of reticence or guilt reflected in this brash declaration of self-commodification will offend many critics, but if it is accepted that feminism ushers in an era of feminine self-determination, the key issue here is one of agency.

> I am a sexually healthy young woman … I take pride in the liberation of female sexuality. As a sex symbol with an intellectual stance, I am and will continue to be vilified, and I am okay with that … In fact, I am content; it gives me the opportunity to shed light on the darker areas of sex and validate the insecurities of sexually repressed women. The days of victimised, disturbed porn stars are fading away. I am the new breed.[30]

One writer observed in 2002 that women are quite heavily involved in the porn industry, 'subverting the notion that women's erotic power can only be located in their role as paid-for sexual objects, rather than as active sexual subjects'.[31] Addiction theorist Wendy Maltz (see Chapter 5), while warning of the public health problems posed by pornography on the one hand, also acknowledges its allure to women. Referring to her own personal experience as a schoolgirl, she recalls that

> porn offered a far more compelling view of sexuality than the cryptic sex education materials I was shown in health class. In spite of how the images degraded women and portrayed men in a position of sexual power, porn gave me a vision of sex that validated sexual passion and pleasure.
>
> *(2010, p.12)*

On making DIY porn, one woman quoted in the *Guardian* observed that: 'it felt like a very safe thing to do. It also showed a deep level of intimacy and trust in the relationship. It was really good fun, and we both laughed a lot.'[32] Writing in the online *CarnalNation* journal, editor-in-chief Theresa Ikard declared that:

> Women like porn. Women watch porn. Women are making porn. Yes, women are part of the pornography industry now more than at any other time in history – and not just as performers or consumers either. Women are gaining power and asserting their influence in the adult entertainment industry as directors, producers, and distributors.[33]

Australian porn-performer Angela White is an example of this emerging cohort of women who participate enthusiastically in the industry, for business and pleasure, and feel no need to apologise for it. Indeed, she used her practitioner's knowledge of the porn-production sector to write an Honours thesis at the university of Melbourne, which explored the motivations of female performers and the positive benefits they gained from their involvement. As part of that work she interviewed six of her co-performers, finding that 'pornography unexpectedly emerged as a kind of queer space in which female performers were able to imagine and experience new sexual possibilities and becomings' (2010, p.4).[34]

White's thesis recounts some examples where female performers have been threatened or abused, and she acknowledges that participation in the porn industry is not without its risks. But neither, for a young woman in search of advancement, is working as an intern in the White House, nor in the same building as Herman Cain,[35] nor in many other jobs and professions which are rarely condemned in the same terms as the porn industry. White concludes, as have many other women who work in the porn industry, at least in countries which have regulatory structures and health and safety systems in place, that it is a satisfying and reasonably low-risk job, which many women choose as a way of finding outlets for their sexuality.

If women increasingly produce porn, they also consume it in ever greater numbers. *Queendom* notes survey evidence that 23 per cent of women view pornographic images several times a month.[36] Producer Erika Lust declares it to be 'a prejudice to say that women don't like porn. Sex images make you hot, but pornography has been made by and for men. In mainstream pornography everything is about male pleasure'.[37] Porn for women, on the other hand, describes 'a curve of arousal' and

> credible female performers. To get excited women want to see something that looks like us. We want to see independent women exploring their sexuality, who are not afraid, but are not sex heroines either. We want to see [in porn] attractive men who share our lifestyles, our ideas.[38]

In the same article, Petra Joy talks about what 'the porn revolution' means to her: 'porn that is made by and for women, that focuses on female pleasure and features male sex objects'.

Clarissa Smith's book-length study of female readings of pornographic fiction found that 'readers approach the porn story as a dramatisation of the sexual moment and the possible pleasures of surrendering to sexual delight' (2007, p.28). Elsewhere she remarks that 'pornography holds particular pleasures for female subjects, and its use can be understood as transgressive of heterosexist norms rather than supportive of them' (p.51). Referring to the persistence of the pornosfearic view that porn is inherently bad for and damaging to women, Smith observes that 'the pathologising of sexual relations between men and women as always turning on women's vulnerability is a key theme of anti-porn theorising' (2009, p.25).

Abandon this assumption or premise, as contemporary circumstances allow, and women are free to indulge in the instrumental excess of the pornographic in the same way as men have long done. Free too, to abstain. To state that some women enjoy porn is not to say that all women do, or should. Kath Albury makes the important point that 'it's a personal choice', and that 'feminist responses to porn reflect the diversity of feminist responses to sexuality in general'.[39]

Self-styled feminist stripper Lily Burana, promoting her book *Strip City* in 2002, argued that 'the increased sexualisation of Western culture is an unfortunate side effect of increased liberty', demonstrating that it is possible to be supportive of some of the trends affecting sexual culture identified in this chapter without necessarily endorsing them all. The important debate for feminism is not, therefore, about who is pro- and who is anti-porn (or anti-sexualisation), and the moral or ethical implications of one's position on that issue. It is about the right of women to choose for themselves whether they consume, or produce, pornographic images.

For this author, the fact that they do both, and in growing numbers, makes the world a better place for two, related reasons. First, it inevitably dilutes the hetero-sexist, often misogynistic content of traditional, pre-feminist porn (as does gay porn – see Chapter 7). Porn for women need not be 'vanilla', or any less transgressive than that produced for straight men. But the mere fact that it *is* by and for women, whatever its content, changes its meaning.

Second, and more broadly, a world in which women are empowered to make and view porn expands the possibilities of what porn is and can be. Porn, understood in this context, becomes part of the evolution of female sexual culture and practice in post-feminist societies, rather than a barrier or obstacle to that evolution. Philosopher A.C. Grayling observes that 'one of the marks of the age is the sexual liberation of women, whose magazines never fail to discuss aspects of it, and for whom elegant sex shops and subtle pornography are now mainstream'.[40] Grayling suggests that in embracing the pornosphere and porno chic (my terms not his), women are merely behaving as nature intended, now that they are free of patriarchal bonds:

> If women's potential investment in sex is reduced by effective contraception and greater economic independence, their behaviour changes. Wherever women attain equal status in business and the professions, their sexual behaviour comes increasingly to resemble that of men.[41]

In this analysis pornography, and other forms of sexual culture, once viewed as essentially male are now recognised as the vehicle for female sexual gratification rather than the instruments of patriarchal subordination.

7

PORNOGRAPHY AND THE POLITICS OF SEXUAL INCLUSION

In March 2002 UK *Pop Idol* winner and emerging superstar Will Young announced that he was gay. Commenting on this, then still rare, example of a celebrity self-outing, manager of boy band Take That, Nigel Martin-Smith, noted matter-of-factly that 'there's an awful lot of gay and lesbian people out now, and most people know gay people. Times have just moved on.'[1]

One year earlier writer Mark Simpson had noted a general homosexualisation of mainstream culture, in that 'habits previously associated with gays are all the rage with straight people'.[2] More recently British playwright Tim Fountain, in his account of *Rude Britannia: One Man's Journey Around the Highways and Byways of British Sex* (2008) noted how commonplace gay culture had become in the United Kingdom. Fountain expresses some nostalgia – albeit laced with the wry humour one might expect of the man who shocked the Edinburgh Festival with his 2004 play *Sex Addict*[3] – for a time when gay men were required to live like sexual outlaws, their preferences and practices hidden and mysterious.

A society growing more accepting of homosexuality, and so quickly, is one in which attitudes are clearly becoming more humane, liberal, tolerant and relaxed towards sexual matters. That such a change should be occurring in parallel with the pornographication of the mainstream tells us, at least, that the widespread availability and consumption of pornography is no barrier to the spread of ethical thinking and progressive sexual politics.

The mainstreaming of homosexuality is, we can agree, a welcome trend in sexual culture and politics, notwithstanding the qualms of those in that community who, usually with a tongue in cheek, lament the loss of their outsider status. It has occurred over a period of only four decades, accelerating from the late 1980s and into the 1990s as the gay-friendly work of Madonna, and of queer artists such as Keith Haring and Robert Mapplethorpe were impacting on public awareness. That period also coincides with the most dramatic expansion of the pornosphere, which followed the emergence of the internet as a mass-media platform. It is my argument in the first part of this chapter that the two trends are connected.

This is not to say that the expansion and diversification of the pornosphere *caused* the mainstreaming of homosexuality, any more than it can be said to have caused the ascendancy of feminism and the remarkable transformation in women's socio-economic and political status noted in Chapter 6. Rather, it is to say that the two trends have proceeded in parallel, with both being outcomes of changing attitudes towards public sexuality, features of an evolving cultural ecology. The growing visibility of gay porn in particular, following the milestone Stonewall 'riots' in New York in June 1970, has been one manifestation of a broader liberalisation of sexual culture which permitted growing tolerance of homosexual practices and a reduction in societal homophobia.

The expansion of the pornosphere, insofar as it has included a proliferation of pornographic texts made for and by gay men, lesbians and other sexually marginalised groups, has made the world a better place by opening up cultural space for the articulation and satisfaction of sexualities and desires which previously existed clandestinely, or only underground, on the fringes of mainstream visibility and respectability.

On the assumption that the advance of gay and other sexual minority rights is a good thing, pornography has had an important and positive role in the formation of minority sexual and cultural identities in conditions where, until quite recently, those identities were at best stigmatised, and at worst harshly policed.

The mainstreaming of homosexuality: 2002–12

As many authors have observed, the period before the sexual revolution was one of deep illiberalism in sexual politics.[4] The sexual arena in the 1950s – including the then still embryonic pornosphere – was largely monopolised by heterosexual men, as a recent news story reminds us. At the end of December 2011 it was announced by the UK government that World War II code-breaker and computing pioneer Alan Turing was to feature in one of ten new postage stamps devoted to 'Britons of Distinction'. Turing had been a homosexual who, despite his war-time record and other service to Britain, was prosecuted for being gay in 1952. He was convicted, and required to have hormonal treatment as an alternative to prison. He died of cyanide poisoning in 1954, and is believed to have killed himself.

Turing's fate exemplifies the way things were, as recently as half a century ago. The combination of sexual liberalism from the 1960s, then the articulation of feminism and gay liberation ideology from the 1970s, produced a climate in which access to sexual culture began to be extended to hitherto excluded groups, and the existence of alternative modes of sexuality, relationship and family structure made visible.

Accompanying that trend has been a mainstreaming of homosexuality in culture. My previous books on mediated sexuality identified key moments in this process, which has continued with popular TV formats such as *Will & Grace*, the globally successful sitcom launched in 1998 and a global hit until the show ended in 2006. Taking this and other shows into account, Avila-Saavedra believes that the 2003–4 US network prime-time schedule could be 'considered a breakthrough with eight leading gay characters' (2009, p.5). For one observer, 'no TV show has ever served up such a palatable version of homosexuality'.[5] This writer articulated the connection between popular culture/entertainment and perceptions of homosexuality thus:

> Mainstream Americans welcome out gay men into their homes where once they would have protested to the network until advertisers withdrew their support and the show folded. They've been won over, not by confrontation, not by politics, but by stealth.

In late 2004 it could be noted that 'gay men have become TV's newest and most bankable playthings',[6] seen regularly in US sitcoms such as *Modern Family*, which featured a gay male couple as part of the cast. At the same time shows such as *Queer Eye For the Straight Guy* and *Boy Meets Boy* were attracting large audiences. At its peak *Queer Eye* achieved seven million viewers for NBC. As a result, 'the show is hailed by mainstream media as a revolution for American attitudes to homosexuality on TV'.[7] Critic Mark Lawson observed the prevalence of gay participants in British reality TV makeover shows such as *Fairy Godfathers*. 'The whole series screams the idea that what women really want is a straight man with a wardrobe and the bathroom cabinet of a gay stereotype.'[8] In *The Sunday Times* Bryan Appleyard noted that in reality TV shows gay men were being represented as interpreters, counsellors, therapists and style gurus for heterosexuals.[9]

Public attitudes were being revolutionised too, appearing to show a steady decline in homophobia. As recently as 1991, 77 per cent of Americans surveyed by the General Social Survey of US Attitudes felt gay sex was always wrong. By 2006 this number had fallen to 56 per cent. In 1988 73 per cent of Americans surveyed disagreed with gay marriage. In 2006 the figure had fallen to 51 per cent (Smith, 2008). Since then evidence suggests that mainstream public opinion has continued to warm to the presence of homosexuality in American society and culture. The most recent survey data obtained before this book went to press showed that US support for civil liberties for homosexuals[10] increased from 63 per cent in 1988 to 83 per cent in 2010 (Smith, 2011).

In the UK similar trends have been evident, as reality TV and other popular forms increased the visibility of gay and lesbian people, placing them in contexts where homosexuality was not an 'issue' so much as an unremarkable character trait. In the *Guardian* Libby Brookes observed that 'it would appear that the limits of outrage are being stealthily withdrawn'.[11]

Around this time, too, Matt Wells marked the tenth anniversary of *Attitude*, the lifestyle magazine published for gay men by Northern & Shell (publishers of soft porn for straight men and often derided as the worst offender in the UK soft core market). 'Today', wrote Wells, 'gay lifestyle is firmly in the mainstream, with homoerotic imagery used by everyone from footballers to perfume manufacturers.'[12] Wells quoted one of *Attitude*'s founders, Pas Paschali, remarking that at the magazine's launch in 1994 that

> we were working within a political climate that was only just beginning to understand that banner-waving wasn't the only way to be political; you could be just as effective, perhaps even more so, by becoming a desirable socio-economic group, one that major companies, and political parties, want to target.[13]

Representations of female homosexuality on US popular TV also became more common over this period than they had ever been: in reality formats; in sitcoms such as *The L Word*, which ran from 2004 to 2009; and on chat shows such as *The Ellen DeGeneres Show*. Women's growing visibility in sexual culture has included expressions of what used to be known as 'lesbian chic' (McNair, 2002), and a growing interest in the recreational possibilities of bisexuality. One 2004 study found that 'as many as four in ten young women have had a bisexual experience while, according to the magazine *Cosmopolitan*, at least 65 per cent admit to fantasising about women'.[14]

Which is not to suggest that all is well, and that campaigners for gay rights can go home and rest on their laurels, nor that all media representations of homosexuality are satisfactory to all people. There continue to be legitimate criticisms made of the caricaturing and stereotyping of gay and lesbian people in popular culture, although such criticisms often start from the false premise that there is such a thing as an ideal, politically correct representation, or that such representations of gayness, or 'queerness' in popular culture have a duty to 'disrupt the heterosexual social order' (see for example Avila-Saavedra, 2009).

My own view is that progress can be measured by the emergence of a range of representational tropes of a hitherto marginalised or stereotyped group (such as blacks in America, or gay men), which are neither good nor bad in some idealistic or mythical way (positively or negatively stereotyped, that is), but merely *representative* of what people are, warts and all. In short, a gay man can be portrayed as a bad person so long as there are positive representations of gay men as good people elsewhere in the culture. After all, heterosexual men are regularly portrayed as 'bad', and villainous, because some of them are. The important point to note is that the days when gay men were in the main portrayed as 'mad, bad or sad' are gone, replaced by a mix of images and texts which depict homosexuality with varying degrees of sophistication, affection, sometimes humour, but rarely with the routine contempt and/or hostility which used to be the mark of cultural homophobia in the liberal capitalist world.

Gay rights: a progress report

Progressive evolution in the representation of homosexuality is welcome, but on its own insufficient to justify the assertion of a broader progress in the achievement of gay rights. However, alongside the increased cultural visibility of gay men and women on TV and other popular arenas there has been a remarkable transformation of the legal status of homosexuality, and the removal of many long-standing inequalities. Highlights include:

- In March 2003 a US Supreme Court judge overturned a Texan law banning sodomy, effectively legalising gay sex in thirteen states where it was still defined as criminal.[15]
- In September 2011, after centuries of prohibition and 18 years of a less severe but still discriminatory policy popularly known as 'don't ask, don't tell', which tolerated gays in the armed forces only if they were not 'out', the Obama administration certified legislation to allow openly homosexual men and women to serve in the military.
- Beginning in 1989, and accelerating in the latter part of the 2000s, a number of countries legislated to permit same sex partners to 'marry' in the form of civil union or civil partnership. Previously, homosexual men and women could not marry (assuming that they wanted to, and many did not), and were thus denied the legal rights and protections afforded heterosexual married couples, even if they had formed life-long partnerships.

  After many years of campaigning, and ongoing resistance from religiously-motivated moral conservatives which continues to this day, civil union legislation was passed in many states of the US, the UK and other European countries, and in December 2011, the Australian state of Queensland (a new conservative government in June 2012 backtracked on the reform, prohibiting state-sanctioned marriage ceremonies). That same month, the governing Australian Labor Party adopted a policy of favouring same-sex marriage at the federal level, and announced support for a free vote in the Australian parliament. At that time an Australian cabinet minister, Penny Wong, was living in a partnership with another woman.[16] In May 2012, as the US general election campaign of that year gathered steam, President Obama declared his personal support for the legalisation of same sex marriage in the United States.

- The right of same-sex partnerships to adopt a child – previously impermissible in almost every country of the world – began to be accepted in the 2000s. The UK allowed same-sex couples to adopt jointly from 2002. In the US, the percentage of same-sex couples who had legally adopted rose by eight per cent between 2000 and 2008, an upward trend constrained by the continuing patchiness of civil-union legislation.

  Here and elsewhere, however, it is increasingly recognised that same-sex partners could and should be allowed to adopt children on the same basis as heterosexual married couples. In April 2011 the Commissioner for the US Administration on Children, Youth and Families wrote to the country's child-care agencies to confirm the Obama administration's view that although only about four per cent of adopted children were at that time with gay couples, 'the child welfare system has come to understand that placing a child in a gay or lesbian family is no greater risk than placing them in a heterosexual family'.[17]

One could devote an entire book to this trend, but here I wish only to emphasise the scale of the transformation in gay and lesbian civil rights, and its speed. After centuries, if not millennia, of systemic, institutionalised homophobia, extending right up to the late 1960s when it was still, in most liberal democracies, a criminal offence to be homosexual and engage in one's sexual preference, many of those countries have now extended full citizenship rights to gay men and lesbians.

As cultural representations have changed, and public attitudes have come to embrace the reality of what gay and lesbian people are in a predominantly heterosexual society, so legal systems have abandoned one prejudice after another. Pinker's timely study of trends in violence in human societies notes that 'tolerance of homosexuality has gone up, and tolerance of antigay violence has gone down' (2011, p.728).[18] And while, as always in the sphere of cultural studies, a direct cause and effect relationship is unprovable, I think it fair to note that there is no example, anywhere in the world, of progressive change in the provision of citizenship rights to gay men and lesbians which has not been preceded by years of progressive evolution in the representation of homosexuality. Culture, and popular culture at that, has been in the vanguard of the process which has led us from criminalisation to gay marriage and adoption in a mere forty years – a heartbeat in human history.

Pornography and homosexuality

What then of pornography and its role in, or contribution to, the process whereby it has become acceptable, even fashionable, to be gay? The moral and legal pressures on homosexual men and women to hide their orientations away from public view, and certainly not to practice their sexualities openly, meant that for decades before the pornographication of mainstream culture began, gay and lesbian porn was key to the sexual expression and satisfaction of these groups.

The gay male eroticisation of images of naked boys and men – swimming, doing gymnastics, and so on – which accompanied the early days of photography has been noted by several historians of queer culture. In Tom Waugh's 1976 interview with the editor of *JumpCut*, Chuck Kleinhams, the latter observed that 'before the days of an openly visible gay movement, the only way for many gay people to discover and explore their own homosexuality was through pornography. That's how they recognised certain things about themselves, that they were not alone' (quoted in Waugh, 2000, p.41). Three decades later Sharif Mowlabocus could observe that

> pornography permeates British gay male sub-culture, together with the identities and practices that it frames. Pornography is written into the code of gay men's lives and it continues to shape understandings of the Self and Other in increasingly powerful ways.
>
> *(2007, p.61)*

The importance of pornography in the sex lives of homosexuals has been true for both men and women. *Lezzie Sluts* was the title of a magazine published by a San

Francisco-based lesbian collective in the 1990s (McNair, 1996). This was before 'slut walk' reclaimed the S-word for feminism, and its use in this context, at that time, was quite challenging. *On Our Backs* (*OOB*) magazine, (subtitled 'entertainment for the adventurous lesbian') ceased publication in 2006, having run stories such as 'Rimming: not just for gay boys' (July 2003) and photosets such as 'Butch on butch action'.

Although these early pioneers of lesbian porn have not survived, the market has expanded alongside porn for gay men. In 2007 *OOB* founder and lesbian porn producer Nan Kinney observed that, in the 1980s, when she had entered the porn production business, 'there was no lesbian porn – none ... Now you have many sex-positive retail stores and a multitude of websites for lesbians to find porn.'[19] Kinney went on to explain how she and her colleagues were required to depart from the dominant anti-porn feminism of the period:

> Back then, the lesbian culture was dominated by the anti-porn, politically correct faction. I met my lover, Debi Sundahl, co-founder of *On Our Backs*, working on the committee which put on the Take Back the Night Rally in Minneapolis! I was teaching street-fighting self-defense courses while Debi worked at the Harriet Tubman Shelter for Battered Women. We were radicalized about women's control of their bodies and their safety. However, once Debi and I became more than just friends, we discovered we both had always enjoyed pornography – *Penthouse*, *Playboy* & such. We disagreed with the Violence-Against-Women movement's increasing focus on pornography as the cause of the violence. Plus, the anti-porn attitude was influencing lesbians in a very negative way around their own sexuality. For example, penetration by any means was perceived as a violent, male-identified, dominant act, and was therefore not to be done. Lesbians were having very limited, politically-correct, side-by-side sex.
>
> It was at this juncture that we split from this anti-porn, anti-sex culture in Minneapolis and moved to San Francisco in the hopes of finding a more open attitude toward sexuality. However, even in San Francisco, only the S/M lesbians were open to and exploring their sexuality, and we joined Samois, the lesbian S/M club. What started as a very personal sexual exploration soon became political. We'd go to the women's bookstore in search of anything about lesbian sexuality and found nothing. It was as if lesbians weren't sexual. But, we knew there were plenty of lesbians [who were] into exploring sexuality. The problem was that the anti-porn lesbians controlled the general lesbian culture, including the press. In response, Debi and I decided to make our own porn. *On Our Backs* started from a very personal need and expression. We got together with our friends, took some photos, solicited erotica, and scraped together money to print the first issue in 1984. We were a bunch of sex radicals expressing ourselves and having a great time.[20]

As noted in Chapter 4, one might have expected the emergence of gay and lesbian porn to weaken the argument that pornography is in itself, always and everywhere, an instrument of patriarchal oppression. It has not. Rather, in publications such as *Big Porn Inc*, where the subject of gay porn is referenced at all it is in the effort to recuperate it for the anti-porn camp. Christopher Kendall's essay in that volume applies the same literalism to gay porn which the same book elsewhere applies to straight male porn. One film, involving a (male) rape fantasy, is read thus:

> the identity sold is one in which violence by one man against another man or men is normalised through sex for the persons involved and for the consumer of these materials.
>
> *(2011, p.58)*

'Violence' is used here to mean the fantasy role-playing of domination and submission, bondage and restraint, perhaps anal fisting. Not to everyone's taste, gay or straight, but part of sexual life's rich tapestry and, in as much as it is entirely consensual, a matter principally of taste and personal preference. To call it 'violence' without such qualification is to devalue that term, and to highlight a key flaw of this strand of anti-porn rhetoric – its insistence on taking literally what is clearly intended to function as fantasy. True of straight porn, the point is even more relevant to gay and lesbian porn, with their extensive repertoires of BDSM and role-playing scenarios. Some lesbians also fantasise about men, for example, and enjoy porn made for gay men, according to lesbian website Lesbilicious. This is a 'guilty secret in the lesbian community', asserts the author, adding:

> the answer to why lesbians enjoy gay man porn could partly lie in how we use pornography as a way to play around with genders and sexualities outside of our usual experience. Watching a gay man having sex on a screen or a magazine is a peek into a forbidden world that we're usually excluded from. It's taboo and exciting, but at the same time totally fake and entirely safe.[21]

Not all gay men and women, or indeed other sexually defined groups such as BDSM specialists, fetishists and 'perverts' (Rosewarne, 2011) of various kinds, have embraced the emergence of their orientation from the margins of acceptability and legality, preferring a strategy of maintaining outsider-ness and a degree of separation from the world of 'vanilla sex'.

But those who did, and who do today, wish to be part of the societal mainstream, and to have legal access to a pornography and a sexual culture which reflects their sexual identities and preferences, now can. The increased accessibility of porn has, to put it quite simply, and as part of that broader extension of sexual citizenship rights I have identified as a consistent political trend, made life better for these groups.

The increasing visibility and indeed routinisation of gay- and lesbian-themed material, and of other forms of culture which have been publicly recognised as relating positively to homosexuality – from the sexually explicit 1980s art works of Robert Mapplethorpe to the self-outing of Will Young or the marriage of Elton John to his male partner in 2009 – have contributed to the formation of an environment in which deviations from, and variations to, mainstream heterosexuality have steadily become more normalised. Through these images and texts, and the public declarations accompanying them, the nature of 'deviant' sexualities has become better understood, and thus has come to seem less threatening, and thus too more readily integrated into even the most resistant and traditionally patriarchal of institutions, such as the US armed forces and the more liberal Christian churches.

One cannot prove that this or that image or statement made the key difference in this process, although I have referenced some which can be seen as milestones, not least because they have been identified as such in media commentary on the trend. One can, however, describe an emergence of gay-themed texts of various kinds into mainstream sexual culture, of which pornography is one, at the same time as late patriarchy has moved away from mandatory heterosexuality towards a much more diverse and inclusive sexual politics.

As Chapter 1 noted, this process is driven by the rising socio-economic power of the previously marginalised group, and its associated presence in the cultural marketplace. In the February 2005 issue of *Vanity Fair* James Wolcott observed that the fifteen million (or so) gay men living in that country had an estimated annual discretionary spend of $500 billion, a demographic that was 'affluent, entertainment-savvy and starving for greater representation on television'.[22] Wolcott added that Richard Florida's 'creative class', as his 2000 book called the emerging generation of internet-savvy consumers, was multi-ethnic, multifaith and 'omnisexual'. As I noted in Chapter 1, economics were driving the transformation of the cultural marketplace into one that cared less about sexual orientation than about spending power.

Education, mediation, substitution – pornography and everyday life

Porn has played its part in an evolving sexual ecology which has made unprecedented room for homosexuality as an identity and a lifestyle. In the same way it has enabled the articulation of hitherto marginalised or suppressed sexualities, giving strength and comfort to those who harbour them. And by making sex and sexuality visible it has educated, about the mechanics of sex in general, and safe sex in particular.

When *Mediated Sex* was being written in the mid-1990s HIV and AIDS were still catastrophic diagnoses, even in the medically advanced countries of the liberal democratic world. Although combination therapies and other treatments had progressed significantly from the late 1980s, when AIDS killed Robert Mapplethorpe and thousands of other gay men, and was justifiably perceived as a death sentence for anyone with the diagnosis, straight or gay, the disease was still a high-priority public health issue recognised as requiring communicative intervention.

In that book I took some time to show how health services and social advertising bodies in affected countries were using pornography and other forms of explicit sexual representation to educate in the need for, and techniques of, safe sex. Videos were designed to look like pornography, in that they were intentionally arousing, were used to show how condoms should be fitted before penetrative sex, or how sex could be satisfying without being penetrative. Pornography itself began to feature more examples of safe-sex practices such as wearing condoms, and to combine sexual representation with signifiers of healthy living such as exercise and good diet.

In part this trend reflected the importance of protecting porn performers from the risks of HIV and AIDS; in part, in at least some cases, they were intended to educate porn users. I wrote then, of gay male pornography in particular, that 'like other categories of sexual representation, it has adapted to reflect changes in the wider political, cultural and biological environments' (1996, p.134). Porn made for and by gay men and lesbians, bisexuals, transsexuals and other once-marginalised categories of sexual orientation continues to play these pedagogic, as well as recreational functions, addressing communities not merely with images of sex which resonate with their sexualities, but communicating educational and political messages of various kinds.

Pornography and young people

People, and young people in particular, of whatever sexual orientation, learn a lot about sex from the media. Research by Buckingham and Bragg published in 2003 noted, for example, that two thirds of 'children prefer to learn about sex through soap operas or teenage magazines because they are a less embarrassing and even an easy way of learning, at home, in a safe environment'.[23]

As we saw in Chapter 4, one argument used by anti-porn campaigners in recent times is that men, and women – and young men and women in particular, such as college students – learn much of their sexual etiquette from pornography, and that insofar as pornography depicts male exploitation and degradation of women (as it is argued to do by these perspectives) its educational function is deeply damaging. Michael Flood reads the research evidence to show that

> pornography plays an increasingly significant role in boys' and young men's peer cultures and sociosexual relations. Consumption of pornography is exacerbating some males' tolerance for sexual violence, intensifying their investments in narratives of female nymphomania and male sexual prowess, and shifting their sexual practices and relations.
>
> *(2010, p.164)*

Flood does allow that 'some of pornography's impacts are innocuous or even desirable', such as in the provision of information about sex and sexualities. He also notes that pornography consumption 'tends to liberalise sexual attitudes' (p.168), which can also be counted as a good thing. In the main however, Flood and other anti-pornography voices emphasise what they see as porn's harmful educational effects – which rest largely on their belief that the content of pornography is read literally by young men and boys, in the process instructing them in misogynistic or damaging sexual attitudes and practices.

Pamela Paul typifies the 'porn teaches harmful things' perspective when she argues that

> when men view pornography, they absorb messages about what it means for a woman to be sexy. Not only does pornography dictate how women are supposed to look, but it skews their expectations of how they are supposed to act.
>
> *(2005, p.133)*

The example of female depilation was discussed above, in which pornography is blamed for the growth in vaginal shaving or waxing amongst women. I challenged that connection, based not least on my own experience of women (and men, for that matter) who shave or wax but have certainly not 'learnt' to do so from the consumption of pornography. But let us accept that it could happen – that young men and women, relatively inexperienced in the conduct of actual sexual relationships, find in pornography a source of information about sex. Would it be a problem?

Pornography can and does perform this role. It certainly did for me, as a pre-teen, encountering discarded pornographic images in the places we played as kids. Or viewing the porn stashed away by my friends' older brothers and sisters. These were the contexts in which I first saw a naked (adult) female body.

Educated in a Catholic school, and brought up by parents who, although commendably liberal and relaxed in their attitudes to my emerging sexuality as a teenager and a young man, shared the tendency of most parents in those days to avoid the subject of sex, or to euphemise it beyond the point where their advice could be of any practical use, pornography, viewed furtively, accidentally, illicitly, was educational both in revealing the physiology of the female, and in demonstrating the meaning of sexual arousal. Over time, pornography also showed me for the first time sexual techniques and practices, some of which I subsequently adopted. By no means all, however, and never with a reluctant partner. In that respect, and from my personal experience, there is no sense in which pornography 'made' me do things which I regret, or which others have regretted (as far as I am aware).

Neither do I believe, although I can hardly be certain, that this early exposure to pornography distorted what might otherwise have been my 'natural' sexuality, any more than did the heady mix of sadomasochism and moral guilt which lay at the core of the Catholic religion, or the sexual preferences of my first girlfriends. As we will see in the next chapter, Catholicism has been a strong influence on the sexually themed work of many great artists, and can be presumed to have comparable influences on those who are not public performers. Pornography, too, is part of the set of environmental influences which formed the sexualities of many, if not all of us. I do not, for myself, view that as having been a negative influence.

Today, of course, children and young people are exposed to more pornography than those of us brought up in the pre-internet era. As we have seen, this fact drives much of the porno fear currently seen in the academic literature and the public sphere, and does require a response beyond dismissal as moral panic. So far though – and conceding that these are early days in the history of the internet – there is no evidence that young people are having more sex, earlier, or in more risky ways, than they did decades ago.

It may be thought that there are too many unwanted pregnancies amongst young people, too many cases of sexually transmitted diseases such as chlamydia, too much sex happening in general, but the truth is that in many respects things were much worse in the past. When abortions were illegal, for example, many women had them in extremely dangerous circumstances, or had children adopted, or were confined to institutions for 'fallen women' like those depicted in Peter Mullan's powerful and poignant film, *The Magdalene Sisters* (2002).

The sexual habits of young people in the 1950s, for example, are still somewhat obscure, because of the taboos around talking about sex, and the very different legal environment which prevailed at that time, which inhibited honesty and frankness in these matters. But as the memoirs and recollections have emerged of how things were behind the façade of moral rectitude, we learn that people then behaved much as people do now, if without the self-confidence and public visibility that often accompanies much of contemporary sexual life (especially for hitherto stigmatised groups such as gay men and lesbians).

Mediation and substitution

I noted above that many alternative pornographies (that is, alternatives to porn made for straight men) serve an important function by making visible and giving sexual affirmation to the overweight and other categories of person who deviate from the fashion- and style-magazine ideal of the body beautiful, and are rarely seen in mainstream sexual culture. These groups may be laughed at in film and TV comedy, or made the butt of cruel jokes by stand-up comedy stars, but they are rarely depicted in a way that might make them seem sexually desirable. Pornography is one cultural form where these rules do not apply.

Pornography objectifies, yes, but does not limit itself to the objectification of prevailing stereotypes of beauty. Kipnis observes, for example, that

> pornography's celebration of fat, even its 'objectification' of fat women, is in defiance of all societal norms and social controls ... [Fat] pornography provides, in the aesthetic realm, a free zone to defy the dictates and the homogeneity imposed on aesthetics, on sexuality, and on bodies.
>
> *(1999, p.121)*

And as for fat, so for age, ethnicity and disability. 'Many pornographic sub-genres are strikingly contiguous with the central aesthetic preoccupations of our day' (Ibid.). In representing these groups, pornography provides a mediated form of sexuality which may be extremely valuable to an individual.

Pornography's *mediation* function, which I will also characterise as one of *substitution*, applies in general to all those who, for one reason or another, are unable to access the quantity or quality of 'real' sexual experience they would ideally wish for. And that is a lot of people.

Lauren Rosewarne writes that 'we live in a culture saturated with sex', and that 'we seem to intellectually understand that the majority of people masturbate, although there appears distaste with piecing the story together and accepting that *someone* is buying the porn and that masturbation often accompanies viewing' (2011, p.70). Indeed. The majority of people wank, but few admit to it, and the subject is rarely discussed in polite company. Likewise, nearly everyone is interested in explicit sexual representation, whether they choose to call it pornography, or erotica, or prefer not to mention it at all. The expansion of the pornosphere, and the emergence of the internet in particular, has merely made that fact more apparent, less easy to deny, and more problematic for the critics of porn as patriarchal propaganda to explain.

The need for mediation may arise from the simple fact that an individual happens to be in a committed partnership with another, and has no desire to betray him or her with infidelity. Whether married or not, many couples feel genuine and commendable loyalty to each other, even if they are having sex less regularly than in the first flush of romance, or even if they have ceased to have sex altogether, as may arise in the period after childbirth, or after many decades of living together. Frankie Boyle, a Scottish stand-up comedian notorious for his politically incorrect humour, explained with iconoclastic frankness in a press interview some time ago why he, as a happily married man with children, uses porn:

> If you have a very high sex drive, which I do, and you've got a kid, you can't just go and shag people any more. So you watch pornography.[24]

As we saw in Chapter 4, one argument used against the pornographication of mainstream culture, and which has gained currency with the rise of the internet, is that otherwise happy and stable families are at risk of breakdown because husbands (wives are rarely implicated in this practice) spend hours and hours online, masturbating, while their wives sulk in bed. This is a central theme in Pamela Paul's *Pornified*, which cites a number of cases in evidence of the 'porn addict' hypothesis. She interviews 'Andy', for example, 'who is recovering from an addiction to pornography' (2005, p.211). Andy and others are enlisted by Paul to substantiate her argument that 'the majority of sex addicts eventually turn off their wives or girlfriends altogether' (p.232):

> Pornography has a corrosive effect on men's relationship with women and a negative impact on men's male sexual performance and satisfaction. It plays a rising role in intimacy disorders [sic]. More than ever, it aids and abets sexually compulsive behaviours in ways that can become seriously disruptive and psychologically damaging.
>
> *(Ibid., p.266)*

If, however, one assumes that now, as in the past, many marriages are under strain for much of the time, and that unsatisfactory or insufficient sex can be a major cause of what Paul calls 'intimacy disorder', one might just as easily attribute to porn use the survival of a partnership that might otherwise disintegrate as the man goes in search of an affair, or resorts to prostitution. In both cases, the need is for a sex-substitute, not necessarily new love. And in that case, pornography is the safest substitute one will find.

Women, too, and in increasing numbers, leave their husbands and even their children because of unsatisfactory sex lives. The liberalisation of divorce laws – one consequence of feminism's political influence – has made that decision easier for an unhappily married woman to make than it has ever been. But for women, too, despite the assertions of some in the anti-pornography lobby, porn can be a convenient and accessible source of the sex that may be missing in the bedroom, and thus a means of preserving an otherwise loving and valuable relationship. Porn, in short, can be seen as a factor in the defence of marriage and a stable family life, as opposed to the source of its destabilisation.

It is true that, in general (and there are many reasons why one half of a loving partnership might lose interest in sex, or find it difficult to maintain a sexual interest in his or her partner), the mediation/substitution argument applies with even greater force to those whose sexualities deviate from societal norms.

We are all the products of our parental upbringing and childhood education, which often have religious components and may instil certain fears and anxieties around what is acceptable in sexual terms, and what can therefore be requested of a partner. In this case, pornography is the outlet for fantasies and desires which it may not be possible to satisfy at home, and which might otherwise damage a relationship. Clarissa Smith writes that 'porn may offer relief to feelings not met elsewhere, it may offer opportunities for exploration and spicing up one's sex life, it may offer a vision of freedom from sexual hang-ups and much more' (2007, p.123). Laura Kipnis celebrates porn as 'a legitimate form of culture and a fictional, fantastical, even allegorical realm' which 'insists on a sanctioned space for fantasy' (1999, p.163).

If we avoid moral judgements about the appropriateness of these fantasies and 'feelings', and focus instead on what is good for the partners in a marriage, or for sexual subjects in general, whether married or not, then this function of pornography as a safety valve for the release of pent-up desires which might otherwise break relationships apart takes on significant individual and social value. Oliver James, a British psychologist known for his work on 'happiness', notes that

> a high proportion of men use porn as a distraction or to reduce stress ... It serves an anti-depressant purpose for the unhappy. A proportion of both men and women claim that it inspires more fulfilling sex with existing partners, providing new ideas.[25]

From this point of view, pornography is good for individual mental health, and for family longevity. Lauren Rosewarne writes that porn provides 'access to unattainable fantasy ... and an outlet for sex that may not be available'. In this respect, pornography 'is aiding people to experience the extent and extremes of their sexuality. Safely and legally.'[26] Tom Hodgkinson adds that

> pornography has the advantage of involving no one else, no possibility of judgement on our performance. Endless fantasy and no one to please except yourself. Porn removes the nagging anxiety that can sometimes spoil our erotic liaisons: is the other person enjoying it? Am I doing it right? Who cares.
>
> *(2004, p.201)*

To the critics of pornographication such a declaration might be read as selfish irresponsibility. In the new porn studies paradigm identified by Attwood it is a statement of an obvious if long-suppressed truth. Men and women are going to have sex, and will seek out the kinds of sex they prefer, in or out of stable relationships. If pornography can be a means of preventing sexual affairs and recourse to prostitution by one or other of the partners in an otherwise mutually beneficial and healthy partnership, with all the associated emotional and health risks of infidelity, then it can be accepted as a welcome, if not essential, accompaniment to everyday life in the twenty-first century.

And if it is the case, as one US study found, that men who use porn are more likely to have sexual relationships outside of marriage, can we say that porn use causes infidelity? Not necessarily. It is just as likely that the man who is bored with his sex life turns both to porn, and to other women, to spice up his sex life. If access to the former helps prevent the latter, that is good for families, and for societies in which stable parenting is valued.

Porn is pleasure, fucking is fun ...

Finally, and in addition to what we might regard as the public goods of pornography I have set out above, there are also the private pleasures, which may be regarded as good in themselves. Sex has an essential biological function, of course, which over time has acquired mystical, religious dimensions, and a history of attempts to control and regulate its practice by patriarchal authority structures, principally the churches.

For those who are not religious (and perhaps even some who are), and who therefore do not attach mystical or divine importance to the sex act but accept it as one of life's gifts, fucking is fun, and its representation a pathway to pleasure which can be accessed without all the accompaniments of the courting process.

Not that courting and romance are not fun too – but they need not be, all the time, and there may be circumstances where an individual prefers to 'go it alone' in the privacy of his or her own domestic space. In such a circumstance, which may apply to both men and women, gay or straight, bisexual, transsexual or whatever, pornography is simply the means to an end – sexual climax, orgasm, pleasure for its own sake, unadorned and requiring no apology.

8

THE AESTHETICS OF SEXUAL TRANSGRESSION

> I loved porno and I bought lots of it all the time – the really dirty, exciting stuff. All you had to do was figure out what turned you on, and then just buy the dirty magazines and movie prints that were right for you, the way you'd go for the right pill or the right cans of food.
>
> *(Andy Warhol)*[1]

Grace Tuck has observed that 'many of the canonical works of both modern and postmodern art and literature employ explicitly sexual tropes and images' (2009, p.77). Indeed, art through the ages, not least art recognised as great, has always addressed sexuality. Chapter 2 noted that prehistoric cave paintings often depicted early humans having sex, and that all civilisations and societies for which we have records depicted, if not always the sex act as narrowly defined, then aspects of the sexual, whether for sacred or secular ends: the Venus of Willendorf; ancient Roman and Greek pottery and sculpture; the extensive canon of Renaissance nudes; Courbet's *Origin Of the World* (1866).

Anthony Julius notes in his book about transgressive art (2002) that sexuality has always been a driver of the artistic impulse, and the appropriation of pornographic images (even before they were called pornography) has been a tool adopted by artists for centuries. Manet's *Olympia* appeared in 1863, around the same time as the word 'pornography' was becoming familiar to speakers of English, French and German. It subverts the classic nude, and establishes the paradigm for a certain kind of sexually transgressive aesthetic in which, as Julius puts it, 'the subversive project appropriates the pornographic in order to interrogate art convention and the art canon. It used the pornographic as an engine of transgression' (p.61).[2]

In short, the compulsion to make art about sex appears to be a universal of human culture. Sex was certainly 'the big theme of twentieth century art',[3] and looks like being quite important in the twenty-first. Film-maker John Waters has written that 'contemporary art is sex … it's all about sex' (2003). And the director of sexually transgressive icons such as *Female Trouble* (1974) and *Mondo Trasho* (1969) is more qualified than most to say so.

Sex, taboo and transgression

The reasons for this linkage must be speculative, of course, but there is considerable agreement amongst cultural historians and anthropologists that it has something to do with the universality of sexual taboo on the one hand, and the evolved function of art (or one of its functions) as a platform for transgressive cultural production on the other. It is believed that cultural taboos evolved in human society as mechanisms for the regulation and control of the activities of its members, for the greater benefit of the group. Contemporary taboos, such as sex with children, and incest – and those which have been eroded in recent decades, such as homosexuality, or sex outside of marriage – have had, and (in the case of both paedophilia and incest) continue to have, important functions in societies where, for example, the human rights of children are regarded as important.

Taboos exist because otherwise some human beings would engage in activities deemed harmful to society. Some of those harms are significant by any objective standards (child abuse for example), while others may be thought to cause damage only from within a particular moral or ethical framework, which may not be shared by all (the now eroding taboo on homosexuality is theological at core, because it challenges the sacred nature of marriage and heterosexual family structures). Either way – which is to say, whether they are rationally founded or ideological in origin – taboos define boundaries between acceptable and non-acceptable behaviours, and signal to members of a society to stay on the right side of the line if they wish to be fully respected, employed, at liberty and so on.

Nonetheless, in any society there will be those who violate the taboos, or transgress, and who must therefore be punished. When, in 2005, English supermodel Kate Moss was captured on a mobile camera snorting cocaine, her (lack of) morality became a *cause célèbre* of the British and international media. Several of her modelling contracts were cancelled, and her status as an aspirational figure for girls and young women was questioned. In the end, after this symbolic chastisement in the court of public opinion, she was forgiven and carried on with her illustrious career, but not before the transgressive act had been identified, debated and punished before the society as a whole.

Societies constantly evolve, and the management, organisational, and controlling functions of particular taboos may come to appear unnecessary, or even to act as a constraint on the social progress of a society at a given point in its development. This has happened with homosexuality in liberal capitalism, and with the taboo against sex outside of marriage which prevailed in most Western countries until the latter half of the twentieth century.

As sexual politics (and the invention of the contraceptive pill) placed gays and women in newly empowered socio-economic positions after the 1970s, patriarchal and heteronormative prohibitions on their sexual activities became anachronistic and oppressive, and were increasingly transgressed in the period we know as the 'sexual revolution'. Transgression of taboo, then, may have a progressive function in human social organisation, breaking through prohibitions which have been functional for a ruling elite (in patriarchy, men and their property rights benefitted from the longstanding taboo on divorce) but inhibiting or oppressive for other groups who, at a certain point, break through the barriers and assert their right to do things differently.

Sometimes the maintenance of taboos – such as the taboo on murder – is logical and necessary, given the capacity of the human species to do violence to its own. In others, the breaking of taboo is part of the process whereby a higher, perhaps more humane form of civilisation emerges. In the latter circumstance taboo-breaking will often be accompanied by elite resistance and public controversy, even moral panic, before the new boundaries of the acceptable are established as commonsensical. Transgression is rule-breaking thought or behaviour, and is likely to be punished before it is forgiven and then embraced by a society. The ritual of punishment may itself have a positive role in societal evolution, insofar as it can often be the trigger for the debate which dilutes or abolishes the taboo.

Even where a taboo can be seen to retain its usefulness, its violation may be viewed as part of an ongoing process of negotiation and discussion which, even if it ends in the maintenance of the taboo, may still be functional in reminding us of what precisely the taboo is, and why it is necessary. The parameters of a taboo can also be varied, the rules modified, to reflect new conditions. In the twenty-first century the 'sex outside of marriage' taboo has been eroded, as has the rule that marriage must be between a man and a woman. Today, marriage is still preferred in the public domain, but need no longer be an exclusively heterosexual institution, and is certainly not compulsory for family units.

Transgression may be coded as sinful, criminal, deviant or offensive according to the value systems of the society in which it occurs. Chris Jenks is among those who stress its positive role in improving imperfect societies, or in catalysing cultural evolution, at the same time as reinforcing rules which it may be important to maintain for the good of the collective. He notes that 'transgression is not the same as disorder. It opens up chaos and reminds us of the necessity of order' (2003).

For George Bataille, author of some of the most sexually explicit literature of the twentieth century, including *The Story Of The Eye* (1928) – a surrealist work very much focused on the breaking of religious taboos – transgression was viewed as an expression of individual freedom, against the impositions of authority.

Work and submission to social order liberate us from chaos and brutality, Bataille argued, but submit us also to the tyranny of materialism and money. 'And so', writes Anthony Julius, 'we need, from time to time, to free ourselves from the means of our liberation. Hence the need for the transgression of taboos' (2002). The transgression of taboo is here viewed as neither 'bad' nor 'good' in itself, but rather as a dynamic force in cultural reproduction and renewal: it prevents social stagnation insofar as rules are being broken, and in doing so it ensures stability by testing and changing or reaffirming those very same rules.

Taboo anticipates its own negation and, like the transgressive texts of pornography, constantly shifts its boundaries as contexts change and circumstances require. The killing of another human being is acceptable in warfare – indeed, mandatory for soldiers – but taboo in peacetime, for virtually all countries (capital punishment now exists in only a handful of the world's 200 recognised nation states). Hegarty notes that 'transgression is a possibility contained within taboo – or else there would be no need for the taboo. Similarly, there is nothing that is inherently transgressive (and therefore inherently evil)' (2000, p.100).

Moving to the realm of the sexual, Anthony Julius presents a compelling account of why art, transgression and sexuality should be so intimately and frequently connected in human culture. Sex, he notes, is an obvious subject for transgressive art, because it is (or has been) religiously charged, surrounded by prohibitions of various kinds:

> Certain forms of sexuality are expressly proscribed in the Scriptures, because sexual experience itself occupies the extreme terrain of momentary pleasures; because there is an underground literary tradition [now pictorial and visual too] of the erotic that attracts the hostility of the state; because a certain kind of sexual liberation is the principal way in which the modern age defines itself against the preceding age.
>
> *(2002, p.22)*

For Julius, 'the transgressive is the utopian aspect of every art work, the one that offers us glimpses of an existence unconfined by rules and constraints' (p.21). Pornography is transgressive, as argued above, and art is often transgressive (in pushing aesthetic boundaries, for example, or challenging conventions of taste and decency, which are not only based on sexual values). That the two cultural practices should come together in interesting ways is therefore unsurprising.

To transgress is to cross a boundary, to deviate from a norm, to go beyond what a society or community deems 'normal', or acceptable in thought and action. Laura Kipnis observes that '[pornography's] greatest pleasure is to locate each and every one of society's taboos, prohibitions and proprieties and systematically transgress them, one by one' (1999, p.163). The content of a society's pornography reveals its morality and sexual ethics, only to violate them in the representation of erotic fantasy. It is arousing *because* it transgresses, or enables scenarios of transgression to unfold in the mind of the user.

French philosopher Bernard-Henri Lévy provides an intriguing set of connections between the taboo, the transgressive, and the desirable, which are central to both the appeal of the pornographic, and the interest of so many artists in the sexual. Art, like porn, is a transgressive discourse rooted in the violation of taboos, the crossing of boundaries, the exploration of the unknown (because it has been forbidden):

> All theoreticians of eroticism know that when there is no distance, there is no border; when there is no border, there is no taboo; when there is no taboo there is no transgression; and when there is no transgression there is no desire.[4]

Insofar as art *is* transgressive, it is easy to see why sex has been a key theme of artists down the ages, and why they have often been accused by critics and commentators of their time as being pornographic (where that term has had unambivalently negative connotations).

In Australia the work of Bill Henson has been so accused;[5] in England that of Tierney Gearon, and Sally Mann; in the United States Robert Mapplethorpe. All, significantly, have been denounced for photographing children in naked or semi-naked poses. They exemplify the contemporary power of the taboo about children and sex, and also the fluidity of the art/porn distinction, and how easy it is for an artist who deals with the body (and is perceived to be sexualising bodies inappropriately) to be categorised in the public sphere as a pornographer, and thereby rendered vulnerable to sanction in the context of wider political agendas. Giselda Pollock defends Sally Mann's nude photographs of her own children, and her right to make them, thus:

> Independently of whether we personally think she should or shouldn't 'explore', expose, or represent her children (regardless of the question: are they or are they not pornographic), the point is that, in their existence, these photographs provoke our culture to think about the boundaries of sexuality and childhood, public image, authorship and cultural usage or abusage.
>
> *(quoted in Raney, 2003, p.146)*

Here we see nicely summarised the boundary-pushing function of art in the moment of sexual transgressivity. It is not that we wish to see paedophilia legitimised – on the contrary, it is among the worst of crimes and should, after centuries of silence and avoidance, be punished with all the force of the law[6] – but there is nonetheless value in using art to challenge the view held in some quarters that children are never sexual beings, and that all nude or semi-nude images of children, even when taken by their own parents and family friends, are somehow reprehensible or obscene.

There have been cases of parents being investigated and even threatened with prosecution after a commercial photo developer has come across images of children naked in a bathtub or at play, and decides to report them to the police as suspicious. The work of Mann and others is controversial because it has raised the issue of childhood sexuality at a time of widespread moral panic around paedophilia which, without disputing the importance of a public awareness of child abuse, has distorted healthy relationships between adults – particularly men – and children. Mann's work, and work like it, is important because it asks us to step back and think about what such images can mean, and about our own attitudes to the sexuality of children.

In 2009 Richard Prince's *Pop Life* exhibition attracted controversy for one piece in particular, *Spiritual America*, in which a 'found' photograph of a 12-year-old Brooke Shields taken during the shooting of Louis Malle's *Pretty Baby* (1978) – itself a transgressive and controversial cinematic study of a child who is also a prostitute in early twentieth-century New Orleans – is reframed with the benefit of cultural historic hindsight. *The Sunday Times* noted of the controversy that 'sensitivity to images of children that might be construed as sexual has heightened'.[7]

'Might be construed as sexual' is the key term here. Even as it raises difficult questions, art of this kind can help a society discuss issues of definition, limitation and boundaries. Even in being used as the raw material for heated and often hypocritical moral panics by the popular media, such art makes visible complexities and ambiguities around particular types of image that it may be healthy and productive for a society to debate. Art about sex can be transgressive in another sense, which relates to and often exploits the cultural relativism of the concept of pornography. It is part of the function of the artist to transgress, and in so much as they are aware of and interested in the debates about the pornographication and sexualisation of mainstream culture, artists may choose to use their public platform to engage with the issues of cultural sexualisation explored in Chapter 4.

Prince's *Spiritual America* is an example, drawing as it does on the assumed cultural memory of the *Pretty Baby*/Brooke Shields controversy, reworking the image in the context of the contemporary debate about the sexualisation of children. In this work he takes an image which had been pilloried long ago as pornographic, and inserts it within a twenty-first century artwork speaking to the times in which he lives. Is the result itself pornographic? Not by a reasonable person's estimation, I would argue, but we may assume that Prince wishes to stimulate that question, or something like it, and the discussion which might follow.

Jeff Koons takes a similar approach with *Made In Heaven* (1989), deliberately making art that looks like porn, while denying that porn is what it is. *Made In Heaven* comprises a series of large-format photographs depicting him and his then wife Ilona Staller, or Cicciolina, in a variety of sexual acts. At the time of their marriage Cicciolina had been for many years a major European porn-star. She had also dabbled in Italian libertarian politics, standing (unsuccessfully) for election to the Italian parliament.

The marriage, therefore, and the images created by Koons in what he characterised as a homage to it, represented in a quite literal way the union of art and porn. The photographs were beautifully constructed and produced, in Koons' signature post-pop art style, but contained many of the tropes of hard core pornography: come shots, vaginal, oral and anal sex, and exotic sexual postures. Koons denied that they were pornographic because, he said, they were inspired by love (Koons, 1992). But they could not fail to confront the art-gallery viewer as images which intentionally looked like pornography.[8]

In exhibiting them, the artist helped generate many of the early reflections around porno chic which appeared in newspapers and elsewhere in the early 1990s (McNair, 1996). His explicit couplings were, he insisted, not to be read as porn but simply as records of loving sex between a man and a woman, husband and wife, more akin to wedding photographs than dirty books. He could not but comment, however, on the arbitrariness of the art/porn distinction, which is fundamental to the work's success, and a theme which recurs in much artistic porno chic. In doing so, he requires the viewer also to consider that arbitrariness.

It is, as noted in Chapter 3, its particular quality of transgressiveness which makes pornography attractive as a source for cultural artefacts which are not themselves pornographic, but which may present themselves as belonging to the spheres of art, advertising, fashion, or popular film and TV, including journalism. Although these works are not pornography, as it was defined in Chapter 2, they are clearly associated with the pornographic, even when they deny their lineage in the manner of Jeff Koons and Madonna – notable transgressors in their respective spheres of conceptual art and pop music and video.

They both produced work in the 1980s and early 1990s which was undeniably 'porno chic' as defined in Chapter 3, and somewhat playful in its implied stance on the pornographic itself, but shied away from the label to prefer, in Madonna's case, 'erotica' and in Koons', simply 'love'. They, however, like many others, drew overtly on the sexily transgressive qualities of porn, exploiting its capacity to reveal and expose a central element of the human condition – sexuality – and transferring these to artefacts which appeared on the art-gallery wall, the coffee table book, the glossy magazine page, or the MTV video playlist.

Madonna's *Justify My Love* video, and the *Sex* book, appeared not long after the *Made In Heaven* exhibitions, and although I have no evidence that she was influenced by Koons, her employment of the iconography of the pornographic at this point in her career seems more than coincidental.

Madonna, and Koons, and Richard Prince, present examples of artists knowingly transgressing the art/porn boundary. Koons' work in particular may be regarded as a paradigm case of the function of art in this context – to question not just the sexual taboos which are pornography's subject, but the formal boundaries and taste distinctions which have structured the art/erotica/porn/trash hierarchy for centuries.

Let us take a moment, then, to consider this oldest and still most relevant of cultural debates: Is the line between art and pornography real, as opposed to a construction? And if so, where is it to be drawn?

But is it art? Navigating the art–porn interface

The notion that one person's art is another's porn is hardly new. As Mary Kerstin has observed:

> the demarcation between erotic and pornographic representations is closely interconnected with aesthetic, moral and legal standards of the time ... what is seen as art and what as pornographic is based on value judgements and can vary from period to period and from culture to culture.

> *(2007, p.88)*

In some cases the 'art' begins as pornography, or erotica (depending on the maker's own assessment of the cultural value of porn), becoming recognised only later as 'Art' with a capital 'A'. Such is the work of Tom Of Finland (Touko Laaksonen), whose sexually explicit drawings of muscle-bound men have been hugely influential in western gay sub-cultures since the 1950s, helping to challenge stereotypical notions of male homosexuality as 'sissy' and effeminate.[9]

When they first appeared in physique magazines in the United States they were received as homoerotic porn by a community largely starved of eroticised images of itself (see Chapter 7). Today the originals are prized collectors' pieces, having migrated from the pornosphere to the art canon, independently of the artist's original intentions with the work. The work is still what it always was, but its meanings have changed.

Scottish photographer Rankin has engaged regularly with the sexual, in such exhibitions as *Sex Show*, and *Sofasexy*. 'It's not art and it's not porn', argued one observer of the latter, of work that might just as easily be defined as fashion.[10] The difficulty in defining the difference between art and pornography – and then sticking to it in a consistent and sustained manner – is a theme in *Destricted* (2006), an anthology of films about sex and pornography by artists including Sam Taylor-Wood, Richard Prince and Larry Clark.

The film comprises seven short sequences, directed (in addition to the contributions by Taylor-Wood, Prince and Clark) by Gaspar Noe, Matthew Barney, Marco Brambilla and Marina Abramovic. Advertised on its DVD sleeve as 'the most controversial and sexually explicit film ever to receive an 18 certificate from the BBFC', *Destricted* includes meditations on the nature of the porn industry (in a segment by Larry Clark featuring young men auditioning to perform with more experienced female porn-stars); a section called *SYNC* in which Brambilla utilises found images from porn movies to construct a breathless sequence of short scenes which, although pornographic in origin, are here reframed; Richard Prince's re-recording of a 1970s porno reel with his own postmodern take on the subject matter; Taylor-Wood's depiction of a solitary man somewhere in Death Valley California, masturbating on the dry earth to the accompaniment of moody western guitar; and Gaspar Noe's mash up of a contemporary porn reel, viewed from within a woman's (and a man's) masturbatory fantasies.

All are sexually explicit works. They play with the tropes and conventions of pornography, or explore its meanings, or embed actual porn in their content, but are read as 'Art' rather than 'Porn' because they are authored by individuals recognised as 'Artists'. Their self-identification, and our acceptance of that status as viewers, removes them from the pornosphere, even if the content of the work is denotatively the same as porn (as in Richard Prince's piece).

As soon as we identify a text as art, it appears, we can no longer view it as porn. In the act of labelling it loses its pornographic qualities, because there is now a distance between the image and the response, which requires that we reflect on meaning and purpose. Why is Prince re-recording a 1970s stag reel? Why is Brambilla splicing together these moments from porn movies, and playing them at a speed too fast to properly register their content? The answer is, of course, to make us look anew at the content and find new meanings there. Porn asks no such questions, and requires us merely to be turned on at the point of consumption for its cultural work to be done.

So, I will answer the 'Is it Art?' question thus: 'Art' is never 'Porn', and 'Porn' cannot be 'Art', at least not at one and the same time. Sexually explicit art *can* be defined as porn in the public sphere, often against the will of the artist, and policed and punished accordingly, before becoming accepted as art at a later stage in a society's evolution. But this is a political act having little to do with the content of the work, as seen in the Chinese authorities' branding of work by artist Wei Wei as 'pornography' (see Chapter 9).

Further, 'Art' can borrow copiously from the conventions of pornography to produce its effects. Art can sexually transgress and perhaps arouse, like pornography, but sexual arousal is not its aim. No matter how explicit or 'sexy' a work of art aspires to be, the very fact that it is viewed as art removes it from the realm of the pornosphere. Our capacity to be aroused by a sexually explicit image is, in this context, overlaid with a metadiscourse of the artistic which asks us to look for meaning and significance beyond the erotic. Art which looks like porn is a text which speaks to us *about* porn, and will be viewed very differently from porn itself. That being so, let me now list the various ways in which the spheres of pornography and art mix, mingle and engage.

A typology of the art/porn interface

Art that looks like porn, and is intended to do so

Chapter 3 on porno chic discussed art which directly and overtly appropriates the codes and conventions of the pornographic, using them in works primarily coded as art to problematise the art/porn distinction, and often too the cultural bias against the latter. Much of this art, however, is paradoxically coy about its relationship to the pornographic, which in itself appears to reinforce the dominant taste hierarchy.

Koons, as we saw earlier, was not comfortable with his work being labelled as pornographic, preferring to focus on its status as a document of 'love' between himself and his wife (Koons, 1992). Madonna's *Sex* book likewise eschewed identification with pornography, preferring to use the term 'erotica' to categorise both its sexually explicit images, and the album of sexually explicit songs she released around the same time. It is as if both artists, despite their power and influence, were simply embarrassed to be associated with the cultural pariah of porn.[11]

Nobuyoshi Araki, on the other hand, the impish agent provocateur of post-war Japanese art, makes both pornography and art, and apologises for neither. Moreover, he gleefully celebrates both the former, and the lifestyle of sexual promiscuity and casual encounters associated (fairly or not) with its consumption. If Araki's persona is Rabelaisian, however, the results are in themselves rarely funny, but very beautiful, revealing an expert technician armed with a pornographer's sensibility.

In Japan, sexual culture is in many ways more extreme than in the West, and the often alarming appearance of Araki's work must be viewed alongside the fact that he is hugely in demand as a portrait artist by Japanese women.[12] It is paradoxical that female responses to Araki's persona are very much evidence of the advancing status of women in Japan where – as they acquire autonomy and sexual citizenship – they use their empowerment to request bondage and submission, even if only at the hands of the celebrity artist.

Shamoon's essay on pornographic comics, or *ero-manga*, notes that Japanese women account for around 10 per cent of the market for these notoriously violent, sado-masochistic texts, concluding that 'their very existence denies many common myths about pornography, such as that women are not visually stimulated and that hard-core pornography necessarily proves harmful to women' (2004, p.99).[13]

Araki began experimenting with surrealistically tinged, sexually explicit images in the early 1970s, when he worked as a photographer for the advertising agency Dentsu.[14] Around that time he famously photographed his wife Yoko as they travelled on their honeymoon, in a variety of domestic, everyday poses, including some nudes and sexual scenes. The album of these images, *Sentimental Journey* (1971), launched his career in Japan, although he did not become well known in the west until the era of porno chic was underway, in the 1990s (assisted by the endorsement of celebrities such as Björk, who commissioned him for the cover of an album). Thereafter his work became more explicit and overtly sexual, as in the *Tokyo Lucky Hole* series of photographs documenting the sex workers of the Shinjuku district of Tokyo, taken between 1983 and 1985, and later collected in a substantial Taschen edition (Araki, 1996).

He has explained his interest in making graphic images of female genitalia, seen in those works and since, as 'an attempt to bring to light everything that society chooses to conceal, as an act of liberation from repression' (Miki, 2005, p.15). His interest in sadomasochistic imagery is less easy to explain in terms of liberation, but certainly cannot be dismissed as misogynistic, given the demand for his services as a portrait artist. On the contrary, in the context of the death of Yoko from cancer in 1990 (photographed as *Sentimental Journey/Winter*), they take on a poignant quality of sadness and melancholy, framing sex in the context of death and the end of love.

His entire output since that time, when one knows that context, can be read as a coming to terms with the loss of a soulmate, and a search for sexual substitution through his encounters with, and photographing of, his female subjects' naked, exposed and available bodies. As he has written: 'when one creates a work, in principle it should be an expression of one's affection, a dedication to the person you love most' (quoted in Watkins, 2005, p.24). Yuko Tanaka suggests that 'his intention is to create relationships. Rather than distancing himself emotionally from his subjects, he strives to deepen his relationship with them as he takes his photographs and to incorporate the subsequent emotions into his work' (2005, p.547).

> In Araki's nude and bondage photographs, as in the *shungo* tradition, there is invariably someone else there, unseen but watching, in addition to the subject herself. Although depicted alone, she is never alone; awareness of the proximity of another person is evident in her eyes.
>
> *(Ibid.)*

In the most comprehensive anthology of his work available in English, *Self, Life, Death* (2005), the argument is made by one observer that

> among all those countless photographs of women in bonds, not a single one conveys an atmosphere of violence. There is no inherent sadism in them. Nor is there any trace of loneliness or isolation in the women depicted in the photographs; indeed [they] emit a mysterious aura of serenity.
>
> *(Jeffrey, 2005, p.547)*

As noted above, many of the subjects of these images are volunteers who paid large sums to be so photographed. These women are participants in Araki's art, not victims. Their collusion, or complicity in his work testifies to the affection with which he is held in Japanese society, and the outlet he appears to provide for female transgression of that society's traditionally conservative gender roles.

Art which declares its nonchalance as to the art/porn distinction

At this point let me restate a distinction made in Chapter 3, between those artists who, while making work that looks like porn, resist the application of the label to their output – they include Madonna and Jeff Koons – and those who embrace pornography as a legitimate cultural practice. Araki an artist of the latter type, and so is Robert Mapplethorpe.

Mapplethorpe was a consumer of gay porn in the 1960s and 1970s, and allowed its tropes to inspire and inflect his art. While it *was* presented to the world by him as art, and not pornography, Mapplethorpe was never shy of the role played by porn in his subject matter and aesthetic. For him, growing into sexual maturity in the era before gay liberation (like Andy Warhol, whose interest in porn is referenced at the beginning of this chapter), pornography's representation of explicit gay sex was a scarce resource to be consumed, and a source of inspiration in his production of sexually explicit homoerotic images, which differed from pornography principally in their quality of technique and creative vision.

In an interview included in James Crump's 2007 documentary on the artist and his patron, Sam Wagstaffe, Mapplethorpe explains his relationship to porn in the following terms:

> There was a feeling I could get through looking at pornographic imagery, and I thought if I could somehow retain that feeling, if I could get that across, and make an art statement, do it in a way that reached a certain kind of perception, that I'd be doing something that was uniquely my own.[15]

Mapplethorpe bathed his images of fetishistic and sadomasochistic acts in a master photographer's knowledge of light and composition (as does Araki), and if he intended them to be accepted as art, he at the same time had no objection to them being used in the same way as the pornographic images which inspired him.

He, like Araki and others, lacked the judgementalism about pornography which qualifies the porno chic phase of Koons and Madonna. Mapplethorpe was not ashamed to declare that pornography was the inspiration for a large part of his work, and to produce photographs which, although undeniably conceived and in the end received as art, advertised their connection to porn, and ignored the boundary between the two categories. Where Koons made work which looked like porn, but rejected the label because of its trashy associations, Mapplethorpe as a gay man in the exuberant post-Stonewall decade drew on the same erotic motifs and tropes as he had found in gay porn, and proudly so.

Despite criticisms directed at some of his more graphic and extreme images from moral lobbies and others at the peak of his visibility in the 1980s and after his death – Mapplethorpe was a key figure of contention in the so-called 'culture wars' around arts funding in the US during those years – his work achieved broad acceptance, associated as it was with the emerging gay rights and liberation movements.

Mapplethorpe's sexually explicit images were mainly of same-sex subjects. They documented sadomasochistic acts performed by men on each other, of the type routinely practiced in that sub-sector of the gay scene to which Mapplethorpe himself adhered. They were often bloody and wince-inducing to those not involved in those scenes, but were also both evidence of, and inspiration for the emergence of an 'out and proud' gay male community able to indulge in its sexual preferences with an unprecedented degree of freedom and tolerance from the mainstream community.

Mapplethorpe's artistic porno chic thus had a connection with the sexual politics of the period, even if he himself avoided association with the more didactic elements in the gay rights movement. In documenting and celebrating what gay men did sexually through the medium of art photography, and in persuading the consumers of art – gay and straight – to view these images as 'Art', and also to engage with moral conservative critics of his work (who also criticised the galleries which showed it), Mapplethorpe's images became part of the 'making visible' of homosexuality which was a feature of the sexual politics of the time.

Paradoxically, this visibility was both encouraged and made necessary by the HIV/AIDS crisis, which put sex, and same-sex behaviour in particular, in the public sphere as never before. Mapplethorpe himself died of AIDS, and his images came to have a poignancy which, despite their extreme sexual content, contributed over time to the enhanced public understanding of and empathy for male homosexuality.

His photographs represent and document 'unsafe sex' of the type which killed him and thousands of others, practised without precaution before anyone understood the risks. They are a memorial to that early flowering of gay sexual culture, even as they remind contemporary viewers of the limitations and dangers associated with it, and why there had in time to be an acceptance of safe sex techniques in an environment of relatively liberal sexual relations.

To this extent, I would suggest, Mapplethorpe's work played a significant role in the complex process of cultural diffusion which led to the mainstreaming of homosexuality in the Western world in the 1990s and 2000s. Utilising the more liberal sex-political environment of the 1980s Mapplethorpe was able to find acceptance for work which *made present* gay sexual identity, unapologetically and unredacted, where hitherto it had been absent – first to the elites of the art world and gay sub-culture, then gradually trickling down to the high street and the realm of the popular. By the time of his death in the late 1980s Mapplethorpe's images were on coffee mugs, mouse mats and t-shirts – like those of his contemporary Keith Haring. He was by then no longer a 'gay artist', merely an artist of rare grace and vision, who happened to photograph gay men in sexualised poses inspired by the pornography of his sub-culture.

Like Haring with his naïve, graffiti-ish pictures, Mapplethorpe penetrated popular consciousness with transgressive images which somehow connected with audiences far beyond the gay community. Mapplethorpe's beautiful pictures of gay men having sex made the subject of same sex activity something that could be talked about by anyone.

Even in its denunciation by moral conservatives, his work provoked conversation. This was possible because of Mapplethorpe's artistry, which can be seen not only in the sex pictures of gay and straight subjects, but also the flowers, the still lifes and the portraits. Unlike Warhol, who as the immigrant 1950s product of a conservative Catholicism felt obliged to mask his homosexuality in public, and in his work, Mapplethorpe was fortunate in that his most creative years coincided with the first major advances of the gay liberation movement. His art, and their politics, combined to give the former a particular relevance and meaning, and the latter humanity. For all the necessary militancy of the gay rights movement in its early years, Mapplethorpe's images were about *people*.

Let me at this point say more about Andy Warhol, one of the greatest artists of the twentieth century, whose comment on pornography sits atop this chapter. Warhol's art predates the era of second-wave porno chic, and he never engaged with the pornographic in such direct terms as, say Jeff Koons or Robert Mapplethorpe.

Unlike Mapplethorpe, Warhol was reared in a time when it was much more difficult for a gay man to be 'out', and although his sexuality – or his interest in pornography – was never much of a secret to those who knew and worked with him, the conventions of his time dictated a more obtuse approach to his treatment of these subjects. Warhol could never have gone to the places so enthusiastically and guiltlessly travelled by Mapplethorpe. But his groundbreaking films of the 1960s are often sexually explicit, or at least represent and discuss sex in what were for the time transgressive ways. Sex was represented as an everyday, even banal activity, like sleeping, eating, arguing, talking, which he approached with curatorial interest rather than participatory enthusiasm. In his own words:

> What I was actually trying to do in my early movies was show how people can meet each other and what they can do and what they can say to each other. That was the whole idea: two people getting acquainted. And then when you saw it and you saw the whole simplicity of it, you learned what it was all about. Those movies showed you how some people act and react with other people ... In *Tub Girls*, for example, the girls had to take baths with other

people. While we were doing *Tub Girls*. They met in a tub. And the girl would have to carry her tub to the next person she'd have to take a bath with, so she'd put her tub under her arm and carry her tub … We used a clear plastic tub.

I never particularly wanted to make simply sex movies. If I had wanted to make a real sex movie I would have filmed a flower giving birth to another flower.

(1975, p.48)

Warhol made two films which are widely viewed as referring to pornography: *Blow Job* (1964) and *Blue Movie* (1969). The former is a famously elusive depiction of what we presume from the title to be a male blow job, happening outside of the frame. On screen we see only the face of the recipient as he (we presume) achieves orgasm. One observer regards the work as the first attempt by a modern artist to problematise the art/porn distinction, made at 'a historical moment ripe with formal transgressions and sexual transgressors' (Osterwell, 2004, p.433). It is not pornography, but a voyeuristic experimentation with what *might have been* a pornographic scenario.

Blue Movie, like *Tub Girls*, featured Factory superstar Viva, having sex with Louis Waldon. Here the act of intercourse is visible, but interrupted with mundane dialogue about the Vietnam war and other issues. Many of Warhol's films were pioneering in their representation of gay and other still-marginal sexualities, and he took 'cock shots' on polaroid in his latter years, though not for publication.

Warhol's 'great' work, which some date to the 1966–8 period and thus includes these experimental films, was influenced by the photography of David Bailey, who in 1973 made a film for the BBC about the artist. The film was banned – the first TV programme ever to be so in the UK – because of its sexually and morally transgressive content, deemed 'shocking, revolting, offensive' by the British press of the day,[16] although no journalist had actually seen the film.[17]

Porn that aspires to be art

If there is a growing corpus of art that has, or aspires to have, many of the qualities of the pornographic, so there is a category of pornography which aspires to be 'Art'. Such efforts seem to be doomed to failure, however, for the reason given above. A given text cannot be both 'Art' and 'Porn' at the same time, no more than advertising can be art. Not because porn cannot be made with skill and attention to aesthetics, but because the function of porn is inimical to that of art. Advertising is for selling, porn is for arousal, art is for contemplation. If the latter two objectives coincide in the same text, that is accidental.

John B. Root, children's author turned porn producer, defends the legitimacy of pornography as an artistic genre, and states his own desire to make 'quality' porn films, by which he means films with 'a real story, with real characters, where the sex scenes either advance the plot or play a key part of it'.[18] Quality defined in these terms does not equate to art, however. One can make art about porn, and there have been attempts to make porn within cultural frameworks which claim the status of art, such as narrative cinema. Several hip-hop artists have worked with the spirit of porno chic in producing promotional videos that are as explicit as hard core porn. But insofar as pornography is defined by its function, and succeeds in facilitating arousal, it militates against the detached mode of the artistic.

Making porn that would be recognised as art was, of course, the sincere and well-intentioned aspiration, the creative Holy Grail, of the characters in Paul Thomas Anderson's Oscar-winning film *Boogie Nights*, about the 1970s porn industry in Los Angeles and the era of the feature-length, properly-scripted porno movie, inspired by the success of *Deep Throat* and *Behind The Green Door* (see Chapter 3).

Porn failed as art then, and fails now, because in becoming conventional narrative, a sexually explicit text inevitably distances the viewer from its erotic purpose. Rather than being aroused to the point of masturbation, such a text wants you to become immersed in the story, and struggles to achieve either plot or arousal with any conviction. One objective distracts from the other, perhaps because the pariah status of pornography has hitherto constrained the involvement in its production of skilled artists (writers, actors, etc.).

Deep Throat may be admired as a cult classic four decades after its release and reception as the first porn movie to become a cultural event, but no-one seriously suggests that its script or acting or lighting are the reasons for its twenty-first century reputation. It remains to be seen if the removal of the stigma associated with porn will attract more artistically gifted talent to its production in the future, and if that may allow for the creation of a pornographic text that is also accepted as 'Art'. I have suggested that it is difficult to imagine such a text, but who can say it is impossible?

However, even if we agree that art and porn are two different things and that porn cannot be art, this does not mean that the latter is without cultural value. As I have argued throughout this book, pornography can be analysed in the same way as other cultural forms, and not 'discursively sequestered' (Kipnis, 1999) from art. Porn contains narratives, meanings, interpretations, and political messages which, if they lack obvious aesthetic value, nevertheless have social and cultural significance.

Art that is as sexually explicit as porn, but is intended to be read as art

One causal factor in the rise of cultural sexualisation was the liberalisation of censorship and regulatory rules governing the representation of sexuality, particularly after the emergence of the internet in the late 1990s made traditional mechanisms of censorship much more difficult to implement. The 2000s, therefore, was a period in which artists – and film-makers in particular, who had always been the main target of twentieth-century censors because of the perceived power of their medium – produced work of unprecedented explicitness. Sometimes the work contained references to and borrowings from pornography, without presenting as 'porno chic'; at other times the graphic nature of the sexual content could be read as a by-product of the pornographication of mainstream culture, and the associated acceptance of work that might have been denounced as obscene or pornographic in an earlier period.

In John Cameron Mitchell's *Shortbus* (2006), for example, set in New York, there are graphic scenes of straight sex, gay sex, bi-sex, masturbation and sadomasochism, all in the service of what is at root a rather sweet story about relationships and the resolution of emotional crises through sexual exploration. *Shortbus* is not porno chic, but it could not exist, or at least could not have been screened in mainstream multiplexes all over the liberal capitalist world without fuss or controversy, had those societies not become used both to the presence of more, and more explicit, pornography in their media environment, the sexualisation of culture in general, and the accompanying discourses of sexual health and confession which I have called 'striptease culture' (McNair, 2002). Pornographication, in this sense, made *Shortbus* possible.

Michael Winterbottom's *9 Songs* (2004) has a quasi-pornographic structure of episodes of escalating sexual explicitness, interspersed by scenes from live performances (the nine songs of the title) attended by the film's two protagonists. These punctuate the narrative, and interrupt the sex, in a story about the evolution of a heterosexual relationship from passionate beginnings to exhausted end.

Despite the echoes of pornography to be found in the film's structure, the work was positioned rather uneasily by its producers in the cultural marketplace as *not-porn*. Billed, like *Baise-Moi* and others before it, as 'the most sexually explicit film ever made in the history of mainstream cinema', and therefore in receipt of welcome publicity on its release (art-house movies of this type need all the publicity they can get, although in this case the result was a meagre £200,000 at the British box office) Winterbottom and his producers insisted that *9 Songs* was 'not some kind of kinky porno flick', but 'a love story' told through 'physical encounters'.[19] We can accept that distinction, I think, given the understated tone of the film, and its sex scenes, which if explicit are rarely arousing (at least to this viewer).

Art and culture critic Mark Lawson endorsed Winterbottom's dissociation of his film from the realm of porn by arguing that 'it qualifies as pornography in at least two ways: it is likely to cause arousal (and could be employed solely for that purpose) and the sex is not pretend'.[20] But *9 Songs* was not porn, in Lawson's view, because 'the performers do not seem to have been exploited, nor has their health been put at unreasonable risk'. These are questionable criteria, it seems to me, since many people are exploited and their health put at unreasonable risk in mainstream movie production, not to mention the unregulated corners of just about every other industry in the capitalist economy.

Lawson is right in his main point, however: *9 Songs* is not pornography, in the same way that Patrice Chereau's *Intimacy* (2001) – an earlier example of the new sexual frankness in culture – was not pornography. That film was notable for its inclusion of a scene where lead actress Kerry Fox gives her leading man Mark Rylance a blowjob. The point of this scene, and other explicit scenes in the film, was not to arouse, but to portray a loveless, anonymous affair between two strangers who, in their anonymity, could find some brief escape from their domestic routines through transgressive sexual encounters.

Catherine Breillat's films often, if not always, address and represent sexuality in terms so explicit that the word 'pornography' is used by critics. Her best-known work, *Romance* (1999), attracted much media attention when it was released, although it came out at a time when liberalisation was well under way, and was not subject to any kind of panic. In the UK film monthly *Sight & Sound* Louise Felperin noted that '*Romance*'s reception so far is an index of how much times have changed. Today, art films have almost lost their ability to shock.'[21] Breillat herself distinguished her work from the pornographic thus:

> Pornography doesn't exist. What exists is censorship, which defines pornography and separates it from the rest of film. Pornography is the sexual act taken out of context and made into a product for consumption. [*Romance* is not porn because] the image portrays an idea and the characters experience emotion.

As is often the case when artists seek to distinguish their work from pornography, Breillat is over-generalising when she asserts that characters in the latter display no emotion, or that a porn film can have no room for ideas. What she means is that pornography will rarely, if ever, have access to the creative skill-sets required to produce authentic emotional range, or coherent ideas. They may try their well-intentioned best, like Burt Reynolds' producer in *Boogie Nights*, but they will fail. Breillat is correct to suggest, however, that as soon as 'real' acting and writing enters the arena of explicit sexual representation, the audience is inevitably distracted from the business of being aroused, and required to focus instead on the meanings within the text. 'Art' and 'Porn' do not mix, even if there is ample room for creative interplay and engagement between the two forms. Perhaps some porno-auteur will come along to prove me wrong on this point, but he or she has not done so yet, and plenty have tried.

This discussion is not one which can be resolved definitively, because: (a) the category distinctions are subjective from the outset – 'Art' is just as subjective and culturally relative a concept as 'Porn'; (b) examples of both 'Art' and 'Porn' are subject to misreading and incorrect designation; (c) audiences bring their own sexual histories and desires to texts, and impose their own meanings independently of what producers want them to see, read or hear; and (d) times and tastes change, as boundaries are pushed and cultures evolve, so that work perceived as one thing today can be read very differently tomorrow.

Can sex be the subject of great art?

In 2001 art critic Waldemar Januszczak was inspired by the *Erotic Picasso* exhibition then showing in London to suggest that 'the sex act is conspicuously difficult to make art about'.[22] And of course there are many examples of indisputably bad art about sex, and bad sexual culture in general, by which I mean work agreed to lack aesthetic value or quality even on its own terms. But his assertion is questionable as a generality. No art of lasting value is easy to make, presumably, and art about sex is no more nor less difficult than art about, say, war, and a good deal easier than art about politics.

In support of Januszczak's assertion, the UK *Literary Review* periodical makes an annual award for the worst sex scenes in a novel – the Bad Sex in Fiction Award.[23] Usually the award is given to popular fiction – 'potboilers', 'bodice rippers' and other genres of pulp novel writing which are not intended to be taken too seriously by their authors – but not always. Martin Amis has been nominated, as has Salman Rushdie.

The award is given, and usually received in good humour, but its public resonance reflects the perception of many that it is difficult to write about sex credibly or authentically. More precisely, it is perceived to be difficult to represent the *sex act* in literary terms, because the writing so often descends into cliché and stereotype.

As it happens, I am sure I'm not alone in being able to bring to mind many examples of literary fiction in which sexual representation is a component element, and successfully executed so as to arouse the reader. It may be difficult, but it is not impossible for a writer to conjure up in the mind of the reader images associated with transgressive desire which do in fact arouse. With a few exceptions – Nicholson Baker's *The Fermata*, for example, where a 'pornographic' interlude of sexual fantasy appears to be a commentary on the then-emerging trend of porno chic, within a novel which is all about fantasy and the male gaze – these sex scenes are not coded pornographically, but are embedded episodes of sexual activity which despite their context work on the reader's imagination, sexuality and emotion in ways perhaps not even intended by the author.

Januszczak was not referring to literature when he wrote about Picasso's erotic drawings, of course, but to the visual arts. And here his point is perhaps even more contestable. Art about sex is universal, as we have noted, and often great, if by that we mean work which lasts and is recognised for its greatness beyond the time and place in which it was made. If the representation of the sex act – out of context, as Breillat puts it – is principally the role of pornography, addressing the sexual in all its breadth and complexity is very much the business of art (including popular culture).

Artists have always made art about sex, and through their art have engaged their publics, and their societies, in thinking about and discussing the sexual. Good art is difficult, yes, and no less so when it comes to sexual subject matter. But it is the key cultural space where sexuality can be addressed in its biological, emotional, aesthetic and political dimensions. Steve McQueen's *Shame* (2011) starring Michael Fassbender and Carey Mulligan, is a powerful, poignant and extremely graphic study of the consequences of sexual dysfunction on adult capacity for healthy relationships.

Gender, sex and art

Art about sex, like pornography, reflects the structures of socio-economic and political power within which it is produced and consumed. And since the history of art has been, until quite recently, the history of male art (Greer, 1981), the great majority of art about sex has expressed what has justifiably been described as a male gaze – incorporating male presumptions about beauty, about the role of the female in art, and about masculinity.

For this reason, much art about sex has been guilty of the same flaws as ascribed to male heterosexual pornography – misogyny, or at least dismissal of and contempt for women's sexuality and perspectives. The history of art is packed full of 'great men' who, if they undoubtedly made great art, were not so great as human beings, treating their wives, lovers and children as accessories or obstacles to the production of their genius.

The Marquis de Sade perhaps exemplifies this model. His late eighteenth-century sexually explicit writings have been acknowledged as art by other artists, including many women (writer Angela Carter, for example, in her book *The Sadeian Woman* (1978); and Susan Sontag in her essay on 'The Pornographic Imagination' (1982) in which she includes Sade with the Surrealists and others in what she calls 'the French pornographic tradition' (p.104)).

Whether one accepts this categorisation or not (and his most obscene works are, let us remember, accorded the status of literary classic by the highly respected publisher Penguin), or the other defence of Sade often made – that his work, with its depictions of sexual abuse, torture and murder, is appropriately read as radical social satire directed at the decadent political and religious institutions of his time – there is little dispute even amongst his admirers that he was a deeply unpleasant man committed to a lifestyle of libertinism which often meant the exploitation and abuse of others over whom he had power.

In this respect he established a template of male artists who regarded the fulfilment of their needs and desires as important above and beyond those of all others. Such men – Picasso is another example – saw themselves as free from the moral laws which governed the rest of society, and sometimes as a duty the violation of those laws. The result was often the suicide of wives and partners (and of children), or at the very least deep and lifelong unhappiness amongst those who fell within their orbit.

It is important, however, to distinguish the personality of the man from his work, and to accept that facility in the production of art is no predictor of ethical or humane personal politics. And in his work, largely unreadable and over-extended as much of it is, Sade has influenced subsequent centuries to an extent matched by few other writers of his time. He revels in the transgression of 'civilised' sexual ethics, and requires his readers to conjure up scenes which would be regarded as atrocities were they to be acted out in reality (as acts very much like them have indeed been perpetrated, in many wars and conflicts, as well as by legislatures and serial killers such as the Moors Murderers).[24]

Sade's key transgression was to eroticise atrocity, and to embed it in a philosophy of libertinism and the supremacy of free will which directly challenged the proclaimed ethics of France's ruling aristocratic and religious elites. He also, by combining sex and violence as he did, constructed at the level of the imagination that zone of psychological or emotional conflict often encountered by users of pornography today. The reader knows that the behaviours about which he or she is reading cannot be moral, but is aroused nonetheless by the very transgressiveness of the acts depicted.

It is hard to defend the status of Sade as a great literary artist, but his transgressive, fantastic approach to the sexual was a key influence on surrealism – 'the principal, programmatic transgressive art project of modern times' (Julius, 2002, p.160). Working mainly in post-World War I Paris, the surrealists paid homage to the Marquis in many works. Man Ray (Emmanuel Radnitzsky, born in the United States in 1890), indeed had a habit of requiring his lovers (such as Lee Miller – see below) to read *100 Days Of Sodom*, presumably as a test of their commitment to his own interest in the breaking of taboos. Some of his best-known works are direct references to Sade, often focusing on the Marquis' defiantly blasphemous rejection of religious ideas and symbols. He made *La Prière* in 1930, for example, with Lee Miller believed by many to have been the model:

> Inspired by Sade's predilection for sodomy, it shows a nude bent forward on her knees, her feet beneath her buttocks and her hands cupped to shield her anus. Man's ambiguous title, Prayer, hints that she offers what is hidden as orifice for exploration. As in much of Man's erotica, the image plays with ideas of cruelty and worship while raising questions about whose desire is on display ... [*La Prière*] uses the woman's body to stage fantasies of domination and submission, along with their entanglement in the sexual imagination.
>
> *(Burke, 2005)*[25]

Most of the surrealist artists were men, of course, although the few women who produced surrealist art also employed sexual transgression as a strategy. Meret Oppenheim's *Lunch In Fur* is one of the best known. For Julius:

> the work stimulates a complex and untotalisable mixture of sensations of pleasure and disgust: at the prospect of rubbing one's face against fur and the coincident prospect of eating fur. There is an erotics and an anti-erotics at play in this work which provokes a certain perplexity, and divides its audience by the subtlety of its sexual challenge.
>
> *(2002, p.159)*

Lee Miller was another exception to the maleness of surrealism, and a muse of Man Ray, who became a respected artist and photo-journalist. Miller (1907–77) is believed to have been abused as a child. She became a fashion model in the late 1920s, moved to Paris and became Man Ray's lover. She was a strong personality in her own right, however, and challenged the patriarchal assumptions of the surrealist movement. Throughout her life she pursued a fiercely independent, unsentimental sexuality.

She was sexually transgressive in her life and her art, as for example in *Untitled (Severed Breast from Radical Mastectomy)* (1930), a diptych comprising two images of a severed human breast obtained from a Parisian hospital where she worked for a time as a medical photographer. Argues Mark Haworth-Booth:

The presentation of the breast, on an elegant dinner plate, twists and scrambles familiar messages. As with other images of hers, Lee's turns a stereotype inside out. The photographs remind us that their author was a woman of remarkable daring and capable of challenging the most forbidding taboos.

(2007, p.88)

It was following the end of their sexual relationship that Man Ray made his *Object Of Destruction* piece, which came with the following, notably 'Sadeian' instructions to the user:

Cut out the eye from the photograph of one who has been loved but is seen no more.

Attach the eye to the pendulum of a metronome and regulate the weight to suit the tempo desired.

Keep going to the limit of endurance.

With a hammer well-aimed, try to destroy the whole at a single blow.

Lee Miller is described by one art historian as a 'spiritual godmother to the modern "Bad Girl"' movement of women who have employed the sexualised body in their work, such as sculptor Helen Chadwick (Haworth-Booth, 2007, p.145). Germaine Greer's important book on *The Obstacle Race* (1981) explored how female artists were for much of patriarchy's existence hidden from history. By the early twenty-first century she was wondering why it was that so many women artists used their own, often naked bodies in their work.[26] In 2007 an exhibition of naked portraits contained many examples of bad girls' work, such as photographs by Frances Woodman, Tracy Emin, Jemima Stehli and Rachel Steirs, who have used sexualised body imagery (often their own bodies) to address aspects of patriarchy and sexual culture (Hammer, 2007).[27]

German author Charlotte Roche authored *Wetlands* in 2008, a graphically confessional account of a woman's inner world (sexually, emotionally and physically) as she recovers from illness in hospital. Roche illustrates in literature Helen McDonald's observation that feminist artists have increasingly 'challenged the patriarchal ideal [of female beauty] in art, as well as commercial norms' (2001, p.2).

9

DROP PORN, NOT BOMBS!

Anthony Julius expresses the view that 'to violate the taboo is to strike a blow for political freedom', and that sexually transgressive art 'attacks "taboos" in the name of reason and public education, and also of compassion, or of moral outrage' (Julius, 2002, p.152). Laura Kipnis writes in similar terms of pornography, that it 'devotes itself to thwarting aesthetic conventions wherever and whenever it can, to disrupting our precious sensibilities at every turn. It's the anti-aesthetic. This is a social undertaking not without philosophical and political significance' (1999, p.92).

As one observer puts it, 'pornography's proliferation of perversions can be understood as subversive insofar as the prevalence of pornography has also meant a proliferation of sexual contradictions' (Gaines, 2004, p.35). On the other hand, for Stallybrass and White, 'it would be wrong to associate the exhilarating sense of freedom which [sexual] transgression affords with any necessary or automatic political progressiveness' (1986).

Both viewpoints are valid. Sexual expression, of any kind, can be but *is not necessarily* a force for good. All depends on the context. Forcing someone to have sex against their will is a violation of their human rights, and properly a crime in most jurisdictions. Preventing someone (a consenting adult) from having sex with another consenting adult when they wish to do so is also a kind of violation, if not of fundamental human rights then of the individual autonomy which in the liberal democracies we claim to value.

So too with sexual culture, which draws its political meaning and significance from the surrounding environment. Like the rawer form of pornography, sexually transgressive art can be, and often has been, politically subversive insofar as it threatens the boundaries which societies necessarily build around aspects of their organisation and culture. Insofar as human societies have maintained social relations which are unequal, exploitative or oppressive, transgressive sexual culture can subvert these too, with at least the potential for progressive political outcomes. Sexually transgressive art can threaten oppressive cultures by dropping into their midst images which present alternative ways of thinking about and regulating sexual behaviour, or which expose injustices in the sexual arena.

I argued above that the photography of Robert Mapplethorpe performed a progressive role in the late 1970s and early 1980s, as gay liberation politics were gathering momentum. His explicit images of sadomasochistic sexual practices were not in isolation the spark for, or cause of, progress in the long campaign for gay rights in the United States, but alongside the campaigning activities of such as Harvey Milk (the first openly gay mayor of an American city – San Francisco) and the growing visibility of gay men and lesbians in popular culture, his work made gay male sexuality visible and contributed to a climate in which the politics of homosexuality could be addressed in ways they never had been before.

Keith Haring, inspired by both Warhol and Mapplethorpe, frequently mixed cartoon, animation and other child-like motifs with explicit sexuality.[1] His art also had a pedagogic and campaigning side, in that he used it to communicate important public-health messages about safe sex, homophobia and the need for empathy and understanding towards those who had been affected by HIV/AIDS (he himself died of AIDS in 1989). His work was often critical of Reagan-era AIDS policies.

Renowned 'queer' artists Gilbert and George rose to prominence in the 1990s in the UK, as homosexuality was going mainstream and porn was becoming chic. Their work has not played with the pornographic in the directly referential manner of Mapplethorpe or Koons, but it has often been transgressive, and sexually explicit. Much of their work – the *Piss* and *Shit* paintings, for example – reflects the anxieties and tensions of the worst of the HIV/AIDS years in the west. Like Haring they pushed important but delicate topics such as the nature of body fluids and the importance of sexual honesty into the public domain.

Acknowledging the controversial nature of their work and the debates it provoked Gilbert and George declared in one press interview that:

> Our art is capable of bringing out the bigot in the liberal, and the liberal inside the bigot.[2]

This is a concise way of expressing the relationship between sexual culture and politics. Art and culture become the foci for debates within the public sphere about sexuality and, as we saw in the previous chapter, push the boundaries of the acceptable and the 'normal' further, and in a positive or progressive direction. There is no inevitability about that process, and it could also operate in reverse. Given the dynamics and direction of change in sexual politics in capitalism since the 1970s, however, the outcomes of most of these debates has been to make things better for groups previously marginalised or disadvantaged by their sexuality or gender.

Sexual culture has also been a vehicle for the discussion and transformation of traditional straight masculinity. Rankin's nude male images, for example, often of celebrities, were part of a movement in photography which utilised the liberalisation of sexual culture to explore the body in newly politicised ways. In the 1990s many observers had recognised a 'crisis' of masculinity in response to the rise of feminism, gay liberation, and the concomitant challenges to straight male heterosexuality (McNair, 2002). By the 2000s, artists had moved beyond merely noting the crisis, to engaging with its aftermath. The *Typical Men* exhibition staged in 2001 at the Djanogly Art Gallery in Nottingham, UK, articulated the liberatory dimension of this exploration:

> The fact that in recent years the male nude body has been made publicly – and often provocatively – visible in photography is indicative of a radical shift in attitudes towards masculinity and is facilitating the establishment of new multiple concepts of male identity.
>
> *(Worton, 2002, p.9)*

Martin Hammer's monograph on *The Naked Portrait* exhibition (2007) devoted a chapter to 'A Crisis Of Masculinity?' and the often explicit, self-revelatory, self-deprecatory work of such as John Coplans, Steven Tynan and Lucian Freud. Sam Taylor-Woods' series on *Crying Men* depicted celebrities such as Dustin Hoffman and Robert Downey Jr. in tears (they were not all nude or semi-clothed, but these too were transgressive images, merely in depicting men crying).

By the early twenty-first century, then, the art of the male body was both expressing and promoting the breakdown of what we might refer to as hetero-hegemony, or straight male stereotypes, to be replaced by a more diverse and arguably representative set of masculinities.

Transgressive sexual culture in the authoritarian world

So much for the liberal West. But what of the rest? Can sexual culture play a similar role in the progressive reform of authoritarian regimes where feminism and homo-sexuality remain prohibited or punished, and sexuality is strictly controlled? In some of the latter, such as Afghanistan, Iraq and Libya, bloody wars have been fought in recent times, with the defence of women's rights among the stated goals.[3] The broader 'clash of civilisations' unleashed by 9/11 has been a conflict not least between opposing views of who should have access to sexual citizenship, and which forms of sexual expression should be permitted. As journalist Mark Lawson wrote in July 2007, 'the targeting of nightclubs in Bali and now in London suggests that disgust at the degeneracy and sexualisation of western culture is one of the terrorists' motivations'. Lawson asserted in response that 'resistance to Al-Quaida forces us into a position where we must suffer [cultural sexualisation]'.[4]

I suggest that we should not merely 'suffer' but *advocate for* and *promote* cultural sexualisation as a potentially powerful tool in the struggle against all forms of author-itarianism and religiously inspired misogyny and homophobia. Drop porn, not bombs, on those societies whose patriarchal ruling elites wish to dictate the sexualities of others.

Some will regard this as an outrageous suggestion, although it is hardly more out-rageous than the state of affairs which exists for women, homosexuals and other sexually defined groups in many countries where extreme religious ideologies hold sway. In these societies, where data is available, the indicators for rape, spousal abuse, domestic violence and so on, remain as high as they were in the advanced capitalist world centuries ago (Pinker, 2011). Robert Jensen's claim of a porn-fuelled epidemic of routine violence against women (see Chapter 4) applies much more to autocratic societies where pornography is likely to be prohibited and punished severely. In a *Vanity Fair* piece from 2005 the late Christopher Hitchens reported how, in the Iranian city of Neka in August 2004:

> A sixteen-year-old girl named Atefeh Rajabi was hauled into a court for having had sex with a man. She might possibly have gotten away with one of the lesser punishments for offences against chastity, such as a hundred lashes with a whip (that's what her partner received). But from the dock she protested that she had been the object of advances from an older man, and she went as far as to tear off her *hijab*, or headscarf. The judge announced that she would hang for that, and that he would personally place the noose around her neck. And so, in the main square of Neka, after the Iranian Supreme Court had duly confirmed the ruling, poor Miss Rajabi was hanged from a crane for all to see.[5]
>
> *(Reprinted in Hitchens, 2011, p.462)*

In a piece for the UK *Independent* newspaper, based on a ten-month investigation and published also in *The Australian*, veteran reporter on the Middle East and Islam Robert Fisk described in harrowing terms a 'murder wave [against women] that shames the world'.[6] Fisk noted that every year the UN records some 5,000 cases of women 'beheaded, burned to death, stoned to death, stabbed, electrocuted, strangled and buried alive for the "honour" of their families'. He cited the views of women's groups that the true figure may be as high as 20,000 a year. The article goes on to list a number of horrifying cases which defy belief in the extent of their cruelty, inflicted on women for the 'crimes' of adultery, independent thinking, being raped, or wearing revealing clothes:

> It is difficult to remain unemotional at the vast and detailed sadism of these crimes. How should one react to a man – this has happened in both Jordan and Egypt – who rapes his own daughter, then, when she becomes pregnant, kills her to save the honour of his family.[7]

We in our 'pornified', sexualised societies react with anger and revulsion. As do many within the countries where such crimes routinely occur.

Of Iran, Nobel Peace Prize winner Shirin Ebadi has written that 'criminal laws adopted after the revolution took away a woman's identity and turned her into an incapable and mentally-deranged second-class being'.[8] The journalist to whom she gave this view observed of Iran circa 2009 that 'despite some advances in women's rights over the past decade, and the fact that 60 per cent of the country's university graduates are now female, legally and socially, women are still considered far inferior to men'.[9]

Statistics for the incidence of violence – be it institutionalised, individual or community inflicted – against women in countries such as Iran, Saudi Arabia and Pakistan are, by the nature of those societies, difficult to obtain. While violence against women in the liberal capitalist world is on the decline (if still too high for anyone to be complacent) we do not know in what direction the trends are moving in less liberal societies. What we do know is that the number and severity of laws controlling women's behaviour, and the punishments laid down for transgression of those laws, are closer to the state of medieval Europe than twenty-first century liberal capitalism.

We know too that porn is far from chic in these countries. We inhabit an increasingly globalised sexual culture or pornosphere, which has provoked not just a terrorist response from Al Quaida and its affiliated groups, but control strategies of varying severity and effectiveness by authoritarian regimes. Theocratic Iran, reported Christopher Hitchens for *Vanity Fair* in July 2005, 'today exists in a state of dual power and split personality'.[10]

> The huge billboards and murals proclaim it an Islamic republic, under the eternal guidance of the immortal memory of the Ayatollah Khomenei. A large force of Revolutionary Guards and a pervasive religious police stand ready to make good on this grim pledge. But directly underneath those forbidding posters and right under the noses of the moral enforcers, Iranians are buying and selling videos, making and consuming alcohol, tuning in to satellite TV stations, producing subversive films and plays and books, and defying the dress code.
>
> *(Reprinted in Hitchens, 2011, p.457)*

Hitchens describes the country, and its capital city in particular, as 'more or less uncontrollable by anybody', and describes how many of its people defy the regime to access porn on satellite TV (among other gestures of cultural rebellion). In other Muslim societies, forms of sexualised popular culture take on a reforming, oppositional nature, not least because of the reaction they inspire from local patriarchs. In December 2011 Pakistani actress Veena Malik was in the global news over a legal action she had taken against the Indian edition of *FHM*. The magazine had put a nude photograph of her on its cover, which she claimed to have been 'doctored'.[11] While the authenticity of the image was being resolved, the author of the article, Nosheen Iqbal, observed that Malik was:

> No stranger to the wrath of Pakistan's conservative, religious right, she was vilified earlier in the year for her appearance on Bigg Boss, the Indian Big Brother. Her crime? According to Mufti Abdul Qavi, whom she memorably slaughtered on a live TV debate, she shamed all Pakistan and Islam by dint of appearing on the show at all. As Malik passionately pointed out, national

disgrace has little do with a female entertainer appearing on TV. 'What about the politicians? What of the corruption, robbery, murder and terrorism committed in the name of Islam?' she asked. 'Why are you picking on Veena Malik? Because she's a girl? Because she's a soft target?'[12]

Acknowledging that Malik's position was 'subversively political' in challenging the theocratic presumptions of her home culture, Iqbal also expressed the view that 'a woman using her body as the battleground to make an empowered feminist statement is redundant and clichéd: whichever way you cut it, there's little intellectually liberating about getting your rack out for the lads'. On the other hand – if one accepts that the institutionalised, religiously-decreed sexism of Pakistani society is a bad thing for women in general, and that this particular woman is challenging it head on by the assertion of her right to do whatever she likes with her body, sexually self-objectifying or not – one is more inclined to welcome Malik's intervention.

Transgressive sexual culture of the type practiced by Ms Malik cannot on its own bring an end to Islamic theocracy (or any other kind of authoritarian control); but anything which challenges institutionalised misogyny, the religiously-legitimised oppression of women and gays which characterises so many authoritarian structures, can make an important contribution to progressive reform. Just as pornographic images played a role in the French revolution's overthrow of a decadent aristocracy, sexual culture can contribute to the demise of patriarchal political regimes.

As I have noted above, there is no easy way to prove a positive cause and effect relation between the liberalisation of sexual culture and advance in women's socio-economic status in advanced capitalist societies. What we can say with some confidence is that where one exists, the other usually does too. And where women's rights are under-developed, as in some Muslim societies, access to popular, sexualised culture (participation in, or consumption of, by women especially) is increasingly a point of tension with resistant male elites. In March 2004 a version of the successful reality TV format *Big Brother* was staged in Bahrain, to great success amongst many viewers across the Middle East. Because of the transgressive nature of the format, however, allowing men and women to share the same space (albeit no sex), Islamic fundamentalists protested on the streets and the programme was abandoned.[13]

In the Arab world, reality TV genres, with their transgressively sexual tone, have continued to be highly popular. According to one observer, the reason is the 'participatory nature and appeal [of reality TV] to a people long denied freedom of expression and representation in other spheres of life'.[14] In particular, the freedom given to women in Arab countries to perform without the strict constraints of male clerics has been an important dimension of the appeal of these formats.

Marwan Krairly analyses the popularity of the Lebanese-based reality TV show *Star Academy* (a variant of the *Fame Academy* format successful in the UK in the 2000s), concluding that it was successful in countries such as Saudi Arabia (if controversial) because 'the show subverted the religious bases of Saudi social order by promoting women's agency' (2009, p.345). Insofar as TV shows of this kind involve sexual performance of varying degrees of transgressiveness within the context of conservative Islamic societies, they can be argued to have contributed to the slow but steady erosion of state-sanctioned sexism.[15]

Krairly's study noted that 'the fact that some within the Saudi elite supported the show suggests that there are contradictory forces at work in Saudi Arabia and undermines the view that Saudi society is arch-conservative across the board' (p.347). On the political power of pop culture more broadly, she adds: 'recurring controversies over popular culture have become prolonged public contests that draw a large number of clerics, intellectuals, journalists and royals and, most importantly, affective involvement by the Saudi public' (p.348). To adapt Lenin's old adage about the subversive potential of words, one might say that pop culture is more powerful than bombs and bullets.

The voices quoted above demonstrate that many women in the Muslim world wish to see progress in sexual politics, and also that at least some of them wish to access and participate in a sexualised culture of the type that they are currently denied by men clutching holy books. Just as the Arab spring of 2011 exposed the long-standing myth (propagated by left and right alike) that Arabs are not ready for democracy, and do not need or want it, the courage of women like Veena Malik indicates that all over the Muslim world there is a growing demand – often associated with overtly feminist politics – for all forms of sexual culture, be it racy reality and talent shows, pornography or the kinds of confessional cultures we see in western daytime talk shows.

Not all authoritarianisms are religious, of course. But all authoritarianisms are equally hostile to pornography and the free expression of sexuality. Catherine Hakim notes that 'George Orwell rightly depicted sex as a politically subversive act in the totalitarian state of *1984*, an expression of defiant autonomy, a garden of private pleasure that could not be controlled by the state' (2011, p.74). Orwell's dystopia was based on the Stalinist Soviet, and applies to this day to authoritarian 'socialist' regimes such as China and Cuba. North Korea, though no longer even pretending to be socialist, was founded on an extreme interpretation of Marxist-Leninist principles, and controls its population accordingly. Christopher Hitchens' short articles on North Korea, reprinted in *Arguably* (2011), observe that there

> every person is property and is owned by a small and mad family with hereditary power. Every minute of every day, as far as regimentation can assure the fact, is spent in absolute subjection and serfdom. The private life has been entirely abolished.
>
> *(p.554)*

To abolish private life, one must abolish sexual freedom and autonomy, which is why every authoritarian regime, secular or religious, goes to such lengths to control its subjects' sex lives (although the elite rulers, from Stalin to Mao and no doubt Kim Jong-Un, impose no such restraints on themselves).

In China, as this book was being completed, the artist Ai Weiwei was defending himself against the authorities' accusation that he was a 'pornographer' because he had produced nude images. Following the announcement of an investigation by the Chinese authorities into alleged spreading of pornography – a photograph of the artist and four women, all nude, was the offending image – Weiwei's supporters began tweeting nude photographs of themselves into Chinese cyberspace, challenging the authorities' attempts to silence the artist.[16]

Weiwei's is a paradigmatic case of how authoritarian political structures use the label of pornography to police dangerous thoughts and images, and how in return campaigners and reformers can use 'pornographic' images to fight back. By definition, in this and similar cases, sexual culture, sexually transgressive art, pornography or whatever we wish to call it are acting as reforming pressures on systems visibly struggling with internal dissent. Laura Kipnis writes that 'pornography can provide a home for those narratives exiled from sanctioned speech and mainstream political discourse, making pornography, in essence, an oppositional political form' (1999, p.123). In Weiwei's case, the intentions of the accusers were to justify police and legal action against a politically troublesome artist.

Of China (in a parallel to what Hitchens observed of Iran in 2005) Katrien Jacobs observes that 'the [Chinese] government fears unrest and social instability' and that 'sex is a major source of instability' (2010, p.188). As of this writing it was engaged in what appeared to be an increasingly futile effort to restrict the circulation of pornography amongst its hundreds of millions of internet users (or 'netizens').

The Chinese system has developed an uneasy and ambivalent relationship with porn, as it has with the internet as a whole (Hughes and Wacker, 2003). In China, notes Jacobs, despite the official ban on its circulation, 'the net-porn industries are surviving and flourishing. It seems indeed that porn cannot be banned and that the PRC government is perhaps even secretly letting it into the country'.[17] Zu et al.'s quantitative study on online pornography use in mainland China shows that despite vigorous state-repression of porn sites, and an anti-pornography campaign which seeks to blame porn-consumption for rising crime and other 'negatives' in Chinese society, they continue to spring up as soon as they are closed down, suggesting that 'China's war against online porn might be endless' (2010).[18]

This ambivalence in its attitudes to the pornographic is not official Chinese government policy, of course, but an unintended consequence of the internet as it weaves around state censorship. Even as the party wishes to ban online porn, it cannot practically do so without severely limiting the people's use of the internet itself, which would do immense harm to other aspects of Chinese development. Observing the release of the Chinese government's Green Dam Youth Escort package for controlling access to internet porn, commentator Zoe Williams wondered in 2009 if it was a tool to control pornography, and dissent in general. It was, and remains, both, because free sexuality is potentially dangerous polity.[19]

Katrien Jacobs' book-length study of pornography on the Chinese internet shows how, despite the official banning of the form since the foundation of the People's Republic in 1949 (with harsh punishments meted out for production, distribution or consumption of porn), 'sub-cultures of user-generated or DIY porn have evolved'.[20]

Jacobs asserts that young Chinese are using online pornography to 'formulate sexual identities'. This 'people's pornography' she defines as:

> iDIY media that exists outside the [commercial] sex industry. For example, a lot of women post stories, confessional diaries or soft-core images. People from the post-1980s and post-1990s generations have started uploading sex movies as well. There is also the idea that people should have access to pornography in general, without the threat of prosecution.[21]

Jacobs is clear that sexual culture is playing an important and progressive role in the campaign for civil liberties in China.[22] She cites several female artists, bloggers and porn producers active in China (some of them based overseas) who work in the terrain of the sexual for overtly sex-political reasons. 'Sister Swallow' is a former sex worker who practices a form of confessional (or 'striptease' culture) online, while identifying as a feminist and a political activist. Another ex-sex worker, Yu Na, 'uses her sexuality and prostitute branding in order to transform her body into a vehicle for art' (2011, p.60). Hong Kong-based Siu Ding 'frequently uploads nude images on her blog … in order to reclaim the female body'. Jacobs notes that:

> both women and men in China are using, and commenting on, sexually explicit media to explore novel tastes, desires, and identities, in order to grapple with edgy and sexually explicit content, and to question the socially-ingrained roles of Chinese morality in the Internet age.
>
> *(p.39)*

Having interviewed many Chinese people for her book Jacobs concludes that 'they agree that [pornography] can be a powerful and important incentive for social change' (p.32). Elsewhere she writes that 'both sex bloggers and activist bloggers contribute to a new sexual individualism in defence of pornography and alternative lifestyles' (p.81). In China, access to sexual culture is 'a matter of civil liberties'.

The disruptive power of transgressive sexual culture can also be seen in the impact of Ang Lee's 2007 film *Lust, Caution*. Banned in mainland China, the film became a much sought-after viewing experience, not only in the PRC but also in Hong Kong and Taiwan, where it became what Jacobs describes as 'a significant force and discourse for the erotic imagination' (p.30). Ang Lee's film is transgressive, from the point of view of its Chinese audience, in at least two ways. First, it dares to present an image of the war-time collaborator Yee (played by Tony Leung) as a man with whom a good patriotic woman could fall in love. Young resistance fighter Mak Tai Tai (Wei Tang) begins the story with assassination of the hated collaborator in mind, and ends up not just sleeping with the enemy but intervening to save his life, a gesture for which she is herself condemned to death.

Second, the sex in the film is violent and sadomasochistic, symbolising the relationship between the two characters, and between their respective loyalties. The transgression arises from the fact that this is what both partners appear to desire – a relationship oscillating between love and hate, domination and submission, liberation and dependency. The film speaks to a Chinese-language audience about the complexity and contradictoriness of human desire, as well as about the confusions and betrayals which emerge when emotion and politics are combined. It avoids the black-and-white morality of party dogma, suggests that love is stronger than ideology, and is thus deeply subversive to a system founded on its people's unquestioning subservience and obedience to a party line.

10
CONCLUSION

To what extent, then, can it reasonably be argued that pornography, and the related forms of sexual culture discussed in the preceding chapters, has changed the world and made it a better place?

- First, the apparently universal human compulsion to represent sex explicitly – up to and especially after the invention of 'pornography' as a recognised category in the nineteenth century – has driven the industries of culture and communication in the direction of innovation. Every technological leap – visual art and sculpture; printing; photography and the moving image; cable, satellite, video recording; digital media and the internet – has been given urgency and application by the demand for sexual imagery.

  In the most recent phase propelled by the invention of the internet, the breakthrough tools required for reliable, secure and anonymous online payment were pioneered by computer geeks such as those dramatised in the film *Middle Men* (see Chapter 3), inspired by the true story of Paycom executive Christopher Mallick, and similar companies such as CCBill. And while, like other online content sectors, paid-for porn fell into crisis in the late 2000s due to the ease of free downloading and sharing, the tools developed by these companies have become ubiquitous all over the internet, as online shopping for everything from holidays to music and houses has become routine.

  It is a cliché, but true nonetheless, that sexual representation has been the killer application for successive waves of communicative technological advance, which then permeate into other, less stigmatised sectors of the culture in ways that benefit a society as a whole.

- Second, and from the very beginnings of human cultural activity as we know it, the demand (or desire) for sexual representation, including explicit or porno-graphic presentation, has inspired some of the greatest works of art and culture.

Chapter 8 explored some of the categorisation issues at stake here, but we can say without hesitation that from the cave paintings of pre-history to classical sculpture, literature and painting, on to the conceptual work of Warhol and contemporary figures such as Koons and Araki, through the most influential pop-music and performance of such as Madonna and Gaga, sexuality and porno chic have been consistent threads. 'Sex, love, passion', as the Pet Shop Boys described it in their 1987 song *Paninaro*, has brought out the best in makers of culture everywhere, working in every medium, through every channel, and for every audience.

- Much of this work has had positive impacts on sexual politics and culture, acting as both a mirror to and a driver of the transformation of patriarchal and hetero-normative structures, as well as authoritarian governance in general (often the three go together).

  Pornography, porno chic, and sexually transgressive art have been effective tools in inspiring popular resistance to theocracy in the Islamic world, to totalitarian party rule in countries such as China, and to the power of patriarchal ideas and structures in the liberal capitalist world. Gaga is a pop star, and the video for *Telephone* a sexually transgressive entertainment. It is also a globally visible, transculturally resonant statement about where feminised women were in the year 2010.

- Pornography in particular, as opposed to sexualised culture in general, has given these same groups access to means of sexual gratification they have had in no other societies, and which had for millennia been monopolised by men as one benefit of patriarchy.

  Pornography was heterosexist, as the anti-porn feminists of the 1970s and 1980s claimed it to be, and still can be misogynistic. But the twenty-first century porno-sphere is unprecedentedly diverse and democratic, in the sense that many more sexual interest groups are represented within it than has ever been the case in the history of the form. The expansion, digitisation and diversification of the porno-sphere has benefitted many groups who were denied access to sexual representa-tion (that is, representation of their sexual desires and needs), not because of their orientation, but because of their physical or mental disability, or simply their emotional shyness. The ease of access to pornography on the internet has pro-vided opportunities for sexual gratification for groups who simply did not have them before, who were indeed actively denied them and expected to live sexless lives as if they had no sexualities to express.

- Preceding the emergence of digital media, but enhanced by them, has been the educational function of pornographic and sexual imagery on young men and women as they enter adulthood and sexual activity.

  Many of us, if not all, received our first introductions to sexuality and the sexualised human body through accidental or illicit exposure to the pornography of parents, older siblings, older friends, or just found images. In the era of HIV/ AIDS, moreover, the need for safe sex education has been a matter of life and death for many. In the age of sexual epidemic, all sexually active people, gay, straight and bisexual, have required as a matter of public health more information about sex than was typically provided by parents or by schools (and certainly by churches). Pornography, and materials influenced by its style and language, have provided at least some of this information, and inspired some of the most effective and highly regarded educational campaigns adopted by the more far-sighted authorities.

• And finally, pornography has increased the stock of human happiness, by giving its hundreds of millions of users access to sexual pleasure they would not otherwise have had. This is true for single people, and also for those in partnerships.

With regards to the latter, where Pamela Paul and others have identified the expansion of the pornosphere as a threat to family life, it can just as easily be seen as a boon to sexual relationships which may be loving and loyal, but lacking passion and novelty, simply because they have lasted for so long. No-one has generalisable statistics on this point, but the capacity of porn to save tired marriages by providing an outlet for otherwise frustrated sexual desires is surely just as great as its potential to break families apart under the pressure of 'porn addiction'. Better porn than the traditional recourse to prostitution, one might argue, particularly in the HIV/AIDS context. Better porn than having an affair, furthermore, if the latter can also be seen as one kind of response to marital stagnation or partner fatigue.

The negatives of pornographication

Of course there are negatives and unintended consequences associated with cultural sexualisation. If the diversification of the pornosphere has enabled the welcome expression of previously suppressed and marginalised sexualities, its expansion has also enabled misogynists and sexual predators to find new opportunities to express themselves. There have always been child abusers, many of them embedded in the most revered of institutions. Some paedophiles *have* made pornography of their crimes, and digital technology provides new ways to produce, share and consume such material (as does social networking). Child pornography is relatively rare, and many perpetrators have been caught using online surveillance and search methods. But they still exist, and no discussion of pornography's impacts can ignore that fact. Rigorous policing of pornographic images of child abuse on the internet must therefore be maintained.

The same point applies to violent pornography. Violence and abuse in pornography should be treated as records of criminal acts, and treated accordingly. Where pornography depicts S&M fantasy and other forms of role-playing activity, on the other hand, it should be permitted for the same reason as individuals are permitted to engage in these activities in the privacy of their own bedrooms – because it is no business of the secular, liberal state to police desire or dictate taste.

Apart from the activities of the sexually criminal, there are important boundary issues around the expanded, digitised pornosphere as a whole which require regulatory responses. Not everyone wishes to be exposed to pornography, or to cultural sexualisation, and no-one should be obliged to. The pornosphere is not everywhere, despite the hysterical titles of some of the anti-porn texts of recent years, but it is in more places than ever before, and easier to access, especially for new generations of net-savvy children and young people.

For adults, the most obvious solution to the risk of unwanted exposure is simply not to go there. People rarely encounter hard core pornography by accident, but as a matter of choice fuelled by curiosity or desire. Free-to-air TV in the US and comparable countries does not carry pornography, nor do mainstream cinemas. When the UK's Freeview digital network was found to be broadcasting a sexually explicit Dutch channel in early 2012, the regulator Ofcom announced an investigation and action to remove the offending images, reported to include 'images of scantily clad women rubbing each other's breasts and simulating orgasm'.[1]

Boundaries on the internet are more fluid, and mischievous or malevolent hackers can catch people unawares, but this is rare. To access pornography on the internet requires, as a rule, that one search for it. For children, on the other hand, increasingly skilled in the use of digital technology, there is a justified expectation of the need for effective parental control within the home, facilitated through tools such as state maintenance of watersheds and other zoning mechanisms in a media environment of collapsing boundaries. It is a valid concern for parents who may not be able to watch over their children's use of computers round-the-clock that there should be some way to prevent their access to sexually explicit material of the kind now routinely found on free websites. The challenge is to come up with mechanisms which do not at the same time restrict the sexual consumption of consenting adults, or any other online content which we would wish to see freely available.

In conclusion, the competing perspectives explored in this book can agree that the pornosphere should not be leaking into the public sphere, unless as a subject of debate. Pornography involving consenting adults should be accessible to those who want it, using the digital communication channels now available. It should not be imposed on those who do not want it, nor an unwanted intruder into mainstream, non-pornographic culture. Although boundary regulation has become more difficult in the digital age, it is certainly not impossible. Clear signposting of pornographic outlets is a good thing, and entirely consistent with the liberalisation of sexual culture which I have asserted to be a progressive transforming influence in this book. Whether this balance can be achieved, in a context of ongoing cultural globalisation driven by the internet and its anarchic qualities, and amidst very different approaches within the world's 200-plus nation states, will be a key challenge of online regulators in the coming years.

NOTES

Preface

1 In her review of *Striptease Culture* in the *Media, Culture & Society* journal, vol.25, no.2, Karen Ross wrote that 'when a new book on sex is published, I'm always interested to see if the author is a woman or a man and as I read through, I ask myself about perspectives, about viewpoints and about experiential understanding' (2003, p.281). The implication of the following review was that, in being a man, I was over-optimistic and naïve in my reading of the trends, including my identification of the rise of feminism, the mainstreaming of homosexuality, the progressive evolution of traditional masculinity and the broader 'democratisation of desire'.

In attempting to refute that optimism (which I admit to, and believe to have been borne out in the decade since) Ross wrote: 'When McNair says that "straight men are learning to be self-critical and reflective, just as gay audiences are learning to embrace negative as well as positive representations and women to exploit and subvert the representational power of their sexuality" I'm left asking, but who *are* these people? Not a lesbian friend who recently had 'dyke' spray-painted on her faculty door in a 'progressive' university, not the women film directors who have never been nominated for an Oscar, not the growing number of men who assault their partners and blame their victims for provoking their attacks' (p.283).

Maybe not them, no (although there is no evidence that domestic violence or abuse is increasing in Western societies – see Chapter 6), but my argument in *Striptease Culture* was not that there was *no* sexism, homophobia or misogyny left in the advanced liberal capitalism of the early twenty-first century – merely that it was in noticeable decline, and that trends in sexual culture were indexical of that trend.

2 Writing in the top-selling Scottish red-top tabloid newspaper the *Daily Record*, shortly after the book was published, 'agony aunt' Joan Burnie wrote that 'Sex has been brought into the mainstream, according to Stirling academic Brian McNair. Gosh. I didn't realised [sic] it had ever been a minority activity. But then I'm not a smart sociologist, am I? Anyway, McNair says we're now all into something called porno chic thanks to the likes of modern icons such as Madonna, Demi Moore and Sharon Stone. Modern? That lot are more stringy boilers than spring chickens ... But McNair is in favour because he says his porn chic is evidence of "a greater humanity in society". Come off it, chum. Porn isn't ever chic. It isn't new either. It's still what it always was – the same stale excuse for

dirty old men everywhere to get a cheap thrill' (Burnie, J., 'Boffin is just a sad porn loser', *Daily Record*, April 22 2002).

3 I first used the term 'porno fear' in print in an essay for the art magazine *Bridge*, August/September 2004 ('Not some kind of kinky porno flick').

4 Arrowsmith, A., 'Porn is good for society', *Guardian*, October 12 2011. http://apps.facebook.com/theguardian/commentisfree/2011/oct/12/porn-society-government-opt-in

1 Introduction

1 The commercialisation of sexuality is a key theme in the narrative of decline around sexual culture. Critics since D.H. Lawrence (1936) have typically equated it with debasement, degradation, 'doing dirt' on authentic sexual experience, although never with any coherent rationale beyond the vague notion, refuted by all of human history for which we have evidence, that sex is somehow too sacred to be sold, too precious to be reduced to monetary value. This is the view of some, but not all. The debate on pornographication and cultural sexualisation is driven by this clash, and competing attitudes to the question of what sexuality is and what it is for.

2 In a statement curiously at odds with the rest of her thesis, Hennessey declares that these sexual niches 'support neoliberalism's mystifications'. The term 'neo-liberal' has become meaningless through over-use (Flew, 2011). It is not clear to me how living as an out gay man in the Castro district of San Francisco, or in any of the major cities of the liberal capitalist world in the twenty-first century, has anything do with the 'mystifications of "neo-liberalism"', whatever they are.

3 Fisk, R., 'Murder wave that shames the world', reprinted in *The Australian*, September 25–26 2010.

4 Haze, S., 'Enjoying burlesque is part of female sexuality, not a betrayal of it', *Guardian*, June 4 2009.

2 Pornosphere

1 The original German language version of the book appeared in 1969.

2 That said, Australia's 'most famous porn star' Monica Mayhem says in her memoir of life in the industry that good lighting can make a difference to the 'quality' of pornography (2008, p.xi). For an article on Mayhem and her life see Marks, L., 'Who is Monica Mayhem?', *Marie Claire*, no.171, November 2009. pp.94–100.

3 *Eroticism*, as I use the term in this book, refers to a quality of a text – its capacity to arouse the individual who reads or views it – which may or may not be intentional, and may not even have much to do with sex. There is no aesthetic evaluation implied.

4 Usually translated as 'writing about whores', fuelling the anti-pornography feminist position that pornography is by definition demeaning to women, reducing them to sex objects for sale.

5 Ancient Greek attitudes to sexuality were very different from those of the modern era. Although a patriarchy led by a warrior caste, Greek society permitted, even encouraged, sex between men, and did not regard it as a deviation. Sex between old and young was also permitted, and the modern concept of paedophilia absent.

6 Hooper, J., 'Ancient brothel restored', *Guardian*, October 27 2010.

7 From 'A brief history of Chinese porn', on the blog G (James Griffiths), at www.jamestgriffiths.com/post/9330260739/a-brief-history-of-chinese-porn.

8 Brown, A., 'In the lap of the Scots', *The Sunday Times*, April 7 2005.

9 Dines, G., 'All authentic desire is rendered plastic by this multi-billion dollar industry', *Guardian*, January 5 2011.

10 Interestingly, medieval religious books often included sexually explicit representations, the significance of which is not yet understood (Tang, 1999).
11 Steven Johnson observes that the Chinese invented movable type four centuries before Gutenberg, but failed to adapt and apply the technology to the mechanical reproduction of texts. Gutenberg's invention of a recognisably modern printing-press was based on technology used for pressing grapes in wine making. As Johnson observes, 'he took a machine designed to get people drunk and turned it into an engine for mass communication' (2010).
12 Maurice Frizot dates the invention of the daguerreotype to a presentation made to the Institut de France on August 19 1839 (1998).
13 Quoted in 'Porn-again movie has created a reel hassle', Scotsman.com, April 27 2004. www.scotsman.com/news/porn_again_movie_has_created_a_reel_hassle_1_1009937.
14 Johnson, B., 'Microsoft is the new porn', *Guardian*, January 21 2002.
15 Lubove, S., 'See no evil', *Forbes Magazine*, September 17 2001. www.forbes.com/forbes/2001/0917/068_print.htmls
16 Misleading because many of the users who generate the content that news organisations then incorporate into their productions are neither citizens nor journalists in the traditional sense, but technologically able amateurs who happened to be in the right place (or the wrong place) at the right time.
17 Websites, usually free, which act as outlets for a multitude of categories of pornography. YouPorn.com is one of the best known.
18 Brooks, L., 'Lights, camera, phwoar!', *Guardian*, October 29 2002.
19 Ibid.
20 Go to www.altsextube.com for examples.
21 McCurry, J., 'Japan's 77-year old porn actor: unlikely face of an ageing population', *Guardian*, October 23 2011. http://apps.facebook.com/theguardian/p/32z3g/tw.
22 Rushe, D., 'Crumbling *Penthouse* on brink of collapse', *The Sunday Times*, April 7 2002.
23 Burkeman, O., 'Boom and bust', *Guardian*, April 10 2002.
24 Carr, E., 'Shelf-life', *Guardian*, March 17 2002.
25 Patterson, J., 'The *Deep Throat* story has got it all', *Guardian*, February 4 2005.
26 Williams, Z., 'The market beyond porn', *Guardian*, July 25 2007.
27 Kane, F., 'Hard core, hard cash', *Observer*, November 3 2002.
28 Gillespie, Nick, 'Pornocopia deluxe: behind the triumph of erotica', *Reason*, December 2001, http://reason.com/archives/2001/12/01/pornocopia-deluxe.

3 Porno? Chic!

1 The term 'pornification' is also used in this context, and has the same meaning (see for example Paasonen *et al.*, eds, 2007).
2 For a review of the documentary see 'Porn is cool, isn't it? It's just a little harmless fun, yeah?', Redfern, C., on *the F word* website. www.thefword.org.uk/reviews/2001/04/hardcore.
3 I exclude from the category of porno chic texts which do not seek to simulate porn, but exploit the sexual liberalism of the era to represent sex in ways so explicit that they might be accused of being pornographic. Such texts are distinct from porno chic in that they make no claim to the territory, and may even reject the association as embarrassing or trivialising of the work in question (some porno chic does this too, as we shall see – but the latter is distinguished by its appropriation of what can only be regarded as pornographic tropes and styles). Work of the kind which, in its sexually explicit content, reflects the era of pornographication and cultural sexualisation, will be considered in Chapter 8 on the aesthetics of sexual transgression.
4 Benedictus, L., 'Porn to be mild', *The Age*, February 6 2005.
5 In February 2011 she presented a BBC Radio Five Live documentary on the subject of pornography, *Porn Again*, which suggested a softening of what had been her official

stance in government. A BBC news report at the time quoted her saying that 'for purposes of research I did watch the sort of pornography that's available on the internet', Smith tells Nicky Campbell. 'One of the most interesting things … the people that work in the industry, I liked them more than I thought I would.' (www.bbc.co.uk/news/uk-12536230).

6 See for example 'Turned on to porn', *Sunday Herald*, February 24 2002.

7 See my Preface. We should be honest, scholars and non-scholars alike, about why pornography and sexuality interest *us*, as well as why we think they are important to everybody else. Honesty neutralises the suggestions as to ulterior motive which might otherwise have some purchase in criticism of male scholarly work about porn.

8 Key texts in this movement have included Clarissa Smith's study of porn for women, *One For The Girls* (2007), and Feona Attwood's recent edited collections on *Mainstreaming Sex* (2009) and *Porn.com* (2010).

9 Blumenthal, R., 'Porno chic: "hard-core" grows fashionable and very profitable', *The New York Times*, January 21 1973.

10 One might reasonably regard *Playboy* as an earlier example of *porno chic*, except of course that its launch and mass acceptance preceded the first use of the term. *Playboy* was not perceived as pornography by the majority of its readers, but as a men's magazine which combined nude and semi-nude shots of Marilyn Monroe and others with weighty, elegant journalism. Looking at the magazine now, there is indeed little in *Playboy* that can be said to be pornographic by contemporary standards.

11 Corliss, R., 'That old feeling: when porn was chic', *Time*, March 29 2005. Corliss writes in detail about *Mona* at www.fipresci.org/undercurrent/issue_0509/mona.htm.

12 For an account of the film's production and aftermath, see *Inside Deep Throat* (Fenton Bailey, Randy Barbato, 2004).

13 In her autobiography, *Ordeal* (1980) she describes in graphic detail her career in pornography, and asserts that she was coerced into sex work by her husband, Chuck Traynor. Opinions of associates and witnesses differ as to the extent of her victimhood, although there is no doubt that Traynor was a violent and abusive man.

14 A leading pornographic magazine and film producer of the pre-internet era.

15 Tom, E., 'Maybe once in a blue moon', *The Australian*, September 29–30 2001.

16 Brockes, E., 'It's art. But is it porn?', *Guardian*, November 5 2002.

17 I did however write a piece for the *Scotsman* newspaper titled 'The shocking truth about porn', December 8 2002.

18 Brockes, E., 'It's art. But is it porn?', *Guardian*, November 5 2002.

19 Williams, L.R., 'An innocent abroad', *Sight & Sound*, no.19, 2005.

20 Bradshaw, P., 'Why did *Middle Men* sink in the UK?', *Guardian*, July 7 2011. www.guardian.co.uk/film/filmblog/2011/jul/07/middle-men-luke-wilson-porn.

21 Goodwin, C., 'Porn again', *The Sunday Times*, March 4 2012.

22 From an interview contained in the DVD collection of four films by Moodysson.

23 Quoted in Brooks, X., 'Dirty business', *Guardian*, January 4 2005.

24 Ibid.

25 Grey specialises in extreme and 'gonzo' pornography, often involving 'rough' sex.

26 The narrative moves from episode to episode in which she appears, almost fatalistically, to fall in love with a client. She shows no regard for or loyalty to her boyfriend, telling him that 'I met somebody today, and I'm going away for the weekend. It's just something I have to do, you know?' Chris is jealous, understandably, and the relationship falls into crisis. But the weekend away doesn't happen, because the other man fails to show. Chelsea forgives him, however, and the disruptive relationship continues. Chris is seen finally on his own weekend away in Las Vegas, and we may assume that his life with Chelsea has ended because of her lack of commitment. Chelsea is also cooperating with an author who appears to be writing a book about her life and work. In one scene he asks if she would ever consent to have sex with him, and thus reveals his true agenda.

27 Cox, D., 'A Serbian film: when allegory gets nasty', *Guardian*, December 13 2010.
28 Lawson, M., 'He put the sense into censorship', *Guardian*, March 9 2002.
29 Landesman, C., 'Cool it, rude Britannia', *The Sunday Times*, October 31 2004.
30 I discussed this film at some length in *Striptease Culture*, noting its portrayal of porn producers as depraved, sleazy figures, and performers as vulnerable victims. Schumacher's *8mm* updates that scenario to tell the story of a child lost to a 'snuff movie' in 1990s Los Angeles.
31 *Money* was adapted for television by the BBC in 2010. One review noted that '*Money* is a world saturated in pornography … But prominent though they are in Self's life [John Self is the central character] and worldview, pornography and the sex industry in *Money* are relatively inaccessible, deviant, beyond the pale … But since *Money* was published, pornography has gone mainstream; the mainstream has gone pornography' (Thomas, J., 'Filthy lucre', *Guardian*, May 15 2010).

4 Porno fear

1 The performance can be viewed at www.youtube.com/watch?v=U6mm8W4ej2c. Rhianna begins the song wearing a white and black striped robe, before removing it to reveal a bikini-style outfit.
2 Mumsnet (www.mumsnet.com) is a UK-based website for parents intended to act as a forum for debate on parenting issues, and a campaigning focus for such issues as the premature sexualisation of children and young people. In December 2010, for example, the site's home-page featured a campaign to persuade supermarkets not to display sexual images intended for adults in locations where children might see them.
3 See for example the UK-based X-Pole, 'world leaders in pole technology', who list the uses of their 'professional pole exercise and dance equipment' as 'Great for fitness' and 'ideal for parties'.
4 Pearce, D., 'Sick mum: it's only like kids on a climbing frame', *The Sun*, June www.thesun.co.uk/sol/homepage/news/3014180/Sick-mum-teaches-daughter-of-7-to-pole-dance.html.
5 I do not regard burlesque as porno chic, so much as a form of striptease. But the recent popularity of burlesque as entertainment for women by women can be regarded as part of the 'pornographication of the mainstream', in that through the sexual liberalisation of the culture, a kind of sexually explicit performance once regarded as very much part of the adult entertainment world has been incorporated into mainstream popular culture. The movies *Burlesque* and Mathieu Amalric's *On Tour* (2010) echo the trend, and reinforce it.
6 *PM*, BBC Radio Four, December 13. Walters' characterisation of burlesque is more accurately represented, perhaps, in Amalric's *On Tour*. Released around the same time as *Burlesque*, this film concerns a troupe of New Burlesque performers as they tour French coastal resorts. These are real, imperfect women, 'curvaceous and tattooed peroxide blondes' (Darke, C., Review, *Sight & Sound*, vol.21, issue 1, 2011), for whom the troupe is a surrogate family.
7 Walters qualified his defence of burlesque as a form by suggesting that its popularisation in both the film and the *X Factor* performance represented a distortion, or 'burlesquing' of its true dignity, by reducing it to pop star clichés.
8 *Calendar Girls* (Nigel Cole, 2003), starring Helen Mirren and Julie Walters, was based on the true story of an English Women's Institute group who posed nude in a calendar to raise money for charitable causes.
9 Bowditch, G., 'Nudity is not the same as pornography', *The Sunday Times*, July 26 2009.
10 Ibid.
11 Davies, L., 'Pornography conference blasted as "meat market" by protesters', *Guardian*, September 23 2011. www.guardian.co.uk/culture/2011/sep/23/pornography-conference-meat-market-protesters?fb=native&cmp=FBCNETTXT9038.

12 Appleyard, B., 'Save us from sexcess', *The Sunday Times*, April 27 2003.

13 Landesman, C., 'Cool it, rude Britannia', *The Sunday Times*, October 31 2004.

14 Baxter, S., 'Prime America blanks out British TV's naughty bits', *The Sunday Times*, May 16 2004.

15 Freeman, H., 'My favourite album: *Like a Prayer* by Madonna', *Guardian*, August 23 2011.

16 Levy presented the argument for the *Independent* ('Ariel Levy on "raunch culture"') on December 4 2005. www.independent.co.uk/news/uk/this-britain/ariel-levy-on-raunch-culture-517878.html.

17 Dowd, M., 'Having it all gives way to girdle girls', *The Sunday Times*, November 13 2005.

18 Devine, M., 'Losers of the sexual revolution', *The Sydney Morning Herald*, February 22 2007.

19 Paglia, C., 'Lady Gaga and the death of sex', *The Sunday Times*, September 12 2010.

20 Needham, A., 'Camille Paglia's attack on Lady Gaga is way off the mark', *Guardian*, September 13 2010.

21 Ibid.

22 Reported in Jeffries, S., 'Are women human?', *Guardian*, April 12 2006.

23 Baxter, S., 'Raunch culture and the end of feminism', *The Sunday Times*, May 7 2006.

24 Bell, R., 'University challenge', *Guardian*, February 9 2007.

25 Knight, I., 'Weak on the inside', *The Sunday Times*, November 16 2003.

26 Bindwell, J., 'The hardcore truth about women in porn', *Guardian*, July 14 2011. www.guardian.co.uk/culture/2011/jul/14/hardcore-abuse-of-women-in-porn.

27 Walters, N., 'What has love got to do with it, Mum?', *The Sunday Times*, January 17 2010.

28 Raven, C., 'Strike a pose', *Guardian*, March 6 2010.

29 Freedman, M., 'Me versus raunch culture. Or not', *Mamamia*, April 10 2010. www.mamamia.com.au/weblog/2010/04/sex-pop-culture-raunch-culture.html.

30 For the Inquiry report and all submissions, go to www.aph.gov.au/senate/committee/eca_ctte/sexualisation_of_children/index.htm.

31 Adams, P., 'The real pornography', *The Australian*, March 20 2011.

32 For a discussion see 'Invasion of the prostitots', Kerry Howley, *Reason*, July 2007 http://reason.com/archives/2007/07/01/invasion-of-the-prostitots.

33 Barbie was based on the German *Bild Lilli* doll, described as 'a working girl who knew what she wanted and was not above using men to get it'.

34 The report also found that children and teenagers are sophisticated media consumers, and 'have a very literate approach – they know that television production is a process and that they are not watching reality. They also recognised that sex is used to sell things and is a device to build up audiences' (Brown, M., '"The less you wear, the more you sell"', *Guardian*, November 8 2003). They also found that 'children debated at length the motivations that led characters to engage in sex and the consequences of their behaviour for others, and they placed a strong emphasis on the need for trust, fidelity and respect.'

35 Brown, M., '"The less you wear, the more you sell"', *Guardian*, November 8 2003.

36 Papadopoulous elsewhere contradicts this assertion, by stating that 'there is strong evidence linking consumption of pornography with sexual behaviour' (p.46).

37 The report, published in June 2008, can be downloaded at www.aph.gov.au/senate/committee/eca_ctte/sexualisation_of_children/report/report.pdf.

38 Round-table statement by Linda Thompson, Scottish Women's Aid.

39 Somewhere between the scholarly and the journalistic sat books such as Sarracino and Scott's *The Porning Of America* (2008), published as noted above under the auspices of the Unitarian Universalist Association of Congregations, a relatively liberal religious grouping. These authors professed to welcome 'an atmosphere of sexual freedom', but were motivated to write by anxiety about 'a culture increasingly being shaped by the dominant influence: porn' (p.x).

40 Dines, G., Long, J., 'Moral panic? No, we are resisting the pornification of women', *Guardian*, December 2 2011. www.guardian.co.uk/commentisfree/2011/dec/01/feminists-pornification-of-women?CMP=twt_gu.

41 Being left-wing is, however, no predictor of support for women's rights. As noted above (and again in Part II), 'socialist' regimes in the twentieth century were amongst the worst oppressors of women and homosexuals, and they remain so. History demonstrates that the pornography debate is not a left–right issue.

42 Cochrane, K., 'The men who believe porn is wrong', *Guardian*, October 25 2010.

43 We note here that pornography is one of the few industries in which female performers receive higher remuneration than male.

44 Quoted in 'Is porn damaging to society?', *Times*, August 5 2010.

45 Bindel, J., 'The truth about pornography', *Guardian*, July 2 2010. Dines' views have been influential in the resurgence of anti-porn discourse, and regularly surface in writing such as an essay in *The Monthly* of September 2011 by Cordelia Fine on 'the dehumanising effects of smut'. In 2010 and 2011 Dines followed up her *Pornland* book with articles critical of the pornography industry. In one she reported from the Las Vegas Adult Entertainment Expo – describing its participants as the 'predatory capitalists' of an industry which produces more than 13,000 films a year in the US alone and makes billions of dollars, including $500 million for big hotel chains which allow customers to pay for porn in their rooms (these figures are estimates, based on imprecise and variable premises). In an edition of the Australian TV debate show *Q&A* Dines cited the size of the global porn industry as $96 billion. No evidence for this estimate was provided.

46 There *is* some evidence – qualitative interview and focus group evidence – that people who view sexual culture, including children and young people, understand that it is not 'real' (Knudsen *et al.*, 2007). Buckingham and Bragg's 2003 study found that the young people they surveyed had a sophisticated, contextual understanding of the sexual material they viewed on TV.

47 Dines, G., Long, J., 'Moral panic? No, we are resisting the pornification of women', *Guardian*, December 2 2011. www.guardian.co.uk/commentisfree/2011/dec/01/feminists-pornification-of-women?CMP=twt_gu.

48 Ibid.

49 A good example of this phenomenon was observed in January 2012. The BBC drama production of *Sherlock*, broadcast in the UK over the Christmas season of 2011, featured a 'naked dominatrix' in its plot. Broadcast before the 9pm watershed, when programmers are supposed to schedule with an audience of children in mind, the programme drew criticism for its sexual content in newspapers such as the *Daily Mail*. Helpfully, the newspaper published a full colour photograph of the nude actress involved, Lara Pulver. www.dailymail.co.uk/tvshowbiz/article-2081486/Lara-Pulver-naked-Sherlock-Holmes-BBC-raunchy-pre-watershed-scenes.html.

50 Quoted in 'Is porn damaging to society?', *Times*, August 5 2010.

51 Thomas Frank, 'Porn didn't give Bernie Madoff his start', *The Wall Street Journal*, April 28 2010. The author of this piece noted that 'It's fun to blame everything on pornography. And so, it is suggested, porn is the reason Bernie Madoff got away with it; porn may be why Lehman Brothers failed; with enough effort we can probably figure out ways to blame porn for every federal foul up from Toyota to FEMA.'

52 Marriott, E., 'Men and porn', *Guardian*, November 8 2003. He also noted that 33 per cent of internet users reported using pornography, and that the porn industry in the US was worth an estimated $15 billion per annum.

53 Carey, T., 'Why more and more women are using pornography', *Guardian*, April 7 2011.

54 Sithartan, G., Sithartan, R., 'Don't get worked up: you can beat your porn addiction … if you want to', *The Conversation*, May 25 2011.

Preface to Part II

1 McNair, B., 'No need for moral panic: we can protect children's innocence in the age of Gaga', *The Conversation*, July 6 2011. http://theconversation.edu.au/no-need-for-moral-panic-we-can-protect-childrens-innocence-in-the-age-of-gaga-1809

2 Rosewarne, L., 'Living vicariously: porn provides a tasting plate for our unspoken fetishes', *The Conversation*, May 30 2011. http://theconversation.edu.au/living-vicariously-porn-provides-a-tasting-plate-for-our-unspoken-fetishes-1438; Albury, K. 'Porn and feminism: not strange bedfellows after all', *The Conversation*, May 27 2011. http://the conversation.edu.au/porn-and-feminism-not-strange-bedfellows-after-all-1446.

3 Goodforher.com hosts the Feminist Porn Awards.

4 www.onlineopinion.com.au/view.asp?article=12567&page=0. See also her piece for the same outlet on 'The woman and the octopus, or how anti porn activists sabotage their own message', *Online Opinion*, September 14 2011. www.onlineopinion.com.au/view.asp?article=12609.

5 Arrowsmith, A., 'Porn is good for society', *Guardian*, October 12 2011. www.guardian.co.uk/commentisfree/2011/oct/12/porn-society-government-opt-in.

5 What has pornography ever done for us? The argument from evidence

1 The killer, Armin Meiwes, was sent to prison for life for killing Bernd Brandes, 'who was obsessed with being eaten'. www.spiegel.de/international/zeitgeist/0,1518,511775,00.html.

2 Sutcliffe was active in the 1970s and 1980s in the north of England. He was convicted of killing thirteen women, many of them prostitutes, or whom he assumed to be prostitutes. At his trial in 1981 he claimed that 'the voice of God' compelled him to carry out his attacks. Novelist David Peace's *Red Riding* quartet of books gives a fictionalised account of the Ripper story, including the religious symbolism which drove Sutcliffe.

3 In January 2012 a UK court found that materials distributed between consenting adults could not by definition 'deprave or corrupt' them, calling into question the entire basis of the Obscene Publications Act as it had been implemented in Britain since the 1950s, 'Not guilty verdict in DVD obscenity trial', *BBC News* online, January 6 2012. www.bbc.co.uk/news/uk-16443697.

4 For a short summary of Pinker's thesis see his article in the *Guardian* of November 1 2011, 'If it bleeds, it misleads: on violence and misery the Cassandras are wrong'. www.guardian.co.uk/commentisfree/booksblog/2011/nov/01/violence-misery-wars-steven-pinker.

5 Pinker argues that cultural trends such as anti-establishment, anti-war activism may explain a lack of trust in and respect for political authority in the 1960s and 1970s which led to increased levels of violence in the period following. Others have suggested that a spike in the population of baby boomers may account for the temporary deviation from what he characterises as a millennia-long decline.

6 As this book was nearing completion at the end of 2011 news emerged of the execution of a woman for 'sorcery' in Saudi Arabia. According to the BBC, in an online story posted on December 12 2011, 'Saudi Arabia does not actually define sorcery as a capital offence. However, some of its conservative clerics have urged the strongest possible punishments against fortune-tellers and faith healers as a threat to Islam.' www.bbc.co.uk/news/world-middle-east-16150381.

7 The issue of the *International Journal of Law and Psychiatry* in which Kutchinsky's article appears contains a number of articles exploring the pornography effects debate. In an earlier piece on the same data, Kutchinsky observes that 'while no one claims it was pornography which led to the decrease [in the recorded incidence of rape in Denmark, Sweden and Germany in the period after the introduction of pornography], these developments leave hardly any doubt that that pornography does *not* cause rape' (1990, p.245).

8 He notes that 'junk statistics from advocacy groups are slung around and become common knowledge, such as the incredible factoid that one in four university students has been raped (the claim was based on a commodious definition of rape that the alleged victims themselves never accepted; it included, for example, any incident in which a woman consented to sex after having had too much to drink and regretted it afterwards)' (2011, p.647).

9 For an account of the award-winning 2001 *Brass Eye* special on media and public perceptions of paedophilia see http://en.wikipedia.org/wiki/Brass_Eye#Paedophilia_special_.282001.29.

10 Lecture delivered at TED 2007. www.goodreads.com/videos/show/2503-steven-pinker-a-brief-history-of-violence.

11 Arrowsmith, A., 'Porn is good for society', *Guardian*, October 12 2011. http://apps.facebook.com/theguardian/commentisfree/2011/oct/12/porn-society-government-opt-in

6 Gaga-ing for it: the feminisation of pornography and sexual culture

1 www.guardian.co.uk/lifeandstyle/2012/mar/05/annie-lennox-world-more-sexualised

2 Dines, G., Long, J., 'Moral panic? No, we are resisting the pornification of women', *Guardian*, December 2 2011. www.guardian.co.uk/commentisfree/2011/dec/01/feminists-pornification-of-women?CMP=twt_gu

3 Faludi's *Backlash* was a misreading of the direction of the trends (McNair, 1996, 2002), and of the pop cultural texts she critiqued. The early 1990s was *not* the start of a male backlash against feminism, unless we are to dispute all the evidence on women's socio-economic and political progress since then. For example, the UK-based Women and Work Commission produced a report in 2009 showing that the gap between women's and men's pay – as measured by media pay per-hour rates – had reduced by 18 per cent in a decade. The report also showed that in 1998 media pay per-hour for women was 27.5 per cent less than in the equivalent work for men. In 2008 this gap had fallen to 22.6 per cent (*Shaping A Fairer Future*, Women and Work Commission, July 2009).

4 For a review see Zoe Williams in the *Guardian*, November 4 2011. www.guardian.co.uk/books/2011/nov/04/why-be-happy-jeanette-winterson-review

5 Baxter, S., 'Women, the true winners at work', *The Sunday Times*, January 11 2004.

6 Krum, S., 'No more faking', *Guardian*, May 15 2006.

7 Penny, L., 'Stop this slut shaming', *Guardian*, August 9 2011. The supportive tone of this article for the slut walk movement contrasts with Penny's dismissal of burlesque as a 'misogynist sham' quoted elsewhere in this chapter.

8 The references to this article are for a version available online at http://esr.oxfordjournals.org/content/26/5/499.full.pdf+html. A shorter statement of Hakim's argument can be found in 'Erotic capital', *Prospect*, March 23 2010 and her book, *Erotic Capital*, was published in 2011. The controversy sparked by her views is reported in *The Sunday Times*, January 9 2011.

9 Williams, Z., 'The market beyond porn', *Guardian*, July 25 2007.

10 Haskell, M., *Guardian*, November 7 2003.

11 Mills, E., 'Women's twisted revenge', *The Sunday Times*, June 20 2010.

12 Campbell, D., 'Body image concerns more men than women, research finds', *Guardian*, January 6 2012. www.guardian.co.uk/lifeandstyle/2012/jan/06/body-image-concerns-men-more-than-women

13 Reported in Hoby, H., 'So much for Lady Gaga's feminist credentials', *Guardian*, February 28 2010.

14 The promotional video is at www.youtube.com/watch?v=i3Jv9fNPjgk

15 For a profile of *Burlesque* star Cher, published to coincide with the release of the film, see Smith, K., 'Forever Cher', *Vanity Fair*, December 2010.

16 For a review see Chris Darke, *Sight & Sound* January 2011. www.bfi.org.uk/sightandsound/review/5787

17 Penny, L., 'Burlesque laid bare', *Guardian*, May 15 2009.
18 Haze, S., 'Enjoying burlesque is part of female sexuality, not a betrayal of it', *Guardian*, June 4 2009.
19 A YouTube video of Starla Haze performing a piece called *Seduction of the Virgin Princess* can be found at www.youtube.com/watch?v=3vlWjyKzXws
20 February 6 2010. www.guardian.co.uk/lifeandstyle/2010/feb/06/burlesque-dancer-really-thinking-interview
21 Edmonstone, E., 'A feminist act', *The Sunday Times*, February 8 2004.
22 Quoted in Carey, A., 'Stripping laid bare', *Sunday Herald*, May 12 2002.
23 Brown, A., 'In the lap of the Scots', *The Sunday Times*, April 7 2002.
24 Landesman, C., 'Cool it, rude Britannia', *The Sunday Times*, October 31 2004.
25 Walsh, H., 'Pornography is far too complicated to distil into a smart t-shirt slogan', *Guardian*, August 29 2009.
26 Ibid.
27 In a newspaper article at the time she explained: 'Since news of my selection broke on Thursday, many people have asked me why I want to be an MP. The answer is: for exactly the same reason I decided to start making pornography for women more than 12 years ago. Someone had to do it and it didn't look like anyone else was going to – at least not with the drive, enthusiasm and determination that I could offer' (Span, A., 'Why I've gone from porn to politics', *The Observer*, March 10 2010). www.guardian.co.uk/commentisfree/2010/mar/14/anna-arrowsmith-pornography-politics
28 Span, A., 'Why I've gone from porn to politics', *The Observer*, March 10 2010. www.guardian.co.uk/commentisfree/2010/mar/14/anna-arrowsmith-pornography-politics.
For a debate on the merits of pornography for women see Arrowsmith's engagement with Gail Dines in the *Guardian* of March 5 2011 ('Can sex films empower women?' www.guardian.co.uk/commentisfree/2011/mar/05/conversation-gail-dines-anna-arrowsmith?INTCMP=ILCNETTXT3487).
29 Quoted in Sullivan, D., 'I am the new breed', Adult Video News, March 5 2009. http://business.avn.com/articles/video/Sasha-Grey-I-Am-the-New-Breed-306226.html
30 Quoted in the *New York Post*, March 8 2009.
31 Brooks, L., 'Lights, camera, phwoar!', *Guardian*, October 29 2002.
32 Brooks, L., 'Lights, camera, phwoar!', *Guardian*, October 29 2002.
33 'women.power.porn.', *CarnalNation*, a 'sexuality news magazine' which ceased publishing in October 2010.
34 She adds that 'pornography, as a work environment, creates a queer space in which performers are able to experience sexual pleasures disinvested from their sexual desires and what they feel to be their own sexual identity' (2010, p.4).
35 Briefly a Republican presidential hopeful in the 2012 campaign, until he was accused of sexual harassment at work by a number of women and forced to withdraw.
36 Sweeney, C., 'But what happens when the fun stops?', *Sunday Herald*, February 2 2003.
37 Quoted in Catalina, M., 'Porn made for women, by women', *Guardian*, March 22 2011.
38 Quoted in Catalina, M., 'Porn made for women, by women', *Guardian*, March 22 2011.
39 Albury, K., 'Porn and feminism: not strange bedfellows after all', *The Conversation*, May 26 2011.
40 Grayling, A.C., 'Sex and sensibility', *Guardian*, February 9 2002.
41 Ibid.

7 Pornography and the politics of sexual inclusion

1 Addley, E., 'Glad to be gay', *Guardian*, March 12 2002.
2 Simpson, M, 'Think pink: soon you will have to', *Guardian*, November 11 2000. Simpson's book, *The Queen Is Dead* (2000) articulated this argument in greater detail.

3 Described thus on his website: 'Each night Tim went live on the worldwide web in search of a sexual partner. The audience decided which person he should have sex with and he duly cycled off on his electric bike to do the deed. He made a video diary of all his encounters and reported back the next night. Surprisingly controversial, *Sex Addict* premiered at the Assembly Rooms Edinburgh in 2004.' In *Rude Britannia* Fountain explains that 'my aim in creating the show had been to make the audience think about their sex lives and how they conducted them in an internet age' (2008, p.2). www.timfountain.co.uk.

4 Sarracino and Scott note in *The Porning Of America* that when the eponymous author of the Hays code (which was used to restrict the sexual content of cinema in the United States until the 1960s) was taken to the divorce courts by his wife in the 1950s, 'she cited his inability to distinguish between her navel and her clitoris' (2008, p.50).

5 Smith, R., 'Amazing Grace', *Guardian*, April 7 2003.

6 Flynn, P., 'Straight choice for a gay man', *Guardian*, November 1 2004.

7 Teather, D., 'Gay team flings TV closet door wide open', *Guardian*, August 11 2005.

8 Lawson, M., 'The generalisation game', *Guardian*, April 26 2004.

9 Appleyard, B., 'It's a queer thing', *The Sunday Times*, May 9 2004.

10 Defined in this survey as the 'average percentage saying [homosexuals] should be allowed to speak, teach and have books in library'.

11 Brooks, L., 'Without prejudice', *Guardian*, December 12 2003.

12 Wells, M., 'Mag that made it cool to be gay', *Guardian*, April 26 2004.

13 Ibid.

14 Cochrane, K., 'The B-Generation', *The Sunday Times*, April 18 2004.

15 The states in question were: Texas, Kansas, Oklahoma, Missouri, Alabama, Florida, Idaho, Louisiana, Mississippi, North Carolina, South Carolina, Utah and Virginia.

16 For a study of UK media coverage of same sex marriage see Jowett and Peel, who argue that although there was by 2006 an expanding quantity of coverage of this subject in the mainstream British news media, 'the heteronormativity of the coverage provided little space for more radical constructions of same-sex relationship recognition' (2010, p.206).

17 Tavernise, S., 'Adoptions by gay couples rise, despite barriers', *The New York Times*, June 13 2011. For a scholarly analysis of mass mediated representations of same-sex parents in the US media around 2004–5 see Landau, 2009.

18 Pinker observes that the incidence of anti-gay homicides in the USA since 1996 has stabilised at around three per 100,000, which is much less than the rate for US adults in general.

19 Silverberg, C., 'An interview with a pornographic lesbian', about.com:sexuality, October 14 2007. http://sexuality.about.com/od/eroticentertainment/a/nan_kinney.htm

20 Silverberg, C., 'An interview with a pornographic lesbian', about.com:sexuality, October 14 2007.

21 www.lesbilicious.co.uk/community/why-do-lesbians-love-gay-man-porn/#ixzz1gTbIhBta.

22 Wolcott, J., 'The Gay Divide', *Vanity Fair*, February 2005.

23 Brown, M., 'The less you wear, the more you sell', *Guardian*, November 8 2003.

24 Frankie Boyle, Scottish comedian, quoted in *The Herald*, September 18 2011.

25 James, O., 'Family under the microscope', *Guardian*, August 15 2009.

26 Rosewarne, L., 'Living vicariously: porn provides a tasting plate for our unspoken fetishes', *The Conversation*, May 30 2011.

8 The aesthetics of sexual transgression

1 Quoted in Hickey *et al.*, 2006, p.33.

2 Anthony Julius suggests that Manet is the first transgressive artist of the modern period, who in works such as *Le Dejeuner Sur L'Herbe* (1863) established 'complex, adversarial relations both with his audience and with the art canon' (2002, p.61).

3   Buck, L., 'Not in front of the British', *Independent*, November 21 1995.
4   http://women.timesonline.co.uk/tol/life_and_style/women/celebrity/article1288676.ece
5   In May 2008 an exhibition by Henson in Sydney provoked public condemnation with its inclusion of a nude photograph of a 12-year-old girl. Kate MacNeill explores the case in *Media International Australia*, noting that although Henson was an established and distinguished photo-artist, 'the news media consistently reported the events within the familiar framing of child pornography' (2010, p.82). She attributes this focus to the growing panic around sexualisation of children visible in Australia and other countries at this time.
6   I make this assertion in the knowledge that many paedophiles have themselves been abused as children, and require properly resourced rehabilitation and support as well as punishment for their crimes.
7   Woods, R., 'Censors and sensibility', *The Sunday Times*, October 4 2009.
8   Stuart Jeffries in the *Guardian* observed of *Made In Heaven* that Koons' 'properly ironic po-mo statement about the work was that it would initiate spectators into the "realm of the Sacred Heart of Jesus". Koons had created a Baudrillardian system of simulacra of sexual passion, religious ecstasy, semiotic overload and voguish kitsch, while suggesting that to the blank-eyed stiff who has it all, nothing, not even Viagra, will get him going any more. Such is the postmodern male condition.' 'Postmodernism: the 10 key moments in the birth of a movement', *Guardian*, September 20 2011.
9   For a well-regarded documentary on Tom Of Finland see *Daddy and the Muscle Academy* (Ilppo Pohjola, 1991).
10 Bowditch, G., 'It's not art or porn – just sex', *The Sunday Times*, September 15 2002. For examples of Rankin's work in a variety of genres and themes, go to http://rankin.co.uk/overview/.
11 Madonna, at least, was vilified in any case, depicted in the popular media of many countries as a 'slut' (McNair, 1996).
12 The documentary *Arakimentari* (Travis Close, 2004) shows some of these portraits in progress, as does the 1995 film *Fake Love*, broadcast by Channel 4 in the UK as part of its *Red Light Zone* series of documentaries on sexual themes.
13 Araki's work, and the response of Japanese women to it, reinforces the argument made above about the possibility of multiple interpretations being placed on even the most 'violent' sexual imagery. In this case we see, sometimes with disturbing clarity, that one woman's sadomasochistic submission is another's statement of sexual autonomy and transgressive desire.
14 One such early work was called *Sur-Sentimentalism Manifesto no. 2* (1970).
15 From *Black White + Grey* (James Crump, 2007).
16 In October 2009 BBC Radio broadcast a documentary on this incident in Warhol's and Bailey's careers, called *When Warhol Met Bailey*.
17 Moral campaigner Mary Whitehouse, again without having seen the offending work, declared that 'we don't want obscenity in our sitting rooms'.
18 Quoted in Henley, J., 'There's no reason why a porn film can't also be a good film', *Guardian*, August 28 2002.
19 Higgins, C., 'Why I made that film', *Guardian*, May 20 2004.
20 Lawson, M., 'A tale of two 18 certificates', *Guardian*, October 23 2004.
21 Felperin, L., 'The edge of the razor', *Sight & Sound*, vol.9, no.10, 1999.
22 Januszczak, W., 'The joy of sex … ', *The Sunday Times*, March 4 2001.
23 Winners have included Tom Wolfe (2004), Melvyn Bragg (1993) and Wendy Perriam (2002).
24 Sade wrote at a time when in Europe the gruesome, prolonged torture and sexual mutilation of condemned criminals was a popular public spectacle, described by Michel Foucault amongst others in his *Discipline and Punish* (1977). Steven Pinker's study of violence (2011) also provides many examples of the routine lack of compassion and apparent joy in inflicting pain which characterised eighteenth-century Europe.

25 Man Ray contributed sexually explicit or 'pornographic' images to a book made with Aragon and others called *1929*.

26 Greer, G., 'The connection between art and exhibitionism', *Guardian*, January 28 2008. www.guardian.co.uk/artanddesign/artblog/2008/jan/28/theconnectionbetweenartand.

27 I delivered lectures on *Striptease Culture* at that exhibition as it travelled around the UK, linking the photographic work of Emin and others to the pornographication of mainstream culture I had identified as a trend in that book.

9 Drop porn, not bombs!

1 His work, notes one critic, 'can be re-imagined as part of the renaissance of figurative painting, known as the trans-avant-garde or Neo-Expressionism, that blossomed in New York at this time. Such painting transgressed humanist depictions of the body, revisioning the body as the site of polymorphous sexuality, of pleasure and violence' (Sussman, 1997, p.20). Kolossa adds that in his work 'the theme of sexuality ... nearly always has a threatening, violent and obsessive side' (2004, p.57).

2 Quoted in Jeffries, S., 'At home with Gilbert and George', *Guardian*, June 25 2009.

3 In Afghanistan as late as January 2012 the defence of women against such violations as being imprisoned for having been raped was being cited as a rationale for the maintenance of a strong military presence in the country. Wyatt, C., 'What future for Afghan woman jailed for being raped?', *BBC News* online, www.bbc.co.uk/news/world-south-asia-16543036

4 Lawson, M., 'Bombers read the arts pages', *Guardian*, July 16 2007.

5 Hitchens, C., 'Iran's waiting game', *Vanity Fair*, July 2005.

6 Fisk, R., 'Murder wave that shames the world', *Australian*, September 25–26 2010.

7 Ibid.

8 Toomey, C., 'Can Iran's young ring the changes?', *The Sunday Times*, June 7 2009.

9 Toomey, C., 'Can Iran's young ring the changes?', *The Sunday Times*, June 7 2009.

10 Hitchens, C., 'Iran's waiting game', *Vanity Fair*, July 2005.

11 Iqbal, N., 'The fuss over Veena Malik's "nude" FHM cover is Pakistan's real shame', *Guardian*, December 6 2011. www.guardian.co.uk/commentisfree/2011/dec/06/veena-malik-nude-fhm-cover-pakistan?fb=native&cmp=FBCNETTXT9037&#start-of-comments

12 Ibid.

13 McNair, B., 'Why Arab BB's demise should be mourned', *The Scotsman*, March 7 2004.

14 Mackenzie, T., 'The best hope for democracy in the Arab world: a crooning TV "idol"?', *TBS*, no.13, 2004.

15 In Saudi Arabia there is, let it be noted, some evidence of progress in women's rights. In 2009 it was reported that the Saudi media company ROTANA was now allowing women to wear skirts and trousers to work, and to work alongside men. This was still very much the exception, however, made possible only because of the reported protection of (relatively) liberal Prince Alwalad Bin Tala Bin Adbulazziz al-Saud. In the country as a whole, women were still compelled to wear the *abaya* (black cloak) or the *niqab* (a gown covering everything but the eyes). 'Women still cannot drive and legally cannot even leave the home to shop, let alone get a job, without a male family member's permission' (Butters, C., 'Something is going on in Saudi Arabia', *Guardian*, October 16 2009). 'We are not really free', one Saudi woman is reported to have said, 'but it is possible for women to express themselves as never before.' In 2011 it was reported that women in Saudi Arabia would be allowed to vote in local elections – not yet, stressed the official who made the announcement, but someday.

16 Branigan, T., 'Ai Weiwei supporters strip off as artist faces "porn" investigation', *Guardian*, November 21 2011. http://apps.facebook.com/theguardian/world/2011/nov/21/ai-weiwei-porn-investigation-naked

17 Quoted in a *Wall Street Journal* report on an interview given by Jacobs on the Danwei website ('Sex scholar: China losing war on porn', August 24 2011). http://blogs.wsj.com/chinarealtime/2011/08/24/sex-scholar-china-losing-war-on-porn/

18 The study can be accessed online at http://journal.webscience.org/306/2/websci10_submission_44.pdf. It is based on analysis of some 93,000 web pages drawn from 1,826 web sites monitored over a ten-month period.

19 Williams goes on to suggest that 'the Chinese think they can prevent social unrest by controlling pornography. We [Western observers] think this must surely be a smoke-screen for preventing explicit political content, since sexual content is itself a form of control. There is no better way on earth to castrate collective protest than to have everyone sitting in their bedroom, atomized and alienated, doing things they want to do in private' (Williams, Z., 'Beijing may fear it, but porn means passivity not protest', *Guardian*, June 11 2009). This probably overestimates the cunning of the Chinese Communist Party. It is much more likely that, like the Bolsheviks in the 1920s, and the Cuban and North Korean regimes today, the Chinese authorities understand that their need for rigid conformity and submission to the austere work ethic of a centralised authoritarian economy, bankrupt as the official ideology is, requires control of this area of human existence as much as it does control of the political sphere. Totalitarianism, as Orwell understood, must reach into the bedroom, as much as it must control political speech and thought.

20 For an interview with Jacobs in which she sets out the main arguments and findings of her book, see Leese, S., 'Sex: the Chinese perspective', *CNN GO*, April 29 2011. www.cnngo.com/hong-kong/life/katrien-jacobs-522084

21 Ibid.

22 She believes that 'people should be able to use pornographic texts and images to express their identities. People should have the freedom to pursue pleasure and to define themselves sexually' (Ibid.).

10 Conclusion

1 Laughlin, A., 'Ofcom contacts Dutch regulator over Freeview "porn"', *Digital Spy*, March 9 2012. www.digitalspy.com.au/media/news/a370009/ofcom-contacts-dutch-regulator-over-freeview-porn.html

BIBLIOGRAPHY

Agustin, L.: *Sex At the Margins: Migration, Labour Markets and the Rescue Industry*, London, Ed Books, 2007.

Albertozzi, D., Cobley, P., eds: *The Media: An Introduction*, 3rd edition, Harlow, Pearson, 2010.

Albury, K.: 'Reading porn reparatively', *Sexualities*, vol.12, no.3, 2009, pp.647–53.

Albury, K., Lumby, C.: 'Introduction: children, young people, sexuality and the media', *Media International Australia incorporating Culture & Policy*, no.135, 2010a, pp.56–60.

——'Too much? Too young? The sexualisation of children debate in Australia', *Media International Australia incorporating Culture & Policy*, no.135, 2010b, pp.141–52.

American Psychological Association, Task Force on the Sexualization of Girls: *Report of the APA Task Force on the Sexualization of Girls*, Washington, DC, American Psychological Association, 2007.

Araki, N.: *Tokyo Lucky Hole*, London, Taschen, 1996.

Attwood, F.: 'Reading porn: the paradigm shift in pornography research', *Sexualities*, vol.5, no.1, 2002, pp.91–105.

——'Pornography and objectification: re-reading "the picture that divided Britain"', *Feminist Media Studies*, vol.4, no.1, 2004, pp.7–19.

——'Fashion and passion: marketing sex to women', *Sexualities*, vol.8, no.4, 2005, pp.392–406.

——'Sexed-up: theorising the sexualisation of culture', *Sexualities*, vol.9, 2006, pp.77–94.

——'The paradigm shift: pornography research, sexualisation and extreme images', *Sociology Compass*, vol.5, no.1, 2011, pp.13–22.

Attwood, F., ed.: *Mainstreaming Sex: The Sexualisation of Western Culture*, London, IB Tauris, 2009.

——*Porn.com: Making Sense of Online Pornography*, London, Peter Lang, 2010.

Attwood, F., Smith, C.: 'Extreme concern: regulating "dangerous pictures" in the United Kingdom', *Journal of Law and Society*, vol.37, no.1, 2010, pp.171–88.

Avila-Saavedra, G.: 'Nothing queer about queer television: televized construction of gay masculinities', *Media, Culture & Society*, vol.31, no.1, 2009, pp.5–21.

Bailey, R.: *Letting Children Be Children – Report of an Independent Review of the Commercialisation and Sexualisation of Childhood*, London, Department of Education, 2011.

Barcan, R.: *Nudity: A Cultural Anatomy*, New York, Berg, 2004.

Barss, P.: *The Erotic Engine: How Pornography has Powered Mass Communication from Gutenberg to Google*, St Lucia, University of Queensland Press, 2010.

Bataille, G.: *The Story Of The Eye*, London, Penguin, 1982.

Boston, R.: *The Essential Fleet Street: Its History and Influence*, London, Cassell, 1990.

Boyle, K.: 'The boundaries of porn studies', *New Review of Film & Television Studies*, vol.4, no.1, 2006, pp.1–16.

——'Introduction: everyday pornography', in Boyle, ed., 2010 pp.1–13.

Boyle, K., ed.: *Everyday Pornographies*, London, Routledge, 2010.

Bridges, A.: 'Methodological considerations in mapping pornography content', in Boyle, ed., 2010, pp.34–49.

Brookes, F., Kelly, P.: '*Dolly* girls: tweenies as artefacts of consumption', *Journal of Youth Studies*, vol.12, no.6, December 2009, pp.599–613.

Brownmiller, S.: *Against Our Will: Men, Women and Rape*, New York, Simon and Schuster, 1975.

Bruns, A.: *Blogs, Wikipedia, Second Life and Beyond: From Production to Produsage*, New York, Peter Lang, 2008.

Buckingham, D., Bragg, S.: *Young People, Sex and the Media: The Facts of Life?*, London, Palgrave Macmillan, 2003.

Burana, L.: *Strip City*, London, Virago, 2002.

Burgess, J., Green, J.: *You Tube: Online Video and Participatory Culture*, Cambridge, Polity Press, 2009.

Burke, C.: *Lee Miller: A Life*, New York, Alfred A. Knopf, 2005.

Calvocoressi, R.: *Lee Miller*, London, Thames and Hudson, 2002.

Carnes, P., Delmonico, D., Griffin, E.: *In the Shadows of the Net: Breaking Free of Compulsive Online Sexual Behaviour*, Minnesota, Hazelden, 2005.

Carter, A.: *The Sadeian Woman: And the Ideology of Pornography*, New York, Pantheon, 1978.

Castells, M.: *Communication and Power*, Oxford, Oxford University Press, 2009.

Ciclitira, K.: 'Pornography, women and feminism: between pleasure and politics', *Sexualities*, vol.7, no.3, 2005, pp.281–301.

Cokal, S.: 'Clean porn: the visual aesthetics of hygiene, hot sex and hair removal', in Hall and Bishop, *Pop-Porn: Pornography in American Culture*, 2007, pp.137–53.

Cornell, D., ed.: *Feminism and Pornography*, Oxford, Oxford University Press, 2000.

Dawkins, R.: *The Selfish Gene*, Oxford, Oxford University Press, 1989.

De Luigi, S., Amis, M.: *Pornoland*, London, Faber & Faber, 2004.

Dines, G.: *Pornland: How Pornography has Hijacked Our Sexual Culture*, Boston, MA, Beacon Press, 2010.

Dines, G., Thompson, L., Whisnant, R., Boyle, K.: 'Arresting images: anti-pornography slide shows, activism and the academy', in Boyle, ed., 2010, pp.17–33.

——'The new Lolita: pornography and the sexualisation of childhood', in Reist and Bray, eds, 2011, pp.3–9.

Doggett, P.: *The Man Who Sold The World: David Bowie and the 1970s*, London, The Bodley Head, 2011.

Duits, L., Van Zoonen, L.: 'Headscarves and porno-chic: disciplining girls' bodies in the European multicultural society', *European Journal of Women's Studies*, vol.13, no.2, 2006, pp.103–17.

——'Coming to terms with sexualisation', *European Journal of Cultural Studies*, vol.14, no.5, 2011, pp.491–506.

Eisensten, E.: *The Printing Revolution in Early Modern Europe*, Cambridge, Cambridge University Press, 1983.

Ellis J.: 'On pornography', in Merck, ed., 1992, pp.146-70.

Evans, D.: *Sexual Citizenship*, London, Routledge, 1992.

Faludi, S., *Backlash*, London, Verso, 1991.

Ferguson, C.J., Hartley, R.D.: 'The pleasure is momentary ... the expense damnable? The influence of pornography on rape and sexual assault', *Aggression and Violent Behaviour*, vol.14, 2009, pp.323–29.

Finkelhorn, D.: 'Current information on the scope and nature of child sexual abuse', *The Future Of Children*, vol.4, no.2, 1994, pp.31–53.

Flew, T.: *Creative Industries: Culture and Policy*, London, Sage, 2011.

Flood, M.: 'Young men using pornography', in Boyle, ed., 2010, pp.164–78.

Foreman, A.: *Georgiana, Duchess of Devonshire*, New York, Random House, 1998.

Fountain, T.: *Rude Britannia: One Man's Journey around the Highways and Byways of British Sex*, London, Weidenfeld and Nicholson, 2008.

Frizot, M., ed.: *A New History of Photography*, Koln, Konemann, 1998.

Gaines, J.: 'Machines that make the body do things', in Gibson, ed., 2004, pp.30–44.

Gibson, P.C., ed.: *More Dirty Looks: Gender, Pornography and Power*, London, BFI, 2004.

Gill, R.: 'Supersexualise me!: advertising and the "midriffs"', in Attwood, ed., 2009, pp.93–109.

Greenfield-Sanders, T.: *XXX: 30 Porn-star Portraits*, New York, Bullfinch, 2004.

Greer, G.: *The Obstacle Race*, London, Picador, 1981.

Habermas, J.: *The Structural Transformation of the Public Sphere*, Cambridge, Cambridge University Press, 1989.

Hakim, C.: *Erotic Capital*, London, Thatcherite Centre For Policy Studies, 2010.

——*Honey Money: The Power of Erotic Capital*, London, Allen Lane, 2011.

——*Erotic Capital: The Power of Attraction in the Boardroom and the Bedroom*, New York, Basic Books, 2011.

Hall, A., Bishop, M., eds: *Pop-Porn: Pornography in American Culture*, London, Praeger, 2007.

Hammer, M.: *The Naked Portrait*, Edinburgh, National Galleries of Scotland, 2007.

Hardy, S.: 'The new pornographic: representation or reality?', in Attwood, ed., 2009, pp.3–18.

Harvey, H., Robinson, K.: 'Hot bodies on campus: the performance of porn chic', in Hall and Bishop, eds, 2007, pp.57–74.

Haworth-Booth, M.: *The Art Of Lee Miller*, New Haven, Yale University Press, 2007.

Hegarty, P.: *George Bataille: Core Cultural Theorist*, London, Sage, 2000.

Heineken, D.: 'Toys are us: contemporary feminisms and the consumption of sexuality', in Hall and Bishop, eds, 2007, pp.121–36.

Hennessy, R.: *Profit and Pleasure: Sexual Identities in Late Capitalism*, New York, Routledge, 2000.

Hickey, D., *et al.*, eds: *Andy Warhol: Giant Size*, London, Thames & Hudson, 2006.

Hitchens, C.: *Arguably*, London, Allen & Unwin, 2011.

Hodgkinson, T.: *How To Be Idle: A Loafer's Manifesto*, London, Hamish Hamilton, 2004.

Hogarth, H., Ingham, R.: 'Masturbation among young women and associations with sexual health: an exploratory study', *Journal of Sex Research*, vol.46, no.6, 2009, pp.558–67.

Holborn, M., Levas, D., eds: *Mapplethorpe: Altars*, New York, Random House, 1995.

Holland, S., Attwood, F.: 'Keeping fit in six inch heels: the mainstreaming of pole dancing', in Attwood, ed., 2009, pp.165–81.

Hoskyns, B.: *Glam*, London, Faber and Faber, 1998.

Hughes, C., Wacker, G., eds: *China and the Internet: Politics of the Digital Leap Forward*, London, Routledge, 2003.

Hunt, L.: *The Invention of Pornography*, New York, Zone Books, 1993.

Jacobs, K.: 'The amateur pornographer and the glib voyeur', *M/C Journal*, vol.7, issue 4, 2004.

Jacobs, K.: *Netporn: DIY Web Culture and Sexual Politics*, New York, Rowman & Littlefield, 2007.

——'The new world dream and the female itch: sex blogging and Lolita costume play in Hong Kong, Taiwan, and China', in Attwood, ed., 2010, pp.186–209.

——*People's Pornography: Sex and Surveillance on the Chinese Internet*, London, Intellect, 2011.

Jeffrey, I.: 'Araki in post-history', in Miki, Isshiki, and Sato eds, 2005, pp.257–61.

Jeffreys, S.: *Beauty and Misogyny: Harmful Cultural Practices in the West*, London, Routledge, 2005.

Jenkins, H.: *Convergence Culture: Where Old and New Media Collide*, New York, New York University Press, 2006.

Jenks, C.: *Transgression*, London, Routledge, 2003.

Jensen, R.: *Getting Off: Pornography and the End of Masculinity*, Boston, South End Press, 2007.

——'Pornography is what the end of the world looks like', in Boyle, ed., 2010, pp.105–13.

——'Stories of a rape culture: pornography as propaganda', in Reist and Bray, eds, 2011, pp.25–33.

Johnson, J.: 'To catch a curious clicker: a social network analysis of the online pornography industry', in Boyle, ed., 2010, pp.147–63.

Johnson, S.: *Where Good Ideas Come From: The Natural History of Innovation*, New York, Allen Lane, 2010.

Jones, M., Carlin, G.: '"Students study hard porn": pornography and the popular press', in Boyle, ed., 2010, pp.179–89.

Jowett, A., Peel, E.: '"Seismic cultural change?": British media representations of same-sex "marriage"', *Women's Studies International Forum*, vol.30, 2010, pp.206–14.

Juffer, J.: *At Home With Pornography: Women, Sex and Everyday Life*, New York, New York University Press, 1998.

——'There's no place like home: further developments on the home front', in Gibson, ed., 2004, pp.45–58.

Julius, A.: *Transgressions: The Offences of Art*, London, Thames and Hudson, 2002.

Kaestle, C., Allen, K.: 'The role of masturbation in healthy sexual development: perceptions of young adults', *Archives of Sexual Behaviour*, vol.40, no.5, 2011, pp.983–94.

Kammeyer, K.: *A Hypersexual Society: Sexual Discourse, Erotica and Pornography in America Today*, New York, Palgrave Macmillan, 2008.

Kavadlo, J.: 'Fear Factor: pornography, reality television, and Red State America', in Hall and Bishop, eds, 2007, pp.99–110.

Kendall, C.N.: 'The harms of gay male pornography', in Reist and Bray, eds, 2011, pp.53–62.

Kendrick, W.: *The Secret Museum*, New York, Viking, 1997.

Kerr, D., Hines, C., eds: *Hard to Swallow: Reading Pornography on Screen*, London, Wallflower, 2012.

Kerstin, M.: 'Making porn into art', in Paasonen *et al.*, eds, 2007, pp.87–97.

Kimmel, M., ed.: *Men Confront Pornography*, New York, Crown Publishers, 1990.

Kimmel, M.S., Plante, R., eds: *Sexualities: Identities, Behaviours and Society*, New York, Oxford University Press, 2004.

Kinnick, K.N.: 'Pushing the envelope: the role of the mass media in the mainstreaming of pornography', in Hall and Bishop, eds, 2007, pp.7–26.

Kipnis, L.: *Ecstacy Unlimited: On Sex, Capital, Gender and Aesthetics*, Minneapolis, University of Minnesota Press, 1993.

——*Bound and Gagged: Pornography and the Politics of Fantasy in America*, Durham, Duke University Press, 1996.

Kleinhams, C.: 'Virtual child porn: the law and the semiotics of the image', in Gibson, ed., 2004, pp.71–84.

Knudsen, S., Lofgren-Mårtenson, L., Mansson, S., eds: *Generation P? Youth, Gender and Pornography*, Aarhus, University of Aarhus Press, 2007.

Kolossa, A.: *Keith Haring: A Life for Art*, London, Taschen, 2004.

Koons, J.: *The Jeff Koons Handbook*, London, Thames and Hudson, 1992.

Krairly, M.: 'Reality television, gender and authenticity in Saudi Arabia', *Journal of Communication*, no.59, 2009, pp.345–66.

Krysinska, T.: *Sex and the Cinema*, London, Wallflower Press, 2006.

Kutchinsky, B.: 'Legalised pornography in Denmark', in Kimmel, ed., 1990, pp.233–45.

——'Pornography and rape: theory and practice? Evidence from crime data in four countries where pornography is easily available', *International Journal of Law Psychiatry*, vol.14, 1991, pp.47–64.

Landau, J.: 'Straightening out (the politics of) same-sex parenting: representing gay families in US print news stories and photographs', *Critical Studies in Media Communication*, vol.26, no.1, March 2009, pp.80–100.

Lehman, P., ed.: *Pornography: Film and Culture*, New Brunswick, Rutgers University Press, 2006.

Levy, A.: *Female Chauvinist Pigs: Women and the Rise of Raunch Culture*, London, Simon and Schuster, 2005.

Liljestrom, M., Paasonen, S., eds: *Working With Affect In Feminist Readings: Disturbing Differences*, London, Routledge, 2010.

Long, J.: 'Resisting pornography, building a movement: feminist anti-porn activism in the UK', in Reist and Bray, 2011, eds, pp.259–65.

Lovelace, L.: *Ordeal*, New York, Kensington, Citadel Press, 1980.

McDonald, H.: *Erotic Ambiguities*, London, Routledge, 2001.

McGlynn, M.: 'Marginalizing feminism? Debating extreme pornography laws in public and policy discourse', in Boyle, ed., 2010, pp.190–205.

McKee, A.: 'The aesthetics of pornography: the insights of consumers', *Continuum*, vol.20, no.4, 2006, pp.523–39.

——'Everything is child abuse', *Media International Australia Incorporating Culture & Policy*, no.135, 2010, pp.131–40.

McKee, A., Albury, K., Lumby, C.: *The Porn Report*, Melbourne University Press, 2008.

McKee, A., Albury, K., Dunne, M., Grieshaber, S., Hartley, J., Lumby, C., Mathews, B.: 'Healthy sexual development: a multidisciplinary framework for research', *International Journal of Sexual Health*, vol.22, 2010, pp.14–19.

MacKinnon, C.: *Are Women Human?*, Harvard, Harvard University Press, 2006.

——'X-underrated: living in a world the pornographers have made', in Tankard Reist and Bray, eds, 2011, pp.9–15.

McNair, B.: *Mediated Sex: Pornography and Postmodern Culture*, London, Arnold, 1996.

——*Striptease Culture: Sex, Media and the Democratisation of Desire*, London, Routledge, 2002.

——'From porno-chic to porno-fear: the return of the repressed', in Attwood, ed., 2009a, pp.110–30.

——'Teaching porn', *Sexualities*, vol.12, no.5, 2009b, pp.1–10.

——'Sex acts' in Albertozzi and Cobley, eds, 2010, pp.534–45.

MacNeill, K.: 'When subject becomes object: nakedness, art and the public sphere', *Media International Australia Incorporating Culture & Policy*, no.135, 2010, pp.82–93.

Madonna: *Sex*, London, Thames & Hudson, 1992.

Maltz, W., Maltz, L.: *The Porn Trap: The Essential Guide to Overcoming Problems Caused by Pornography*, New York, Harper Collins, 2010.

Manning, J.C.: 'The impact of internet pornography on marriage', *Sexual Addiction and Compulsivity*, vol.13, 2009, pp.161–65.

Mayhem, M., Lim, G.: *Absolute Mayhem: Confessions of an Aussie Porn Star*, Sydney, Ebury Press, 2008.

Merck M.: *The Sexual Subject: A Screen Reader in Sexuality*, London, Routledge, 1992

Miki, A., Ishiki, Y., Sato, T., eds: *Nobuyoshi Araki: Self, Life, Death*, London, Phaidon, 2005.

Mireshghi, S., Matsumoto, D.: 'Perceived cultural attitudes toward homosexuality and their effects on Iranian and American sexual minorities', *Cultural Diversity and Ethnic Minority Psychology*, vol.14, no.4, 2008, pp.372–76.

Moeller, S.D.: *Compassion Fatigue: How the Media Sell Disease, Famine, War and Death*, London, Routledge, 1999.

Moore, L.J., Weissbein, J.: 'Cocktail parties: fetishizing semen in pornography beyond bukkake', in Boyle, ed., 2010, pp.77–89.

Moran, C.: *How To Be A Woman*, London, Ebury Press, 2011.

Morris, D.B.: *Illness and Culture in the Postmodern Age*, University of California Press, 1980.

Moulton, I.F.: *Before Pornography: Erotic Writing in Early Modern England*, Oxford, Oxford University Press, 2005.

Mowlabocus, S.: 'Gay men and the pornification of everyday life', in Paasonen *et al.*, eds, 2007, pp.61–71.

Muhleisen, W.: '*Baise-moi* and feminism's filmic intercourse with the aesthetics of pornography', in Schubert and Gjelsiuk, eds, 2004, pp.21–38.

Mumford, R.: 'Bust-ing the third wave: Barbie, blowjobs and girlie feminism', in Attwood, ed., 2009, pp.183–97.

Nagle, J., ed.: *Whores and Other Feminists*, New York, Routledge, 1997.

Nathan, D.: *Pornography*, Toronto, Groundwood Books, 2007.

National Centre for Social Research: *British Social Attitudes*, 26th Report, Princeton, NJ, National Centre for Social Research, 2010.

Neely, S.: 'Virtually commercial sex', in Boyle, ed., 2010, pp.90–102.

Osterwell, A.: 'Andy Warhol's *Blow Job*: toward the recognition of a pornographic avant-garde', in Williams, ed., 2004, pp.431–60.

Paasonen, S.: 'Epilogue: porn futures', in Paasonen *et al.*, eds, 2007, pp.161–70.

——'Healthy sex and pop porn: pornography, feminism and the Finnish context', *Sexualities*, vol.12, no.5, 2009, pp.586–600.

——'Repetition and hyperbole: the gendered choreographies of heteroporn', in Boyle, ed., 2010, pp.63–77.

Paasonen, S., Nikunen, K., Saarenmaa, L., eds: *Pornification: Sex and Sexuality in Media Culture*, Oxford, Berg, 2007.

Paglia, C.: *Sex, Art and American Culture*, London, Penguin, 1993.

Papadopoulos, L.: *Sexualisation of Young People*, Home Office, March 2010.

Paul, P.: *Pornified: How Pornography is Transforming Our Lives, Our Relationships, and Our Families*, New York, Times Books, 2005.

Pinker, S.: *The Better Angels Of Our Nature: The Decline of Violence in History and its Causes*, New York, Allen Lane, 2011.

Railton, D., Watson P.: 'Sexed authorship and pornographic address in music video', in Paasonen *et al.*, eds, 2007, pp.115–25.

Raney, K.: *Art In Question*, London, Routledge, 2003.

Reist, M.T., Bray, A., eds: *Big Porn Inc: Exposing the Harms of the Global Porn Industry*, Sydney, Spinifex, 2011.

Ridley, M.: *The Rational Optimist: How Prosperity Evolves*, London, Fourth Estate, 2010.

Roach, C.M.: *Stripping, Sex and Popular Culture*, Oxford, Berg, 2007.

Rosewarne, L.: *Part-time Perverts: Sex, Pop Culture and Kink Management*, Oxford, Praeger, 2011.

Rush, E., La Nauze, A.: *Corporate Paedophilia: Sexualisation of Children in Australia*, Canberra, Australia Institute, Discussion Paper number 90, 2006.

Russell, D.: 'The tumescent citizen', *M/C Journal*, vol.7, issue 4, 2004.

Sarracino, C., Scott, K.: *The Porning Of America: The Rise of Porn Culture, What it Means, and Where We Go From Here*, Boston, Beacon Press, 2008.

Schubert, R., Gjelsivk, A., eds: *Femme Fatale*, Goteborg, Nordicom, 2004.

Shamoon, D.: 'Office sluts and rebel flowers: the pleasures of Japanese Pornogaphic comics for women', in Williams, ed., 2004, pp.77–103.

Shteir, R.: *Striptease: The Untold Story*, London, Routledge, 2006.

Silverman, S.: *The Bedwetter: Tales of Courage, Redemption and Pee*, New York, Harper Collins, 2010.

Simpson, M.: *The Queen is Dead*, London, Arcadia, 2000.

Skinner, K.B.: *Treating Pornography Addiction: The Essential Tools for Recovery*, Utah, GrowthClimate, 2005.

Slade, J.: *Pornography and Sexual Representation: A Reference Guide*, New York, Greenwood Publishing, 2001.

Smith, C.: *One for the Girls! The Pleasures and Practices of Reading Porn for Women*, London, Intellect, 2007.

——'Pleasing intensities: masochism and affective pleasures in porn short fictions', in Attwood, ed., 2009, pp.19–35.

Smith, P.: *Just Kids*, London, Bloomsbury, 2010.

Smith, T.: *Changes in Family Structure, Family Values, and Politics, 1972–2006*, Chicago, GSS Social Change Report, no.53, University of Chicago, February 2008.

——*Trends in Support for Civil Liberties*, Chicago, GSS Social Change Report no.59, University of Chicago, April 2011.

Sontag, S.: 'The pornographic imagination', in Bataille, 1982, pp.85–105.

Stallybrass P., White, A.: *The Politics and Poetics of Transgression*, New York, Methuen, 1986.

Stevenson, B., Wolfers, J.: *The Paradox of Declining Female Happiness*, Philadelphia, University of Pennsylvania, 2009.

Stoner, J., Hughes, D.: *The Social Costs of Pornography: A Collection of Papers*, Princeton, NJ, Witherspoon Institute, 2010.

Struthers, W.: *Wired for Intimacy: How Pornography Hi-jacks the Male Brain*, Illinois, IVP Books, 2007.

Sussman, E., ed.: *Keith Haring*, New York, Whitney Museum of American Art, 1997.

Tanaka, Y.: 'Japan in Araki's World', in Miki, Isshiki and Sato eds, 2005, pp.545–48.

Tang, I.: *Pornography: The Secret History of Civilisation*, London, Channel 4 Books, 1999.

Tankard Reist, M., Bray, A., eds; *Big Porn Inc: Exposing the Harms of the Global Pornography Industry*, Sydney, Spinifex Press, 2011.

Tuck, G.: 'The mainstreaming of masturbation', in Attwood, ed., 2009, pp.77–92.

Tyler, M.: 'Now, that's pornography! Violence and domination in Adult Video News', in Boyle, ed., 2010, pp.50–62.

Vance, C., ed.: *Pleasure and Danger: Exploring Female Sexuality*, London, Routledge and Kegan Paul, 1984.

Walker, A., Flattery, J., Kershaw, C., Moon, D., eds: *Crime in England and Wales 2008–09*, NSO/Home Office, 2009.

Walter, N.: *Living Dolls: The Return of Sexism*, London, Virago, 2010.

Warhol, A.: *The Philosophy of Andy Warhol (from A to B and Back Again)*, New York, Harcourt Inc., 1975.

Waters, J., Hainley, B.: *Art – a Sex Book*, London, Thames & Hudson, 2003.

Watkins, J.: 'Ice that doesn't melt', in Miki, Isshiki, and Sato eds, 2005, pp.21–24.

Waugh, T.: *The Fruit Machine: Twenty Years of Writings on Queer Cinema*, London, Duke University Press, 2000.

Weitzer, R., ed.: *Sex for Sale: Prostitution, Pornography and the Sex Industry*, New York, Routledge, 2000.

Whisnant, R.: 'From Jekyll to Hyde: the grooming of male pornography consumers', in Boyle, ed., 2010, pp.114–33.

White, A.: 'Pornographic becomings: female experiences in pornography beyond the victim/agent divide', Honours thesis, University of Melbourne, 2010.

Williams, L.: *Hardcore*, London, Pandora, 1990.

Williams, L., ed.: *Porn Studies*, Duke, Duke University Press, 2004.

Williams, L.R.: *Screening Sex*, Durham, Duke University Press, 2008.

Winterson, J.: *Why be Happy When You Could be Normal?*, Jonathan Cape, 2011.

Witherspoon Institute: *The Social Costs of Pornography: A Statement of Findings and Recommendations*, New York, Witherspoon Institute, 2010.

Worton, M.: *Typical Men: Recent Photography of the Male Body by Men*, Nottingham, Djanogly Art Gallery, 2002.

Wu, Z., Jiang, L., Zheng, Q., Zhao, J., Tian, Z., Liu, J.: 'A peep at pornography web in China', (n.d.) http://journal.webscience.org/306/2/websci10_submission_44.pdf

INDEX